Joris Ivens and the Documentary Context

D1563533

Joris Ivens and the Documentary Context

Edited by Kees Bakker

Amsterdam University Press

This publication is made possible with the support of the Dutch Film Fund and the European Foundation Joris Ivens.

Cover illustration: Jean Umansky © CAPI Films, Paris
Cover design: Kok Korpershoek, Amsterdam
Typesetting: JAPES, Amsterdam

ISBN 90 5356 425 x (hardcover)
ISBN 90 5356 389 x (paperback)

Contents

Articles by Joris Ivens

Introduction

Photo: Marion Michelle

'Le vent de l'Histoire nous a quelquefois plaqués au mur.
Mais le vent nous a donné des ailes.'
Marceline Loridan-Ivens

Joris Ivens and the Documentary Context

Kees Bakker

Reporter, painter, poet, propagandist, freelance communist, advocate, pioneer, source of inspiration, fellow traveller, teacher, cadger - many qualifications have been used by friends, enemies, colleagues, and writers to
describe Joris Ivens (1898-1989). In isolation, none of these qualifications are
accurate, but together they provide a strange and confusing image, yet
maybe a more accurate one, of one of the most important documentary filmmakers of the twentieth century. Ivens himself, in the preface to the autobiography he wrote with Robert Destanque, sketched two ways to describe
his life: from a historical and ideological point of view, as the life of 'a filmmaker, activist, following the revolutionary movement and serving those
who struggle for dignity and freedom'; in a more romanticized view it's the
life of 'an adventurer, a young Dutchman, breaking with his country and
exploring the world with his camera'. Georges Sadoul labeled him 'The
Flying Dutchman', and indeed, several parallels can be drawn between this
legend and Joris Ivens: both wandering around the world, often sailing
against the wind, and, at least for a while, not welcome in their homeland.
The one being a myth, the other sometimes creating his own myth. Both are
legends in a way: not everything about them is true, but they are both very
intriguing. Most characterizations of Ivens say more about their author than
about Joris Ivens, but they do illustrate the richness and complexity of his
life and work.

On the occasion of Joris Ivens's hundredth birthday in 1998, many activities were organized throughout the world, and especially in Nijmegen, the
Dutch town of his birth. Among these activities was a three-day conference,
'The Documentary Context', organized by the European Foundation Joris
Ivens. The present book grew out of this conference in that most of the con-
tributors participated in it. However, for this book we wanted more than
simply to present the proceedings of the conference. First, because the main
aim of these three days was not so much to focus on Joris Ivens as on the

context in which he, and many others, have made his films. We wanted to learn about Joris Ivens through the documentary context. This volume inverts this aim in desiring to learn about the documentary context through Joris Ivens. Hence, there is a slight shift in focus by concentrating more on Joris Ivens and taking his work as a starting point for reflection on the twentieth-century documentary. Whereas at the conference several aspects of Ivens's life and work remained underexposed, this inversion implies almost automatically that some aspects of the documentary context will remain underexposed in this volume. In fact, while it is impossible to capture all aspects of either Joris Ivens or the documentary context in a single volume, our aim is more modest than it might appear at first glance: we hope that the essays in this book contribute to a better understanding of some aspects of both Joris Ivens and the documentary film in the context of the twentieth century. Another reason for not merely presenting the proceedings is that we wanted Joris Ivens himself to speak through some articles he wrote during his career. In these articles, Ivens presents his ideas about the documentary film, and we can see the evolution in his thinking about the documentary. These texts, clearly written by a filmmaker, offer an inside view of his film practice. But they are also products of the time in which they were written and thus give a particular insight into different aspects of political and documentary film history.

The book is divided into four sections. The first section presents a more general and introductory view on the main theme of this volume: both the documentary context and Joris Ivens. The second section contains more historical perspectives on his life and work, while the third section reflects on some aspects of his work which are related to other works and current debates on the documentary. In the fourth section we assembled some articles by Joris Ivens, which reveal his own thinking and point of view on documentary filmmaking.

José Manuel Costa in 'Joris Ivens and the Documentary Project' opens the preliminaries with a challenging view on the Documentary movement, and Ivens's role in the emergence of this movement in relation to others. With history as the main subject of most of his films, Joris Ivens shaped documentary film history – setting an example for others, sometimes following others, but always maintaining a continuum in his oeuvre.

In his films, Joris Ivens documented major events of the twentieth century, but he did not only film these world events, he also shaped the world by filming them. The relationship between the world, film and the filmed world has always been a point of discussion surrounding the documentary, and Ivens's film practice not only stresses this relationship, but also explores it in a fascinating and illuminating way. In 'A Way of Seeing: Joris Ivens's Documentary Century' this will be studied more closely.

Three essays in this volume relate directly to Joris Ivens's early works. André Stufkens in 'The Song of Movement' explains how Joris Ivens became involved in the avant-garde film movement in the Netherlands, and how avant-gardist values can also be found in his later films. It is interesting to also have the views of Karel Dibbets and Bill Nichols on the same subject: all three have a different starting point for their reflections on the subject, and they all shed a different light on it, but not necessarily with opposing views. Karel Dibbets in 'High-Tech Avant-garde: PHILIPS RADIO' studies the elements in PHILIPS RADIO which make this film diverge from the avant-garde movement. Although Bill Nichols acknowledges a shift in Ivens's work in this same period, his contribution 'Documentary and the Turn from Modernism' looks for the elements that persist in Ivens's later films. Following Schmidt's wave-theory, Nichols draws parallels between the 'supplemental elements' that persist in Kazimir Malevich's later paintings and a similar form of persistence as Ivens moves from a modernist, avant-gardist film style to a realist style in his documentaries after 1930.

In 1947, Joris Ivens began to work in Eastern Europe, making several documentaries for the socialist cause. He also worked for five years for the DEFA, the East German film production company. In 'Between Two Letters' Günter Jordan, who worked for the DEFA himself, discusses this period in Ivens's career by sketching the context in which he had to work, the impact it had on his films, and the impact that Ivens had on the DEFA. Jordan closely examines this particular period of film production in the German Democratic Republic. This view is complemented by Alfons Machalz, a close collaborator of Joris Ivens during that period, and who, in 1963, also made a documentary portrait of Joris Ivens. In 'MEIN KIND – As if it Were Ivens's Child' Machalz describes what a collaboration with Joris Ivens implied, in his presence as well as in his absence ('how would Joris decide?'). A testimony and inside view on Joris Ivens's filmmaking methods.

Michèle Lagny concentrates on the first film Joris Ivens made upon his return to Western Europe. As the title indicates, 'LA SEINE A RENCONTRÉ PARIS and Documentary in France in the Fifties' places this film in the context of French documentary film production of that period. An ambiguous film: is it fiction or 'Kino Pravda' as Vertov defined this? Lagny gives us a close look at how this film project came into being, and how it fits, or not, into the dominant mode of representation of 1950s France.

Virgilio Tosi, who has been a close friend of Joris Ivens since the fifties, takes us to Italy. 'Joris Ivens and the Documentary in Italy' gives an account of Ivens's visits and work in Italy, the reception of his work and the Italian documentary context in which this took place. Tosi gives us a closer look at the realization and the peculiar history of L'ITALIA NON È UN PAESE POVERO.

During the last twenty-five years of his career, Joris Ivens shared the credit with Marceline Loridan. Jean-Pierre Sergent, in 'Joris Ivens and Marceline Loridan: a Fruitful Encounter', reflects on the professional partnership of Marceline Loridan and Joris Ivens, and on their mutual influence on their ways of filmmaking.

Several aspects of Ivens's work reflect the problematics of the documentary film in general: objectivity, reconstructions, engagement, the use of sound, music, and editing, etc. Some of these aspects are reflected in this volume. Brian Winston discusses the practice of staging in documentary films in his 'Honest, Straightforward Re-enactment – The Staging of Reality'. The claim for the real can be endangered by these interactions between filmmaker and reality, and therefore Winston asks the question how far this intervention by the documentarist can go. Joris Ivens's engagement is praised as well as disputed. Thomas Waugh describes the continuous and autonomous history of more than eighty years of committed documentary. 'Joris Ivens and the Legacy of Committed Documentary' discusses the strategies used by artists to intervene in history and make their documentaries change the world – strategies for which Ivens is still an inspiration and example. Claude Brunel reflects more on the poetic aspects of the films of Joris Ivens by focusing on the use of sound and music in his films.

In 'A Special Relation: Joris Ivens and the Netherlands', Bert Hogenkamp analyses the history of Joris Ivens's relations with his homeland. Especially in the Netherlands, Joris Ivens has always been controversial because of his communist sympathies and his position regarding Indonesia. Hogenkamp gives an account of the discussions that occurred, and still occur, over and over again, when Ivens appears in the press.

In his last film, UNE HISTOIRE DE VENT, co-directed by Marceline Loridan, Joris Ivens looks back on his career, the choices he made, and on his experiences in China. Sylvain De Bleeckere explains the character of this autobiographical and testamentary film as an encounter with Chinese culture, as well as a flashback on twentieth-century history, sketching for the spectator a way to understand an intercultural society.

This book also contains nine articles by Joris Ivens, some of which are published here for the first time. Written between 1931 and 1963, they represent Joris Ivens's ideas about the documentary film and the documentary film practice. As I have already stated, these articles are clearly written by a filmmaker and thus give an inside view of his own film practice. On the other hand, they treat aspects which concern almost every documentary filmmaker. But they also reflect the time in which they were written, portraying the socio-political context of documentary film production during a large part of the twentieth century; a valuable addition to the book's other contributions, which we hope, in its turn, will contribute to a more profound knowledge of Joris Ivens and of the documentary film in general.

A short biography, a filmography, and a bibliography complete this volume.

This volume did not come into being without the help of others, especially the authors themselves. Many thanks go to them for their cooperation, patience, and willingness to contribute. Next, I would like to thank Bert Hogenkamp, Frank Kessler, Emile Poppe, and Daan van Speijbroeck who helped program the symposium, and in this way more than indirectly contributed to the compilation of this present volume.

I would also like to thank my colleagues and the board of the European Foundation Joris Ivens: Marceline Loridan-Ivens for her permission to publish the many photos in this book. André Stufkens and Elles Erkens, for their support in the realization of the symposium and this book, and Elles for working overtime on her translations. Many thanks are also due to Kees Bakker, Sr. who also worked overtime to translate some of these essays.

At a very early stage Professor Thomas Elsaesser, general editor of the series in which this book appears, showed his confidence in this project, which was very encouraging. I would like to thank him for this confidence and for leading me to Wardy Poelstra, Peter van Dijk, Françoise Kraaijenzank, and their colleagues at Amsterdam University Press, who were willing to collaborate to realize this book before the end of this millenium.

This project would not have been possible without the financial support of the Dutch Film Fund, for which I want to thank its board. It stresses once again that in the Netherlands too, Joris Ivens is still regarded as an important filmmaker.

Photo: Chris Marker

Preliminaries

Joris Ivens and the Documentary Project

José Manuel Costa

Those who, like myself, have more closely followed the life and work of Joris Ivens over his last ten years, from 1979 to his death in 1989 – his fight to film again, his unfinished or unrealised projects of that period – could not but see his effort to regain his own beginnings. He consciously sought the origins, trying to close the circle and, at the same time, reopen it, out of a deeply rooted belief of Documentary as art and as a laboratory of the whole cinema – a platform of immense formal liberty, a non-conventional land, or, in his own terms, a creative no man's land. He wanted to go back and beyond, and in fact, while doing this, he not only 'came back to his beginnings' but was indeed unveiling the roots and nature of the whole genre.

Key unrealised projects of that period, like the Florence film, were the clearest sign of a larger concept, the concept of Documentary not so much as 'a creative treatment of actuality' but more as a way of forcing reality to reveal its inner sense through a confrontation with it, and as a textual creation and formal invention arising out of this confrontation. Something here immediately reminds us of another 'dialogue with a city' – ...A VALPARAISO, (1963) – a midway film that already pointed back to the origins of his work and of Documentary itself. (...A VALPARAISO, like the unrealised Florence film, was a key example of his unified concept of social meaning as both source and result of a formal approach. In this respect, one has only to think about the incessant movement of the elevators between the two *social* levels of the city, in that film, in order to understand how social commitment was one with the creation of form, and *form* actually seen as *movement* in the precise sense of the avant-garde roots of the late twenties.)

In his later projects, and of course in his last film, Joris Ivens was in fact making his own personal synthesis, building from his own remote origins, while also revealing them. But in that process what we may see are the larger roots of the Documentary movement as we still see it today, what one may call its paradigm.

One peculiar feature of this last Ivens decade was, I believe, the way in which both the 'fight to film' in itself and the experimental mood proved to be an enduring force in his life's work. One may argue that those particular years could have been the last and definitive ideological crisis for a man forged in the strong, clear contradictions of the thirties, and therefore a period of puzzling and interrogation, where he too might have lost faith and gone back to a more formal search, to supposedly lighter subjects, and a 'pure' enjoyment of filming. That is not my view – I see intense interrogation but also absolute resistance to any loss of faith in the process of social change – and, if anything, such an argument shows something else, namely, an incorrect analytical framework. The idea that Ivens could be attracted by the act of filming, and also by 'form', because of any ideological disenchantment is not only objectively wrong but also as wrong as the previous – also common – idea that his cinematic experience had been set in motion primarily for ideological reasons. Some have theorised about his film work (and I quote Carlos Boker[1]) as a 'rhetorical medium' and as something that found its primary rationale in Ivens's 'ideological commitment'. On the contrary, I believe that the concept of Documentary as a *medium*, as a *means* for expressing social commitment, is in fact inadequate to explain his work. What I do believe is that film work was, for Ivens, both a means and a *driving force* in itself – and that we cannot only say that he filmed *because of* his social commitment but also that he even sometimes kept his social and political beliefs (at least longer than one would expect) in order *to be able* to go on filming. One does not need to diminish the major importance of his commitment in order to understand this. Moreover, one does not need to underestimate the *articulation* between that commitment and his contributions to the representational forms of Documentary, in order to understand it. However, in the late eighties or even after Ivens's death, what we have seen is the blindness of many film critics who were unable to understand this. Documentary, in the Ivens conception, was not exactly a *medium* to transmit ideology, or something that *came out of* ideology, but a global impulse where ideology played a structural role. And in order to understand this we must go back to, and appreciate, its very beginnings.

I have always believed that the discussion of the Documentary genre has nothing to gain from an excessive dilution of the concept in the general history of the film medium, out of an intended, but ultimately misplaced theoretical rigour. As much as we must be aware of the fact that Louis Lumière launched an embryonic documentary approach, to see this idea in its right light we should understand that his genial work was an embryo of different film paths where none had a specific identity. The Documentarist approach and the fictional approach were both there, in a latent way, indistinct and unified by a single coherent desire to seek the movement of the world. In the same way, as much as we have to pay tribute to some isolated pioneers of a *realistic* artistic film practice – and especially to the greatness of Robert Flaherty (already evident in his work of the twenties) – we should under-

stand that they also did not achieve the differentiation of the Documentary
as an approach.

Despite the very early tradition of the travel film and these isolated precursors – and they *were* isolated – the Documentary approach was in fact
neither the first nor in many ways the earliest natural development of the
film medium. On the contrary, it was an answer to it and even a *denial* of it.
Early cinema had its first strong developmental momentum, and achieved
its first artistic assertion and paradigm, by stressing its manipulative potential as opposed to its reproductive one. Cinema asserted itself as an art by
learning its power to manipulate reality – a power that it soon overasserted,
or overestimated. By the second part of the twenties, however, precisely in
reaching the peaks of manipulation, it had created room, and in fact a willingness, for something else.

The specific identity of the Documentary movement is part of a larger reaction to the manipulative peaks of the twenties, to the gulf between the
filmmaker and normal daily life, and to the eruption of technical and or-
ganisational complexity that had already occurred by that time in the film
industry. Rather than as a natural development of a supposedly *inherent* nature, Documentary was consciously created as a response to the previous
evolution of cinema. Documentary began to appear at that uniquely rich
moment, between the late twenties and the early thirties, when cinema
looked upon its first extraordinary achievements and trends and opened up
new (and so far underestimated) potentials. Rather than an *aspect* of the
whole cinema (which it also is), rather than the continuation of the early
travel or factual film, Documentary rose as a specific movement with a precise historical context and responding to specific needs. We cannot repeat
this too often, because it is the only way to grasp the very identity of this
movement and to understand its whole further evolution.

Documentary is therefore not the *innocence* of cinema but, on the contrary, something that arose when cinema had already lost its primitive innocence. Documentary is not the lack of power in the face of reality but the
assumption of it – the wish to confront that already conscious power with
the power of those who are seen by the camera. In its origins, Documentary
was the establishing of a new creative balance between the filmmaker and
the people who were filmed, and, in that sense, the first consistent movement (only later to be followed by fiction and by a new theoretical paradigm) to invest in that kind of creative tension between controlled and
uncontrolled reality that is involved in any act of filming.[2]

The cradle of Documentary as a movement is in fact the avant-garde
spirit of that precise period. Documentary is one of the many outputs of the
artistic impatience of that time: it is a way of seeking the renewal of the lan-

guage of film by coming out of the limitations of the studio, opening a new film practice, using reality – and the opposing resistance of reality – in order to achieve a genuinely new creative mood, one that is not overburdened by industrial conventions. In this sense, it uses the road opened by the genius of Flaherty, but it does so with its own new program, which includes confronting contemporary social reality and contradictions, the analysis of our present world. (In another sense, of course, it also uses the path opened by Vertov – another precursor rather than a documentarist, given that his plunge into objective reality was reshaped by him in terms of the manipulative paradigm.) Therefore, we can say that Documentary is not only inseparable from the artistic context, even less something made *against art*, but precisely that it is something that arises at the very core of the evolution of film art. At the same time, as it seeks the renewal of that art by opening it up to the uncertainty of reality, the genre is in fact a crossover between the intrinsic evolution of cinema and the state of the Western world in the same period – a world of growing social and political contradictions, a world of opposing and globalizing ideologies, a world between wars.

On the other hand, in order to characterize fully the emergent Documentary movement in the film context, one has still to add its coincidence in time with the exact period of the sound revolution. The handicap of early sound technology – unable to cope with what would otherwise have been the natural tendency to catch direct sound – had the curious, contradictory result of keeping the camera flexible and free to an extent that was then forbidden to fiction. So Documentary, having had from the start a somewhat contradictory nature, given that it came out of a formalist impulse but tried to face and integrate uncontrolled reality, found these contradictions further reinforced by this audio-visual handicap. In that sense, Documentary in the thirties may be seen as a transitional corpus, almost an anachronistic one, and maybe the only one (except for the straightforwardly abstract cinema) where the avant-garde of the twenties had a chance to develop a bit further. In many of its formal terms, Documentary of the thirties *was* the avant-garde of the twenties transported over the sound period. With its mostly separate system of sound – except in the cases where sound recording actually limited the more radical adventures of the camera and led Documentary to *reconstruction* – it meant that the new confrontation with reality could still go along with formal traces of the previous period. Documentary in the thirties was therefore a mix of past and future, with all the contradictory, but also rich, potential which this brought.

Now, if we accept this, we cannot but acknowledge that Joris Ivens was in fact one of the main proponents of the genre – an *inventor*. Throughout the whole decade of the thirties, in parallel with other genuine but different

approaches (mainly, the Grierson approach and eventually the Pare Lorentz contribution), he led the way and progressively helped to define the
concept. Moreover, his specific path was the one which most clearly embodied the shaping process of that concept from the late twenties to the late thirties, when in many ways it finally reached the representational mode that
we still call Documentary.

All those three *matrices* (Ivens, Grierson, and Lorentz) were responsible
for a common pattern of artistic search and social concern that has been definitely associated with the genre (the latter being what we could call a pattern of *social productivity*). But neither the Grierson *public education* approach
nor the *lyric Rooseveltian* approach of Lorentz identified as clearly as did
Joris Ivens with the very boundaries of that process and with the process itself – that is, the assumption of the avant-garde spirit and its progressive as-
similation into a social, political, and historical intervention.

Many have said – and the filmmaker himself seemed to ratify it, when
talking about the *turning point* of BORINAGE – that what Ivens did was to go
from the avant-garde basis *towards* the political engagement. This is true up
to a point (even if the preciseness of the turning point is more questionable)
but, again, it still implies a sense of dichotomy and succession (*first* the
avant-garde, *then* the political assertion) that allows us to only touch on the
surface of a more complex process. The uniqueness of Ivens's work of the
thirties, in comparison to the other major trends of the same period, was that
he went further in both directions – art and militancy – and also that he built
one new practice and *one* new concept out of both.

There is no better example for understanding this than THE SPANISH
EARTH (1937). In Madrid, Ivens totally changed what was then the normal
approach to the war film. I believe that for the first time in the practice of
non-fictional cinema, an artist came to the front himself and conceived the
film there, while he was shooting. The episode of the abandoned Lillian
Hellman *fiction* script, and all the subsequent experience at the front, was,
however, not just the *confirmation of the Documentary path*, or the opening of a
new kind of *war film*, but something of a larger consequence. Ivens himself
wrote and talked extensively about the extreme uncontrolled situations that
one had to face in that kind of film. More precisely, he frequently expressed
the challenge of war, saying that, in Spain, 'the enemy was co-director', because only the enemy knew exactly when and how he would attack, therefore playing a decisive role in the very basics of the shooting experience.
This was the experience, certainly more than anything ever before in his career, that gave him the final touch in the awareness of Documentary as *the*
representational mode that structurally has to integrate another source of

control, and that is actually built upon that kind of confrontation, or, simply, on partial *lack of control*.

Behind its very pragmatic lesson on the filming of war, the practical and conceptual experience of THE SPANISH EARTH can in fact be seen, metonymically, as a decisive point in the larger development of Documentary. By now, for the first time, Documentary was taking shape as a new *form*, where the personal authorship itself, no matter how strong it was, worked and expressed itself under new rules, demanding a new analytical frame. At last, the avant-garde crucible had become something else, something more definite, but something where the formal search was displaced, rather than overtaken. Formal construction ceased to inhabit the more definable area of *style*, at least as one is used to analyzing it in fiction, being displaced into what we could call a global *attitude*, a mix of *action* and *reaction*, an ethical and aesthetical, unified, *semi-automatic* construction.[3] The strong, assertive, visual construction of the avant-garde, or the straightforward constructivist mood in the use of the camera and in montage were displaced into a personal way of confronting and penetrating an evolving situation. Formal construction identified itself with a drifting process, which could thereafter be the result of plainly uncontrolled situations (THE SPANISH EARTH) or the drifting penetration of a complex urban and social reality (...A VALPARAISO). Documentary, once a mixture of *past* and *future* linguistic elements, was finally detaching itself from its past conceptual components, even if still strongly influenced by them. That is exactly what makes the difference (and at the same time the common bond) between THE BRIDGE (1928), or RAIN (1929), and ...A VALPARAISO (1963).

Documentary eventually had its second great momentum, and certainly its only important major mutation, in the sixties, with the direct sound revolution. Then, Ivens was not an *inventor*, as in fact he could never have been, coming as he did from the original crucible where visual construction played a dominant role. Taking advantage of the new partnership with Marceline Loridan, who started to work in film with the synchronous microphone in hand[4] (a combination that he used significantly to remember as 'the marriage of image and sound'), Ivens entered the new system only in the second half of the decade with LE 17ÈME PARALLÈLE (shown 1968), in which he made the jump simultaneously to codirection[5] and to the new 16mm medium.

It may be that LE 17ÈME PARALLÈLE was another turning point in his career but it was not necessarily linked to this *return to war*, and to another extreme, and extremely *symbolic*, war context. And yet, one sees how close this film was to THE SPANISH EARTH and how evident again is the link between the paroxysm of the situation and the conceptual step forward that it required of Documentary. On a primary, analytical level, LE 17ÈME PARALLÈLE is the *same film* as THE SPANISH EARTH, absolutely coincidental in its subject matter: the people and the war, the challenges of daily life *behind the war*, the food issue – be it bread or rice – under circumstances of war. On the other hand, it is precisely their amazing similarity that makes it easier for us to identify the linguistic evolution from one to the other and how the pair of Ivens/ Loridan finally entered, at least partially[6], the new direct cinema experience. Once more, the evolution had a larger relevance and it came out of the concrete response to the circumstances.

As it had been in the thirties, Documentary in the sixties was again a laboratory of the whole cinema experience, now both embodying the new theoretical paradigm of the late forties and fifties and developing it further, running parallel to the new fictional trends. Once again, the taking over of old formulas and the trial of new ones was more easily done in this less conventional land (the Ivens *no man's land*), where less controlled shooting was an antidote to convention. In particular, the exploration of synchronous sound in Documentary was the platform for a change in the concept of image duration, direct sound having decisively *taught* the image to wait and to prolong the act of looking, therefore also leading to new subject matter. With it, cinema went deeply and decisively, as never before, from the exploration of space to the more complex exploration of time – something that it has continued to do for the rest of the century. This being so, when we look back to that otherwise fabulous momentum of the early direct cinema (Drew, Leacock, the Maysles, and even the French *Rouchian* side to some extent), we cannot but feel that somehow its real object was the shooting experience *in itself*, the pleasure of that new experience, the playing with the camera and the microphone. No matter how exciting it was, early direct cinema included an obvious fetishism of the equipment, addressing its own film universe.

Naturally, by this time, that *sheer pleasure* would have been strange and insufficient to the militant Ivens. But again we should not be misled by an artificial separation between the *moment of formal exploration* and *the moment of militancy*, for the one did not work *against the other*; the latter being rather the way to develop, and in that sense to *consolidate*, the embryonic mutation of the former. In Vietnam, under the permanent bombing, any insignificant gesture had a completely different, unique value. Therefore, in a partial use of direct cinema techniques and the new awareness of duration, Ivens clung to those small, anonymous gestures precisely expressing their *uniqueness*. As the inventors of direct cinema had done, he looked into the other side of normal action (the moments *in between*), only here – again facing the paroxysm of another special war – he was destined to deepen the method, to di-

Joris Ivens and Ernest Hemingway during the shooting of THE SPANISH EARTH, in 1937.

Marceline Loridan and Joris Ivens during the filming of LE 17ÈME PARALLÈLE, in 1967.

gest it, and to reach a new synthesis. In that sense, LE 17ÈME PARALLÈLE was in the late sixties, like THE SPANISH EARTH in the late thirties, a moment of consolidation of a new representational form – a structural step. In fact, until now, Documentary never ceased to evolve from that exploration of direct techniques. And never again did it remain concentrated in its own film universe as much as it had done earlier in that decade. Once more, Joris Ivens was a decisive part of a larger mutation, and by no means only on the subject of war or political Documentary. (See Wiseman, Kramer, and all those who developed the method from that earlier platform on, starting precisely towards the end of the sixties.)

One may remember a very concrete moment of LE 17ÈME PARALLÈLE in order to understand this, and, as a matter of fact, something well beyond it – what I would call the very *system* of the entire Ivens oeuvre. I am referring to the scene where a group of Vietnamese girls come out of the subterranean quarters to wash and comb by the well. On the level of the soundtrack (the *loose* conversation about the planes and the noise of a sudden bomber coming very close to that spot), Ivens deals with that precise historical context. But on the level of what we actually *see* during the first part of the scene (before the approaching bomber compels them to lower and protect themselves, *in the continuity of the shot*), he makes us concentrate on what are, in fact, normal gestures of daily life, those insignificant human gestures of anyone, in whatever place or whatever time, to which the specific context adds such a strong relevance, beauty, and value. So, the true meaning and intensity of the scene does not lie in one or the other of those two levels but rather *on the contradiction between them*. Suddenly, out of that absurd contradiction, the film arises from a localized meaning to something of universal stature, and what we have in front of us are not only – or not anymore – the historical facts of the Vietnam War, but larger features of human nature. By then, what Ivens is really talking about is not just Vietnam, but the ability to survive in whatever circumstances, the need to act as much as the need to forget, human resistance or human endurance in general.

The work of Joris Ivens stands as a unique document of some of the historical events, struggles, contradictions, and human dreams of this century. His real subject was, however, History itself, Time, Man; and it is precisely this which enables us to appreciate the unity of that long and diverse work.

A Way of Seeing: Joris Ivens's Documentary Century

Kees Bakker

The twentieth century has been a century of movement. In all kinds of fields, this movement has been, within a relatively short period, extraordinary and extreme. There have been many wars, including two world wars and more than fifty still going on at present. The twentieth century also experienced a turbulent development in the political and technological arena. The industrialization which was set into motion in the nineteenth century resulted, some decades later, in a globalization of activities: the rise of multinationals, greater mobility of people and information, and an ever increasing technologization. Politics began to cross borders and experience polarization, putting a stamp on a large part of the twentieth century. National revolutions had serious consequences for the rest of the world.

Historians will not have an easy job in describing this century, let alone explaining and understanding it. They, and we, are still too involved in this recent history to find the distance which is needed for thorough reflection. Although there are some similarities between historiography and documentary filmmaking, the films of Joris Ivens (1898-1989) make it clear that he was not a historian, but a conscious part of the history he was filming. However, both historiography and documentary film try to give an account of events in the real world and here they face the same epistemological and hermeneutic problems regarding their relation to reality and the possibilities of describing the world. The lack of temporal distance is one of these problems, especially when it concerns recent history. As Eric Hobsbawm puts it;

> Religious or ideological confrontations, such as those which have filled this century, build barricades in the way of the historian, whose major task is not to judge but to understand even what we can least comprehend. Yet what stands in the way of understanding is not only our passionate convictions, but the historical experience that has formed them.[1]

These seem to me just the elements that, in retrospect, charactarize most of the films of Joris Ivens. His historical experience fed his passionate convictions in a way that the will to understand the world around him was replaced (some might say 'blinded') by a belief that a better world could be experienced if people followed the right way. This was the way of socialism.

In Ivens's films we see a reflection of twentieth century moods and sociopolitical issues. His documentaries have become documents. But like all historical documents, they should not be taken at face value: 'objective' documents, *if* they exist, are rare – history being what historians try to make of it. But it is certain that Ivens's films are not 'objective'. Yet this is not peculiar to Joris Ivens, but probably true of all documentarists. The first objective documentary has yet to be made – if it is at all possible – notwithstanding the pretentions of some filmmakers. Ivens explains it in an interesting way:

> I was surprised to find that many people automatically assumed that any *documentary* film would inevitably be *objective*. Perhaps the term is unsatisfactory, but for me the distinction between the words *document* and *documentary* is quite clear. Do we demand objectivity in the evidence presented at a trial? No, the only demand is that each piece of evidence be as full a subjective, truthful, honest presentation of the witness's attitude as an oath on the Bible can produce from him.[2]

The films of Joris Ivens are openly subjective, truthful, and honest presentations of his interpretations of the world. But is this not contrary to our 'image' of documentary?

Documentary as it is or as it should be?

Documentary film has very often been opposed to fiction film. This is not strange, for the first documentarists saw themselves opposed to the so-called story film in their very different relations to society and with their aims beyond mere entertainment and profit-making. They also had to gain themselves a position equal to that of the dominant fiction film. But in later and more recent thoughts on documentary film, the fiction film has seemed to be the point of reference against which the documentary is defined. Where fiction invents a possible world, documentary is about the real and natural world; where fiction has a narrative structure, documentary draws on arguments; the fiction filmmaker constructs whereas the documentarist *re*constructs.[3]

But a *re*construction is also a construction in itself, and there are many documentaries that use narrative structures (if not all, because narrative structure is not synonymous with fictional structure, if one considers narrativity as the basic characteristic of all discourses, fictional, or non-fictional). In recent years some so-called 'fake-documentaries' have proven that 'documentary structures' can be used to tell fictional stories. Illustrative in this respect is the screening of a film of Lodewijk Crijns at the International Film Festival in Rotterdam. Both his KUTZOOI (1995) and LAP ROUGE (1996) present themselves as documentaries. There was some consternation when, after the screening of the first film, a portrait of wandering school boys, the boy who had lost his arms during a dangerous game appeared with two normally functioning arms. The film appeared to be a 'fake'. Both films use all the dominant characteristics of documentary film, but both were in fact fictional.

It is clear that these kind of films challenge the limits of the genre(s). But they also make clear that what is still the most important, albeit problematic, criterion to distinguish documentary from fiction, is their relation to reality. The natural world versus a possible world. A few scholars have tried to make a distinction between documentary and fiction on the basis of Etienne Sourieau's concepts of the filmic, profilmic, and a-filmic[4]. Since the filmic is the point of reference and the a-filmic is potentially the same for both, the distinction should be made on the profilmic level. But there seems to me no ontological difference between the profilmic of a fiction film and the profilmic of the documentary, for a staged reality is ontologically as real as a non-staged reality (otherwise, how can it leave its trace on the photographic material?).

Eva Hohenberger has redefined and complemented these notions in a more pragmatic way, to include such processes as pre-production, post-production, distribution, and reception.[5] It seems that the difference between documentary and fiction is made in the moments of production and reception. It is probably in the confrontation between the film and the spectator that the distinction is finally made: a confrontation between realities, one constructed in the film, the other by the spectator. The spectator has, or tries to define, an a-filmic reality which is the touchstone for interpreting and reconstructing the profilmic as 'what has been' and what has been filmed. Referring to the use of the terms, Frank Kessler states:

> To become profilmic is a potential quality of every visible (or audible) element of the a-filmic world. The latter can never be grasped as such by the film, for it is what the discourse is about. The a-filmic, however, builds the horizon for the understanding and evaluation of what has been said in the film. It is the horizon, but not a surety for the valuation of the discourse, because the a-filmic is always but an epistemic construction on the basis of other discourses.[6]

This brings us to a more pragmatic and/or phenomenological attempt at defining, or describing, documentary. Both fiction and documentary make a 'proposition of a world'[7] which has to be interpreted by the spectator. But the audience's perception of the world is not just a perception of what is in front of them, but already mediated by their experience:

> That which is given is not only the thing, but the experience of the thing... A thing is thus not *given* in perception, it is re-assumed by the inner self, reconstituted and lived by us, as related to a world of which we carry the fundamental structures and of which it is only one of the possible concrete forms.[8]

So the spectator has his own interpretation of the world, which is for him the starting point for interpreting the world proposed by the film. He confronts this world with his 'image of the world', the 'horizon' which Kessler refers to. This leads us to Gadamer, for the next step in the understanding (and evaluation) of the world proposed, is a 'fusion of horizons'.[9] It is the experience of the spectator that builds the horizon which places the reference that has been made as a reference to *a* world, or as a reference to *the* world, depending on the match that can be made between the world of the film and the world of the spectator. The horizon proposed by the film fuses with the horizon of the spectator, who comes to understand it and is able to explain it. This horizon is also fed by the dominant modes of filmmaking: the spectator 'recognizes' a film as being a fiction film or a documentary, for they follow certain dominant strategies of presentation (e.g. fictive or assertive).[10] However, fake documentaries illustrate that this is not a guarantee.

From the perspective of the spectator, a fiction can be regarded as the experience of an invented, possible world. A documentary then, is not the world represented, but a second-hand experience of the world: the experience of an experienced world. This makes a documentary's relation to reality even more problematic: in the reception of a documentary there are already two stages of interpretation. First, the perception of the filmmaker: he has to translate his interpretation of the world into an audiovisual text. Second, the interpretation of this perception by the spectator, which doubles this process of perception and interpretation. But these are more theoretical problematics and have not prevented filmmakers from making documentaries. In practice documentarists have been conscious of these problematics, which are more or less the same for historians, but they did not stop them from making films about their world.

With this in mind, we can go back to the analogy between the documentary filmmaker and the historiographer. To be convincing the documentarist uses certain strategies to make the spectator believe that what he presents is about the real world and concerns the spectator directly. Like a historian, the documentarist makes explicit reference to the real world, for his film is about a certain aspect of reality. In this respect the two face the same problems of truth and objectivity. Siegfried Kracauer also draws a parallel between the historian and the photographer/filmmaker, seeing their tasks as follows:

> Now whatever questions he [the historian] brings to bear on some portion or aspect of historical reality, he is invariably confronted with two tasks: (1) he must establish the relevant evidence as impartially as possible; and (2) he must try to render intelligible the material thus secured. I am aware, of course, that fact-finding and exegesis are two sides of one and the same indivisible process.[11]

Establishing the relevant evidence and rendering it intelligible means that the 'raw material' has to be 'arranged' to come to a convincing interpretation of the historical reality. This concept matches Grierson's ideas on the documentary very well: '[I]n its use of the living material, there is *also* an opportunity to perform creative work.'[12]

In a continuation of this, Kracauer works out these two sides: 'One might also say that the historian follows two tendencies – the realistic tendency which prompts him to get hold of all data of interest, and the formative tendency which requires him to explain the material in hand. He is both passive and active, a recorder and a creator.'[13] Is this not exactly what the documentarist stands for? Here we can see the different approaches between which the documentary filmmaker can move and has moved during documentary film history. And if we replace 'photography' by 'documentary' in the next quotation from Kracauer, we also see what makes it difficult: 'The thing that matters in both photography and history is obviously the 'right' balance between the realistic and the formative tendencies.'[14]

The balance between these two tendencies is often determined by the intentions of the filmmaker. If he's leaning towards a more aesthetic approach in his film, the result will be a more poetic documentary, like Ivens's RAIN or LA SEINE A RENCONTRÉ PARIS. But if the intention is to inform and agitate the public, he will be more like a 'recorder'. It is interesting to note that Kracauer refers to BORINAGE to illustrate, in fact, that the discrepancy between the realistic and the formative tendency is not always that big. There seems to be a dialectic relation between those tendencies, which is discernable in each individual film: 'They [documentarists] practice self-restraint as artists to produce the effect of impersonal authenticity. Now the salient point is that their conduct is based on moral considerations.' And to continue: 'Human suffering, it appears, is conducive to detached reporting; the artist's conscience shows in artless photography. Since history is full of human suffering, similar attitudes and reflections may be at the bottom of many a fact-oriented historical account, deepening the significance of its pale objectivity.'[15] But this artless photography is in fact a formative choice to stress the realistic aspects of the events portrayed. This seems paradoxi-

cal, but I think it is something we can recognize especially in the films of
Joris Ivens, for he often combines realistic intentions with an aesthetic approach.

We have moved away from the distinctions between documentary and
fiction towards the specific problems of the documentary. These distinctions are made not only by theorists, but also by documentary filmmakers
themselves. They have been fruitful in studying documentary film, but
have also driven fiction and documentary further away from each other
than they in fact are. They are not as opposed as they are often assumed to
be, and the fictionality or non-fictionality of the documentary film may not
be the most distinctive quality about it. It seems to me that the referential
strategies the documentary uses to ascertain its direct relation with the natural world are more characteristic; strategies that can be used by fiction
films (e.g., Woody Allen's ZELIG (1983) or the above films by Lodewijk
Crijns), but that have first and foremost characterized the documentary as
we still know it; strategies thus, which are highly conventional, and which
tend toward a definition of the documentary as a pragmatic one, which in-
cludes the intentions of the maker and/or the reception by the spectator.

In most of the definitions given by the founding fathers of the documentary film, it is presented as a film form in its own right, but which covers a
broad field of film practice. Basil Wright, in 1947, summed it up: 'A documentary would be variously defined as a short film before the feature, as a
travelogue, as a description of how films are made, as an instructional film,
as an aid in teaching, as an artistic interpretation of reality and, by some the-
oreticians in the documentary field, as a film made by themselves.'[16] This
more or less corresponds to Ivens's conception of the documentary: 'On the
one hand you have the fiction or acted film, on the other hand you have the
newsreel, and between those two you have the field covered by the documentary film.'[17] This does not make it easier to define the documentary. As
Wright puts it, 'The first thing to note is that there is, in the end, little need to
define a documentary film. Those two worlds now cover such a multitude
of activities and approaches that the real underlying purpose becomes less
and less clear.'[18]

The purpose of the documentary was quite clear for Grierson and his followers: '[T]he documentary idea was not basically a film idea at all, and the
film treatment it inspired only an incidental aspect of it. The medium happened to be the most convenient and most exciting available to us. The idea
itself, on the other hand, was a new idea for public education.'[19]

If we take these ideas as leading principles to define the documentary,
then we must conclude that the documentary has existed since the early beginnings of cinematography. There are many films made between 1895 and

1922 (or 1927, since Ivens sometimes thought documentary started in that year) that can be included in the fields described by Wright and Ivens, and that match the idea of public education (does public education cover propaganda?). Why then do we usually suggest the twenties as the birth of the documentary came to life?

Joris Ivens and the Evolution of Documentary

If we do not fixate on trying to find the 'first documentary in film history', then I think there are several things to say regarding the documentary's emergence in the twenties – and I am inclined to state the late twenties – especially when we take into consideration the 'purpose' of the documentary: i.e., not only to inform, but to educate, agitate, move, and interpret reality. Robert Flaherty and Dziga Vertov came very close to these notions in a way that makes them the precursors of the documentary. Both showed a certain creativity with their material; to paraphrase Grierson's definition of the documentary as 'the creative treatment of actuality': Flaherty, with NANOOK OF THE NORTH (1922) and MOANA (1926), offered a kind of creative reinvention of a past reality, while Vertov offered a creative arrangement of actuality with his KINO EYE (1924). But the form of the creative documentary as an artistic and political response, as we still know it today, evolved in the late twenties. Paul Rotha, himself one of the early documentarists, puts it neatly:

> What we have come to call 'documentary' did not appear as a distinctive method of filmmaking at any given moment in the cinema's history. It did not suddenly become manifest as a new conception of film in any particular production. Rather has documentary evolved over a period of time for materialist reasons; partly as the result of amateur effort, partly through serving propagandist ends, partly through aestheticism.[20]

This evolution gains momentum at the height of the avant-garde movement in Europe, as well as in relation to the 'Great Depression', the economic crisis of 1929-1933, and the forthcoming political crisis of the thirties.[21] The aesthetic movement came as a reaction against Hollywood dominance, but, for many documentarists-to-be, was superseded by social and political dissatisfactions. This is especially the case with Joris Ivens:

> In the beginning, it was based very much on aesthetics, and most of us were strongly against Hollywood. We thought, especially before the sound films started, that they were emphasizing the sentimental angle of cheap stories, as well as the sex angle. We thought they were too far from reality. There was a very strong and logical reaction

'The Flying Dutchman': Joris Ivens preparing to film ZUIDERZEE, in 1929.

Hans Richter, Robert Flaherty and Joris Ivens, New York, 1940.

Old friends: Joris Ivens and Vsevolod Pudovkin, here with the Russian actor Tcherkov, in 1949.

A gathering of documentarists, Leipzig 1964: (standing, from left to right) Ivor Montague, Alberto Cavalcanti, Henri Storck, Paul Rotha, Annelie Thorndike, Bert Haanstra, Andrew Thorndike; (sitting, from left to right) Basil Wright, Joris Ivens, John Grierson, Jean Lods.

from students, artists, and young people in Europe, who thought we should go against that sort of thing and base our work on reality. So that was the beginning of the documentary film.[22]

If we can believe William Alexander, Ivens's films, which he had brought with him when he came to the United States in 1936, had a major impact on American film directors: 'No documentary films ever shown here before have been as exciting, stimulating, dynamic, tense and as briliant in execution of their purposes;' or '... far more creative than mere reporting... far more exciting and enriching than mere fiction.'[23] His films moved the spectator more than the films of other noted documentarists of that time, but it is difficult to say whether his films were a touchstone for them. Documentarists influenced each other, and the films of Joris Ivens matched the idea of the documentary that emerged in the thirties and was further shaped in the forties and fifties by the great documentary films of that time, like those of Griersons's Film Unit (e.g., NIGHT MAIL), Paré Lorentz with THE RIVER (1937), Flaherty with LOUISIANA STORY (1948), Humphrey Jennings's LISTEN TO BRITAIN (1942) and of course Ivens's own films like THE SPANISH EARTH (1937) and POWER AND THE LAND (1941). But Joris Ivens played an important role in this forming and shaping; more in the thirties and forties than in the fifties, when he became more of a skillful artist than an innovator.

In fact, since the fifties Joris Ivens's contribution to the documentary was less as a creator of new forms of expression, but he remained very important in other ways. With the arrival of new techniques and technology such as the lightweight 16mm cameras with synchronous sound, Ivens was no longer a forerunner, but he still made remarkable films through skillful and professional use of these techniques and technological advances (which were sometimes neglected by other directors). But it is also due to his important collaboration with Marceline Loridan. Initially, Ivens showed some reticence toward these new techniques that were presented by Direct Cinema and Cinéma Vérité:

> [W]e should remain alert to the fact that with the possibility of quick observation and increased mobility comes the danger of remaining on the surface of truth, of skimming reality instead of penetrating it, of showing it without any force, daring or creative power. We need to be aware of the dangers that might make us lose, along the road, the truth we had first set out to express. It is important at the outset to look intensely for the truth in order to express it through an elaborate documentation-process and an intelligent analysis – because real truth is often hidden.[24]

Marceline Loridan and Joris Ivens show this awareness in LE 17ÈME PARALLÈLLLE (1968), which reveals a powerful photography and a skillful combination of direct sound and synchronized sound. In this way they introduced a more conscious use of the new techniques that had become so popular and easy to handle, but which, at the same time, endangered the profession. On the other hand, these new techniques were cheaper and more readily available to more people. This influenced the documentaries of the sixties, and a movement in which Joris Ivens set an example for others (especially in France), because of all of his experience with militant cinema. This time his contribution was not as an innovator, but more as an agitator. With Chris Marker he became one of the proponents of political and militant cinema. Together with Marceline Loridan he formed collectives to make cinematographic statements about such themes as Vietnam (LE CIEL, LA TERRE (1965), LE 17ÈME PARALLÈLE and with, among others, Chris Marker LOIN DU VIETNAM, 1967) and Laos (LE PEUPLE ET SES FUSILS, 1970).

Combining fictive with factual elements in his last film UNE HISTOIRE DE VENT (1988), Joris Ivens, together with Marceline Loridan, contributed once more, but for the last time to the documentary form. Chris Marker had already developed this kind of personal filmmaking, especially in SANS SOLEIL (1984). But UNE HISTOIRE DE VENT extrapolates this in extremis, creating not only a reflection of Ivens's own life and work but on the history of changes in the twentieth century, as well as reflecting on the documentary, truth and the boundaries of the genre.

Joris Ivens's Twentieth Century

Ivens's 'passionate convictions' and 'historical experience' were incorporated into his films only a few films after THE BRIDGE, which together with RAIN represent his avant-garde debut as a filmmaker. In 1929 he made POOR DRENTHE, his first socially-engaged film with Leo van Lakerveld (a Communist Party member), which was probably (for the film is considered lost) a good illustration of Kracauer's statement that human suffering is conducive to detached reporting:[25] 'Unemployment is everywhere. But also those who work have to live in hovels made of sod, pieces of wood, crates, and cardboard boxes. The living and sleeping quarters: a cramped den for ten to twelve people. Lack of the basic nutrition; lameness and tuberculosis. The misery suffered was beyond comprehension.'[26] But was the evolution of Ivens into an engaged, socialist, and revolutionary filmmaker a logical one? It is certainly not his formal education that led him to becoming a filmmaker.

As the second son of the Catholic family of Kees Ivens and Dora Muskens, Joris Ivens enjoyed a protected but liberal education. The Ivenses were a progressive family. Ivens's interest and trade both in Nijmegen and at home was photography. The latest technical developments in the field of film and photography were found in the CAPI shop (CAPI being Kees Ivens's initials: Cornelis Adrianus Peter Ivens), such as the cinematograph. It is therefore not surprising that son Joris (then still called George) came into contact with the film medium at an early age. At thirteen he had already made his first film, WIGWAM (DE WIGWAM), a story about Indians in which the entire Ivens family participated. But for the time being Joris was not thinking of a career as a filmmaker. There was a job in store for him in his father's prospering photo business, and for this purpose he followed the necessary training: economics at the Commercial College in Rotterdam and photo-technology in Berlin, as well as some apprenticeships with Ica, Zeiss, and Erneman.

In Berlin, Joris Ivens met Germaine Krull and came into contact with the experimental film community as well as the left-wing revolutionary movements. In the twenties Berlin was the cultural and political Mecca for the left-wing avant-garde. Germaine Krull got Joris Ivens involved in it, if only so that Ivens could be affected by socialist ideas rather than by his friends' anarchist ideas. In the cinemas they saw German expressionist films and the avant-garde experiments of Walter Ruttmann. Joris Ivens took both these cultural and political experiences with him to the Netherlands where he first worked as head of the technical department and later as managing director of the CAPI branch in Amsterdam.

So far, little had pointed towards Joris Ivens becoming a filmmaker. True, in the twenties he had already made some short family films, but in a family of a photographic materials supplier, where all the equipment was available, this is not surprising. This all changed in 1927, when a movement came into being in Amsterdam to promote art films. In May of that year the Film League was established. Joris Ivens was to play an important role in the League as its technical leader, inviting guests and bringing in films. That same year he began his first film experiments. Upon meeting Walter Ruttmann and seeing his film BERLIN: SYMPHONY OF A GREAT CITY (BERLIN, DIE SYMPHONIE DER GROSSSTADT) Ivens was stimulated to make more serious film plans. Seeing Ruttmann work with an old, inadequate camera and hardly any filmmaking skills, Joris Ivens must have thought, 'I can do that too.'

Although his political ideas evolved at a similar time as his aspirations for filmmaking, Joris Ivens did not combine these developments from the start. In early 1928, Ivens began shooting THE BRIDGE. For him this film was mostly a study in movement, composition, and film language. After its first showing, the film was received with much acclaim and was soon marked as

Still from SONG OF HEROES.

an avant-garde masterpiece. Joris Ivens began spending less and less time on his work for the CAPI enterprise and more and more time filming. Certainly after RAIN his reputation as a filmmaker was established. He received an assignment from the General Netherlands Construction Workers' Union to make a film on the occasion of the tenth anniversary of the union. After finishing POOR DRENTHE, his WE ARE BUILDING became the first documentary by Joris Ivens revealing his involvement with the workers, even though it still focused on their work and not so much on their way of life.

With PHILIPS RADIO, the first Dutch sound film, changes are already noticeable. Ivens was commissioned to make this film after a trip to the Soviet Union: 'We know you just returned from the Reds,' the publicity manager of Philips said. '[W]e have discussed that journey a lot and... Indeed, they are communists, but they make superb films and we thought that when Pudovkin and others invited you to show your films, that you must be worth your weight in gold.'[27] Ivens also wanted to focus on the workers themselves, but Philips did not allow him to film outside the factories to 'disturb the private lifes of the personnel.' PHILIPS RADIO (1931) became one of Ivens's masterpieces, and was baptised SYMPHONIE INDUSTRIELLE by the French. Here, social critique, if evident at all, was very subliminal. But his fascination for industrial progress was very much in evidence, as it already was in THE BRIDGE and in ZUIDERZEE.

Directly after the Philips film Joris Ivens got the chance to combine this fascination for industrial progress with his passionate conviction, his socialist and communist sympathies. His first trip to the Soviet Union let to his being asked to make a film there. With SONG OF HEROES (PESN O GEROJACH, also referred to as KOMOSOMOL; 1932) he was able to represent his political beliefs in the socialist utopia. Cooperating with, among others, Hanns Eisler, who produced the soundtrack of the film, he made a film about the building up of the socialist Soviet state using as his subject the construction of the blast furnace town of Magnitogorsk by the Komsomol youth. 'It was exactly what I was looking for: young people and steel.'[28] The film sparkles with enthusiastic propaganda for the cause of socialism.

In the evolution of the documentary, Paul Rotha distinguishes four traditions: the naturalist (romantic) tradition of which Flaherty is the most illustrative exponent, the realist (continental) tradition, the news reel tradition (Vertov), and the propagandist tradition (Eisenstein, Pudovkin, Grierson).[29] On the basis of Ivens's first films, Rotha placed him in the 'Realist (Continental) Tradition', which springs from the avant-garde with such major works as Cavalcanti's RIEN QUE LES HEURES (1926) and Ruttmann's BERLIN. According to Rotha, Flaherty's idyllic, romantic films are of 'secondary interest', because there are 'larger and more urgent problems in the world',[30] and Vertov's work falls only into a 'broad interpretation of documentary.'[31] Viewing the attention Rotha is gave to the other two traditions (that is, at least, to the films that fall into these categories), the realist and the propagandist, he probably estimates the films in these traditions as falling into a more narrow definition of documentary. They do better represent what Rotha considered the task of the documentary as he states in the subtitle of his book: 'The use of the film medium to interpret creatively and in social terms the life of the people as it exists in reality.' The films of the British documentary film movement, like DRIFTERS (1929), INDUSTRIAL BRITAIN (1933), COAL FACE (1935), NIGHT MAIL (1936), match this notion perfectly, which is not strange since Rotha was himself a part of this movement. But all the films of Joris Ivens, his later films included, also represent this notion.

This is very evident in Ivens's first real social documentary that he made with Henri Storck in 1934: BORINAGE (MISÈRE AU BORINAGE), about the miners strike and the abominable lifestyle forced upon the workers in the Borinage. His social and political engagement reappears that same year in his ZUIDERZEE. Together with a new reel, the stirring music of Hanns Eisler, and the title NEW EARTH, it offered an explicitly social and political message. Joris Ivens became, with his many films made in the short period be-

After filming THE 400 MILLION, Joris Ivens gave his camera to Chinese filmmakers. Here it is used to film Mao Ze Dung (left) in Yenan, 1945. The camera can still be found in the Bejing Film Museum.

tween 1927 and 1934, not only one of the major exponents of Rotha's realist tradition, but also one of the major figures of the documentary movement in general. First inspired by such avant-gardists as Ruttmann, Clair, and Dulac, he himself became an inspiration for other documentary filmmakers. This became even more evident with his next film.

After another stay in the Soviet Union, Joris Ivens in 1936 left for the United States where, after the outbreak of the Spanish Civil War, Contemporary Historians, Inc. was established to enable him to produce what was later to become THE SPANISH EARTH (1937). Recorded on the republican front in Spain, this film is still regarded as one of Ivens's most important works, characterized by powerful photography and editing, sober commentary by Ernest Hemingway, and a clear prejudice against Franco's fascism. This point of view was one of the strong points of this and other films, but also what he was most criticized for.

> I was often asked, why had we not gone to the other side, too, to make an *objective* film? My only answer was that a documentary filmmaker has to have an opinion on such vital issues as fascism or anti-fascism – he *has* to have feelings about these issues,

if his work is to have any dramatic, emotional, or artistic value... If anyone wanted that objectivity of 'both sides of the question', he would have to show two films, THE SPANISH EARTH and a film by a fascist filmmaker, if he could find one.[32]

THE SPANISH EARTH is also a good example of the dialectics between the realist and the formative tendencies that Kracauer had isolated: the film is a truly realistic account of the events on the republican front, but Ivens uses his cinematographic skills to shape this realistic account into an aesthetically very strong, and therefore even more convincing film. Kracauer recognized the interrelationship between the tendencies he placed in opposition - the realist and the formative - and we can regard Ivens's work as the best illustration of this dialectic put into practice. It's a practice we can define as his style, for we can discern it in many of his films, not only in his political films such as LE 17ÈME PARALLÈLE, but also in his poetic films such as ...A VALPARAISO.

A year after THE SPANISH EARTH, Ivens made another anti-fascist film, this time about the Sino-Japanese War, THE 400 MILLION, again supported by the music of Hanns Eisler. Joris Ivens also made a number of films in the United States itself, which alternate his anti-fascist convictions (OUR RUSSIAN FRONT, 1941; ACTION STATIONS!, 1943) with his fascination for industrial progress (POWER AND THE LAND, 1941, a New Deal propaganda film for rural electrification; 1941, and OIL FOR ALADINN'S LAMP 1941, a publicity film for Shell oil company).

Within a relatively short period, Joris Ivens had already put a clear mark on the documentary film and since then has generally been regarded as one of the innovators of this 'movement', as the documentarists called it. But Ivens was also formed by his 'historical experience'; besides having co-developed the language of the documentary, he continued to devote even more passion to his ideals and the progress of society while working against the repression of the weaker groups in society. He was not always thanked for it and in part it helped define the future of his career and his special relation with the Netherlands.

Despite his communist sympathies, Joris Ivens was appointed by the Dutch government to film the liberation of Indonesia as Film Commissioner of the Dutch East Indies. However, in Ivens's opinion, the Netherlands was not concerned with the liberation of Indonesia, but with its recolonization. He considered this a breach of contract on the part of the Dutch; he resigned from his position, and went on to make a filmic pamphlet against the Dutch policy in Indonesia. INDONESIA CALLING (1946) led to a break with the Netherlands; Ivens was considered *persona non grata* by the Dutch government, which for a short period of time took his passport away and offered him only three-monthly renewals. After 1936, he did not officially return to the

Netherlands until 1964. He was offered a film assignment in the Netherlands (not by the government; ROTTERDAM EUROPORT was completed in 1966), but only officially rehabilitated in 1985, when the Minister of Culture, Eelco Brinkman, referring to INDONESIA CALLING, stated that 'history proved you were more correct than your adversaries at that time.' This banishment never hampered his film work, however. He had in the meantime been filming in various corners of the world and was now given an assignment from Eastern Europe to film the reconstruction of the Eastern Bloc Nations after World War II, which were on the brink of a socialist future (THE FIRST YEARS, 1949). Ivens found himself now in the center of a place where his ideals for a better society could be realized.

Joris Ivens continued to work in East Germany until 1957, producing one of the largest productions in the history of the documentary cinema there (SONG OF THE RIVERS (DAS LIED DER STRÖME), 1954). But the films from this period were predominantly characterized as communist propaganda, and less by his artistic qualities. This was not only because Ivens was still following his passionate convictions which partly drowned out his artistic aspirations, but also because he was given less freedom to develop them. He never made explicit his reactions to the events in Budapest, in 1956, but it is likely that the first cracks in his Stalinist beliefs began to appear. This was perhaps enhanced by Khrushchev's process of de-Stalinization. To his brother he wrote: 'What a long, worrisome, and sometimes horrible period is necessary in order to arive at a better world, to change a socio-economic system and to achieve better, more humane relations among people.'[33] He never commented on the events in Prague, in 1968, but his drift toward China and Maoism probably illustrates his dissilusionment with the failing Soviet ideology in which he so believed, and which had determined the historical experience that formed this belief.

In 1957, Joris Ivens returned to Western Europe and made the poetic LA SEINE A RENCONTRÉ PARIS in France. This, however, did not mean he was turning away from his political and social engagement, because his subsequent films are characterized by the alternation between poetry and politics, between realist and formative tendencies, and between free productions and commissioned films. In 1958 he worked as a lecturer at the Beijing Film Academy, and produced both the poetic BEFORE SPRING and the political cinematographic pamphlet 600 MILLION WITH YOU. After his film commisioned by the Italian state oil company ENI (ITALY IS NOT A POOR COUNTRY (L'ITALIA NON È UN PAESE POVERO), 1960), once again revealing his fascination with technology, he made both the pro-revolutionary AN ARMED PEOPLE (PUEBLO ARMADO), as well as the more poetic travel letter to Charles Chaplin, TRAVEL NOTEBOOK (CARNET DE VIAJE), in Cuba (both 1961).

Here he was also asked to teach at the ICAIC (Instituto Cubano del Arte e Industria Cinematograficos), and this invitation, in 1960, also offered Ivens a chance to dive into that fresh revolutionary climate, which promised to be the new hope for the socialist world, especially the Latin American world. It closely mirrored Ivens's ideas and hopes for socialist progress. Cuba also became the temporary center of heightened Cold War tensions with the Cuban Missile Crisis.

Communism was in favor in parts of Asia and in Latin America. The Latin American aspect was especially threatening to the United States. Two ideological blocs faced off:

> Like the USSR, the USA was a power representing an ideology, which most Americans sincerely believed to be the model for the world. Unlike the USSR, the USA was a democracy. Unfortunately, it must be said that the second of these was probably the more dangerous. The Soviet government, though it also demonized its global antagonist, did not have to bother winning votes in Congress, or in presidential and congressional elections while the US government did. For both their purposes an apocalyptic anti-communism was a useful, and therefore tempting tool, even for politicians who were not sincerely convinced of their own rhetoric.[34]

Ivens had already experienced this anti-communism during his stay in the United States in the forties, when he was listed and frequently followed by the FBI.

The possibility of socialist democracies in Latin America, as well as increased American aggression in Asia, led Ivens to follow his convictions and translate them into film. In 1964 he made an election film, LE TRAIN DE LA VICTOIRE, for Salvador Allende to stress the hopeful possibilities of a candidate like Allende. Allende did not win the election, however. In the second half of the sixties he made several militant films in Asia to demonstrate against the politics of the United States, and to support the people of Vietnam (LE CIEL, LA TERRE; LE 17ÈME PARALLÈLE; LOIN DU VIETNAM) and Laos (LE PEUPLE ET SES FUSILS).

For LE 17ÈME PARALLÈLE, Ivens for the first time used a 16mm synchronous sound camera, which was Marceline Loridan's choice, because she already had some experience with it. By this time he was no longer an innovator, instead he used techniques already explored by others while giving them new dimensions through a very specific use. The sixties are furthermore characterized by the two extremes in his work as a filmmaker, for before the abovementioned, starkly militant films, Ivens also made two special film poems: ...A VALPARAISO (1963) and POUR LE MISTRAL, 1965).

His close collaboration with Marceline Loridan dates from le 17ÈME PARALLÈLE, and continued until his death in 1989. This cooperation resulted, among other things, in the monumental twelve-hour series COM-MENT YUKONG DEPLACA LES MONTAGNES (1976), about the influence of the Cultural Revolution on everyday life in China. Ivens had already witnessed the promise of the Great Leap Forward in 1958 (but left China before the great famine of the following two years). In filming the Cultural Revolution, and especially its influence on the daily life of the Chinese people, Joris Ivens and Marceline Loridan wanted to provide answers to the questions of ignorant Westerners by letting the Chinese speak: 'It is important that in this film it is not me or Marceline who does the talking but that 80 percent of it is by the Chinese people.'[35] Sudden changes in China's political situation made it almost impossible to film additional material, but further changes in 1976 – Mao's death and a more moderate political course – made the longing for information on China even greater. YUKONG supplied much of the information longed for, although the films were soon outdated.

Towards the end of his life Joris Ivens distanced himself from the 'passionate convictions' that had largely determined his films. His historical experience and the many changes in the world of this century moved him to a more reflexive position. He was almost nineteen during the October Revolution of 1917 and died just before the final collapse of communism. 'I used to say that communism was not a faith, but there is much of it in it. I stuck too long with my notions of utopias, until I finally saw that History does not develop according to a book that was written at the beginning of this century.'[36]

Ivens criss-crossed a world that underwent many radical changes during his long life. He witnessed and filmed many of those changes, giving his interpretation of reality, and always offering hopes for a better world, a socialist world. His films reflect the beauty and the atrocities of this world, the poetry and the sorrow. They are also examples of documentary film history, of which he was one of its main proponents and characters. And, although subjective, his films have become useful documents.

Together, Joris Ivens and Marceline Loridan made many films, including their last, poetic, contemplative, and sometimes ironic testimonial UNE HISTOIRE DE VENT (1988). A highly-praised pinnacle of his imposing oeuvre, which emerged from five continents and bore witness to much of the turbulent twentieth century.

Perspectives

The Song of Movement

Joris Ivens's First Films and the Cycle of the Avant-garde

André Stufkens

Train journey...

Glittering parallels
Together leading to the end
The wheels sing the song of movement
We all are travelling
To the old?
To the new!
We crawl on the back of the world
(The near turns away from us
The distance moves with it)

Joris Ivens, 14 January 1925, Nijmegen[1]

'You know the speed of your own car, the delight of the speed of movement and you do not want that speed in your own inner life?' Joris Ivens, surprised and worried, asked of Miep Balgerie Guérin, his big love of the early twenties.[2] For Ivens, movement was not only a sign of the times, the speed and bustle of the new metropolises such as Paris and Berlin, the new mechanical and electric inventions; it was also a state of mind and a mental attitude. He continued his letter with 'There should not be any half-heartedness. I would have liked to shout: be complete – strike... You should run, we might be horses.' Renewal and rebellion, not as a purpose as such, but as a way to acquire new points of view and to escape the everyday routine of one's parents and the entire pre-World War I generation.

The avant-garde credo in those years was movement. It called for the adaptation of the imagination and design in the arts to these new states of mind of movement – mechanical, emotional, and psychological. It can also be found in a rare poem written by Joris Ivens. Poetically speaking it is not a good one, for in 1925 he had not yet, as he wrote himself, found 'the right form of expression' to convert all impressions. Yet the central ideas of his later film oeuvre are present: trains, the sensation of travelling and discovering a new world, which at the same time is a spiritual movement and a purposeful search for renewal. And again and again a utopian view travelled with him on the horizon when the transitory impressions had disappeared. It is a personal credo to which he was faithful all his life, from his first film to his last.

In his first successful avant-garde film, THE BRIDGE (1928), a train stops hissing, for the obstacle of an open bridge stops it. During his first years of filming, his father, who forced him into the role of succeeding him in the family business, was also an obstacle, although Ivens himself had long ago chosen to lead the life of an artist and Bohemian. In the film, the bridge closes, the obstacle is conquered, and the train moves on, triumphantly belching out steam. Mechanical and cinematographic movement united with a new pictorial language in a visual rhythm. After it receives the green light, the train disappears to a modern cinematic end with an abstract image of a shining black square in a white background – a horizon that resembles Malevitch's *black square* and is inspired by the abstract pictures of Eggeling and Ruttmann. It was also a symbol of liberty for Ivens himself, for with THE BRIDGE, he made the definitive step towards a film career and away from his father's business.

With a short animated part in SONG OF HEROES (1932), in which futuristic little trains give a flashing idea of a possible, future industrial complex, Ivens expands the connection between cinematographic and technical movement and social and political renewal. It is the young workers however, who should realize this future. There is a similar connection in LE TRAIN DE LA VICTOIRE (1964), where using the straight railroad tracks stretched across the length of Chile, the election train of presidential nominee Allende brings social improvement closer.

In his last film UNE HISTOIRE DE VENT (1988), Joris Ivens and Marceline Loridan find a simple image to symbolize Ivens's surviving major surgery and a near-death experience. He is back among the people, shuffles among playing children with kites, and a few moments later a train moves solemnly through the Chinese landscape. He can travel again, the ultimate sign of life for a man whose suitcases were always packed. The train takes him to a grotto with the magical mask of the wind, which literally and figuratively gives him the key to his oeuvre; the wind is a physical and metaphysical power of continuous change.

Trains and also airplanes, present in THE BRIDGE as well as in UNE HISTOIRE DE VENT, have made the world an accessible unity in a geographical sense. In the same way, the medium of film has made the world an accessible unity in a cultural sense, a world of global cultural migration, whereas the social contrasts and conflicts have never been so extreme and ruthless. That contrast is also essential to his films.

Surprisingly enough, the credo returns once more in one of his last film images, sixty years after THE BRIDGE. When, in China, as the result of bureaucratic short-sightedness, he is forbidden to film the ceramic army of Xian, he puts together an army himself. Playing himself, as director, the old man takes up a position at the head of his troops. The image refers to the military origin of the notion 'avant-garde', which originally was described in French military manuals as a strategy to provoke skirmishes with storm troops and confuse the enemy before the main force could be activated. What nobody had thought possible occurs, the old man puts the masses – having been fossils for twenty-one centuries – into motion with a simple tap of his stick. With a masterly trick, Ivens shows what he as an avant-garde artist had always been about: movement and renewal. It is ultimately the artist's imagination that puts into motion these traditions and firmly rooted ideas, and succeeds in what seems impossible. It makes the cycle of the avant-garde come full circle. It refers both to his early years, in which he sees the documentary film as a cinematic stormtrooper and on into the next century, because without imagination the chance for survival is small. 'The 21st century will be a century of esprit or it will not be,' he prophesied on his ninetieth birthday in Nijmegen.[3]

This chapter describes the way in which Ivens ended up in the avant-garde, the role he played in it, and what the notion of avant-garde meant to him.

The Introduction to the Avant-garde

'How does one become a filmmaker in a country without a film industry?' L.J. Jordaan, the doyen of Dutch film criticism, wondered in his first monograph about Ivens, published in 1931.[4] Even then, four years after his first film, Jordaan called him the most important filmmaker. It surprised him that Ivens's pioneering work met with such immediate success, appreciation, and support. That immediate success, both in Dutch and in international avant-garde circles, points to craftsmanship – especially in editing and photography – with an appealing sobriety and sincerity, which, remarkably enough, had been present from the beginning. Moreover, it came at the right time: 'It knew how to answer many people's vague questions with a positive, concrete answer.'[5]

What was the origin of this apparently sudden craftsmanship, and how is it possible that Ivens became the leader of the film avant-garde? When, in the following sections, Ivens's background – his family, education, and training – is dealt with, we will see that in the fields of technology, politics, and the arts, Ivens had always been in a prominent position, and that his avant-garde role, in which all these aspects come together, only needed the right moment to flourish.

The Technical Vanguard

Joris Ivens grew up in a family in which observing was important, observing with the naked eye and with the camera lens. In around 1867 his grandfather, Wilhelm Ivens, came to Nijmegen from Germany to settle there as a photographer. He made such high quality photographs that he became the house photographer of the Jurgens family (founders of the multinational Unilever) and court photographer of the queen dowager.[6] Three generations of Ivenses studied at the vocational college for photography in Berlin – at the time, the most thorough and modern academy for chemistry and optics: his grandfather, his father, and Joris Ivens. Joris's father, Kees Ivens, convinced of the possibility of making money through the sale of photographic articles, started the first chain of photo shops in the Netherlands, called CAPI. In his field, Kees Ivens was always the first to consider new developments, to demonstrate them and explain them to the public. He wrote about the 'kinetoscope', also called the last forerunner of cinema, and was present at the first performances of the Lumière brothers' 'living photography' in Amsterdam. 'The invention of the bioscopy, the 'living picture', will later attain the same importance for mankind as, for example, the invention of the printing press,'[7] he prophesied. In 1902, he demonstrated the Roentgen X-rays, and in 1907 Lumières' method of colour photography. As early as 1910 he suggested the establishment of a Netherlands Photo Museum.

His son showed a similar dedication to technical innovations when he constructed a life-size model of the first airplane that flew over his birthplace, Nijmegen, in 1911. He was also curious about a Pathé camera on a tripod that he had seen in a shop. After he had seen some films about cowboys and Indians at the fair and in cinemas, Joris Ivens wrote a film script in 1912, which was recorded with a mix of seriousness and hilarity around the family country house. FLAMING ARROW or THE WIGWAM (1912) contains a stylistic device recorded by chance that he was to use repeatedly later: interrupting the rhythm by a pile-up, a minor accident, or some other discomfort. Because Ivens saw that it was the interruption of the rhythm that made the viewer aware of the visual rhythm. His father took a picture of him at the camera with the caption: 'Kinoman', a prophecy he himself could not then foresee.

The CAPI shop sold film projectors made by Ernemann and others, and son Joris accompanied Kees to product demonstrations. During the war years he examined the films that reported on the various fronts in France and Belgium, and he followed the course of the battle on a map. He was right on top of it, because his father showed the press agency photographs in shop window. 'The firm Ivens&Co, active as always, today had in its shop in the Van Berchenstraat some six photographs of the destruction caused by airplanes throwing bombs on Zierikzee.[8] The day after, the family cinema showed the film made by Albert Frères of the same 'fury of war'. 'The film is excellently made and although the notion 'artistic enjoyment' is suppressed when seeing this film, you do not refrain from watching.'[9] The notion of documentary was still unknown, but in the Great War we see large-scale propaganda films for the first time, with pictures that at least pretended to show reality. Later, Joris Ivens was to be present with his camera at five different war fronts, and, as a pioneer and co-founder of the documentary genre, would make a stand against the idea that 'artistic enjoyment' should not be part of this valuable type of film.

After the War, in 1919, father Ivens organized a photo competition with a documentary theme on the occasion of the twenty-fifth anniversary of his business. With the theme 'The Crisis' he wanted to preserve the consequences of the war for everyday life in the Netherlands. Joris was appointed secretary of the competition committee and he endorsed the significance of recording historic moments for future generations. Those who look at the many photo albums and photographs of grandfather and father Ivens with reports on building processes and special events, cannot help but feel that documentary recording in a sober, unpolished style was 'in his blood'.[10]

Father Ivens not only wanted to make a family archive of photographs, but also of film. From 1921, Joris made a few films of family gatherings, which are not very interesting from the point of view of style. Not until 1927 do we notice striking camera work, 'a driver' from a car, with which he filmed his elder brother Wim's Lancia. In the meantime, he had sharpened his view through his long study at the vocational college and during apprenticeships at German optics factories. He worked there in the construction department of the ICA factories on the Kinamo model, a small handheld 35mm camera, with which he was to make his early films in 1927 and onwards. Back in the Netherlands he was nominated for the first lec-

Joris Ivens 'Kinoman' in front of the CAPI photo shop in Nijmegen, about 1910.

tureship in photography at the Technical College in Delft in 1927 and 1929.[11] 'My inclination as well as my study is purely technical-scientific first of all.'[12]

In artistic Amsterdam circles it became increasingly clear to him that he had the advantage, precisely because of his technical knowledge. Film – the new muse – was regarded an 'Art of the Arts', a combination of the old muses, as if it concerned a sacred or superior art form. 'For them film was a great mystery, and that mystery was created by technology. Little by little I began to explain their interest in me and what I represented. In their view I was a master of technology.'[13]

Political Vanguard

In the family's liberal business environment, politics was seen as a logical means to emancipation. In Joris Ivens's later extreme political choices three emancipation movements come together: those of German immigrants in the Netherlands, the emancipation of the Catholic community in the Netherlands, and the global labour movement.

The Ivens family belonged to the Catholic entrepreneurs who had settled in the Netherlands from Germany in the nineteenth century, and after their economic success, had entered social and political circles to improve the centuries-long fallacious position of the Dutch Catholic minority. In all their initiatives, the Ivens family was not only interested in improving the level of prosperity of the Catholic minority, but also the general lot of society. This contrasted greatly with what other influential Catholic families did.

Wilhelm Ivens was a member of the 'Humanitas' central committee, a general society for the care of wandering children of all denominations. His father was appointed chairman of 'Religion and Science', a Catholic debating club with the purpose of setting aside the Catholic diffidence among intellectual and scientific circles. Kees Ivens referred to his basic liberal principles: 'our view should remain uninhibited, thinking liberally about other people to not become fanatical in matters of religion, and knowing what we want and to be open about it. Tolerance is the first principle of community after all.'[14] In 1904, he became a town councillor for the Catholic electoral association 'Recht voor Allen' and startled the town with all kinds of initiatives that would move Nijmegen forward. The winds of change favoured him, for the town was expanding rapidly at the time. He wrote a report on the local situation and pleaded for more council interference to improve the bad state of health and the debts in the housing and industrial sectors. Technical innovation might raise the standard of living. He organized the first exhibition of electricity, the digging of the Maas-Waal canal, and the construction of industrial sites and a large bridge across the Waal river. He had fought for them for decades, and when he succeeded, he wrote: 'Only they who ever did pioneering work and have struggled for an ideal unselfishly for decades, can rightly feel, on reaching a great goal, what someone has on his mind and in his heart.'[15] His motto was 'Frapper! Frapper toujours!' and he wanted to play a historic role with his local innovations. His grandfather's and father's drive and purposeful pioneering spirit were rewarded with a royal decoration at the end of their lives. When Joris was awarded the same honour in 1989, he said that those awards should really be given at a young age, 'for then you do not have to strive after them'.

The belief in technical progress, the pursuit of a great goal and putting one's stamp on history – the main pillars of his dominant father's educational ideal – were handed over to son Joris. This is what the Germans call *Bildung* and it formed the son's career. What father Ivens initiated at a local level, Joris would record on film on a global scale. How many bridges, blast furnaces, dams, factories, and power pylons pass in review when looking at his oeuvre? Ivens's oeuvre seems a perfect illustration of what the English historian Eric Hobsbawm calls the most important revolution of the twentieth century with more far-reaching influences than temporary conflicts between 'communism' and 'capitalism' – a revolution to which both systems contributed in spite of ideological differences: the transition from a seven-thousand- to eight-thousand-year-old agrarian culture to an industrial society.[16] As Ilja Ehrenburg wrote in 1931: the victory of man over nature, which Ivens was called in to film, whether it be Dutch workers reclaiming the Zuiderzee, creating new farmland by hand; young workers who build a town with blast furnaces from scratch on the empty plain near Magnitogorsk; Ohio cooperative farmers who supply their farms with electricity; or the farmers plodding through the mud behind the buffaloes in China and Vietnam: they are all impressive portraits of people changing the face of the world with their own hands. The improbable force of collective labour is shown in Ivens's images with love and respect. 'The power of the weak,' as Anna Sehgers called it. 'This proletarian sentiment is not a matter of political views – it is a matter of inclination, of instinct, of becoming aware by his close relationship to the German proletariat. It gives his oeuvre that striking simplicity, that clarity and straightforwardness,' thus states L.J. Jordaan, referring to Ivens's films made until 1932.[17] That 'close relationship' began in his early childhood in his father's photo shop. The young Ivens had an informal relation with the craftsmen, specialists in precision engineering, optics, and chemistry, and parties were frequent. The staff members formed a harmonious family, although his father was considered to be a domineering man.

The revolution Hobsbawm speaks of, is also connected to old cultures by Ivens. In the film L'ITALIA NON È UN PAESE POVERO (1960), the commentary accompanying the pictures of classic temples in Sicily is 'that since the time of the Cyclops nothing has changed'... till gas was discovered. In THE 400 MILLION (1939) it is the age-old pictures of the four quarters of the compass, and in the Vietnam films, the old Buddhist temples, with which nineteenth century ideas of progress are connected again and again. Similarly, his father never wasted an opportunity to add his actions of technical innovation to the rich past of his home town – the oldest Dutch town with a history dating back to the Batavians and the Romans.

This rigorous revolution realized on a global scale, was shortly thereafter accompanied by more extreme, merciless violence than ever before, both in communist and in capitalist countries. And with many ideals and illusions, he wanted to realize a change in the social arena at the same time as this revolution, in which the human factor would triumph over capital. In 1921, while Ivens was studying at the Rotterdam Commercial College, he read Hegel and Marx for the first time. As chairman of the students' union, being liberal and tolerant, he protected opposition. But he must have recognized a similar, unstoppable idea of progress in Hegel and Marx that characterized his father's entrepreneurial Catholicism, when the latter wrote: 'Only a firm conviction that everything leads to one goal along undefinable roads for the people, can keep us going.' 'Together leading to the goal,' Ivens wrote in a poem as early as 1925. And then again at the end of his life he spoke about the wind as 'the big stream on which mankind goes forward, independent of minor streams, empires, fascism, and of civilisations that have fallen. A stream that I still believe moves in the direction of something better.'[18]

After the weak vibrations in the Netherlands from World War I and the Russian Revolution, Ivens was directly confronted by their tumultuous political consequences in Berlin, where he studied from 1921 to 1924, and trained in the factories. He was completely rattled by the shock of the new and at the time, wrote articles against the narrow-minded morals, money, and materialism of the generation to which his parents belonged. 'It is necessary for people to stick to ideals, for people to put the ideal above the mechanization of our society.'[19]

In the early twenties – first in Berlin and later in Amsterdam and Paris – Ivens associated with a group of artist friends, who agreed about notions of anti-bourgeois morals and the desire for innovation. He embraced vitalism, an expressionistic variant and romantic reaction to the wartime *Menschendämmerung*, with a sincere art and a 'grand and compelling life', whose undoubted leader at the time was his friend, the poet Hendrik Marsman. 'Art and life are one, undivided and undistinguished,' Marsman wrote. This attitude of social involvement is something Ivens remained loyal to all his life. It's a loyalty that can only be understood and explained in the context of the times in which it originated. It is a view that was common in various avant-garde circles at that time, such as De Stijl, of which Piet Mondrian writes: 'What is true in life, must be true in art.' The artist is given a priest-like function, after the bourgeois was finished morally and politically because it had not been able to prevent the war's battlefields. 'The ivory tower of the artist becomes a lighthouse by whose light future generations can find their bearings.'[20] Many artists portray themselves in that period with apostolic pretensions.

Arthur Lehning, anarchist friend of Ivens, also propagated the artist's utopian role in the twenties. There is even mention of Ivens investing money in a project to publish Bakunin's writings, an assignment Lehning was to devote his whole life to. Together they planned to publish an international magazine in which the artistic avant-garde could vent their opinions. When Arthur Lehning indeed published *i10*, the revue of the 'tenth international', Ivens was to remain a modest author and it was to be the contributions by Mondrian, Bloch, Moholy-Nagy and many others that would make it an authoritative journal.

At Arthur Lehning's, Ivens met the German photographer Germaine Krull with whom he started a strained affair, and whom he was to marry in 1927. She had already had a shocking, personal history. As a young student she supported Kurt Eisner's soviet-style republic in München and took pictures of him after he had been assassinated. At an early age, she had had two abortions, fled with left-wing revolutionaries to Austria via Switzerland, was caught, went to Moscow, and after she was arrested during the Third International fled back to Berlin, completely disillusioned with communism. Concerning her attraction to Ivens, she wrote: 'His eyes had a way of seeing things in a different manner... I found myself strangely attracted to him. His simple way of seeing things gave me confidence... as everything was always simple and clean with him.'[21] Her relationship with Ivens was to be the longest relationship of her life, and one based on equality and independence. Ivens was the first to introduce her to the world of the bourgeois entrepreneur. When Ivens and Krull started to live together in Amsterdam, they came into a circle of artist friends where the political contrasts were to loom large, but this did not exclude personal contact and cooperation. Although artists such as Jan Toorop, Erich Wichman, Hendrik Marsman, Pyke Koch, and J.C. Bloem drifted to the political right and were attracted to Catholicism, Mussolini, nationalism, the aristocratic order and fascism, others like Charley Toorop, Henri Pieck, Piet Zwart, Paul Schuitema, and Joris Ivens drifted toward left-wing politics, attracted by the Russian experiment; contacts remained friendly and political points of view were not in such sharp contrast as they were to become after 1929. Not until then did the economic crisis and the inevitable choice – for or against fascism – create a sharp dividing line among artistic circles. Looking back on that period, Ivens said: 'At that time I did not bother about politics and consequently thought I was apolitical in my art, whereas I did support the bourgeois ideology with this kind of unpolitical film, without being aware of it.'[22]

Artistic Vanguard

Although a true businessman, father Kees Ivens was enormously interested in the arts, and the presence of artists in the home was common. Painter and graphic artist Eugène Lücker was a family friend, and Joris discovered something of the avant-garde atmosphere when Henri Pieck exhibited in Nijmegen in 1917, with a poster on which he attacked his linen like a thing possessed. The exhibition caused a scandal because of the five nudes that were hung behind curtains in a separate cabinet. However, it did not prevent Kees Ivens from inviting him to portray his wife and two daughters in a triptych (in which Joris can be seen in the background in the garden). During these years, Henri Pieck produced advertising campaigns for the CAPI photo shop. At the same time he was captivated by communism after he had visited the Hungarian soviet-style republic as an illustrator. Contact between Henri Pieck and Joris Ivens became closer when, at the end of the twenties, the two worked in left-wing cultural circles in Amsterdam and Pieck made posters for the communist party and the films of Eisenstein and other Russians.

Kees Ivens was in touch with various artists. In 1911, he organized the first exhibition in Nijmegen of Jan Toorop, who was welcomed as the great leader of modern Catholic art. In 1916, he hired such famous Dutch artists as Richard Roland Holst, Joseph Mendes da Costa, and Lion Cachet to decorate his Amsterdam photo shop. They had already made a name for themselves, but their *Jugendstil* style was outdated by then.

Joris Ivens got in touch with new art trends in Berlin, where he expressed his interest in art by collecting art books and reproductions of expressionists such as Franz Marc, Dadaists such as Georg Grosz, but also Van Gogh, among others. As a filmmaker, he would later regularly make use of art books as study material. With artist friends, he went to the theatre and cinema, and end the night in the Romanische Café. 'I spent all my time on the new – people's and artists' new passions, because they break with materialisation and decay [...] and sympathize with everything enabling me to conquer old rotten ideas and opinions better.'[23] Artistic callings beckoned, and together with the expressionist poet Hendrik Marsman, he went to see expressionist films by Wiene, Dupont, and others. The use of the subjective camera in VARIÉTÉ (1925) inspired Marsman to write an ecstatic poem:

'I myself made, swinging from trapeze to trapeze, the dizzy salto mortale, and in the indivisible eternity of that second, somewhere flashed – Beneath me? Above me? On which side and in which universe? – beyond the last meteoric shower...'[24] He dedicated it to Joris Ivens, who already had that strong urge to visit the dark projection rooms. It was Germaine Krull who took him deeper into the arts, politics, and life. At first, she took photographs that resembled symbolic *tableaux vivants*, but after using the Ikarette camera – a manageable camera and the photographic opposite of the Kinamo camera – her photographs acquired an artless snapshot character. Her photographs were sometimes out of focus, unaesthetic, and without any message, and her subjects differed strongly from those of other female photographers at that time. After Ivens and Krull had settled in Amsterdam in 1925, she went to the harbours. The large metal structures of the cranes filled her with dread, pervaded as she was with the fear of death after her tragic early life experiences – a fear that she could conquer by controlling the cranes with her camera. By means of the bird's eye view perspective, the diagonal directions, and the subject of the metal structures, Krull achieved a new sort of objectivity, and in doing so, became one of the leaders of the new photography. 'Seeing things with an unspoiled, neutral and unprejudiced eye,' she wrote, and her friend Walter Benjamin wrote about her: 'When photography disassociates itself like people such as Sander, Germaine Krull and Blossfeldt have done, then it becomes creative.'[25] Not prejudiced and unrestrained by dogma or illusion, she photographed tramps, drunks in cafés, markets, political subjects, landscapes, nudes, and portraits. A wide range of subjects indoors and outdoors that we – apart from the nudes – see again in the choice of subject of Ivens's first films. At the beginning of 1927, Ivens was still torn between his Bohemian life among artists and his position as vice-president and successor to his father in the family business. His inability to enter into a conflict and fight it out, made it impossible for him to escape his father's pressure. He was waiting for a chance to be able to realize his still-dormant artistic ambitions.

The Film League and the First Film Year

The night from 13 to 14 May 1927 was the historic moment Ivens had been waiting for. A number of Amsterdam University students, Menno ter Braak, Henrik Scholte, and Dick Binnendijk decided to found a union to enable them to show avant-garde films. Ivens's younger brother Hans introduced him to this group that still wanted to show Vsevold Pudovkin's forbidden film THE MOTHER (1925). With his technical knowledge and CAPI equipment, Ivens projected the incendiary film twice before an enthusiastic audience. It was preceded by an announcement by Henrik Scholte that the Film League was going to be founded. Two days later, Scholte wrote in his well-known Film League manifesto: 'it is about film. Once every one hundred times we see the film. For the rest we see the cinema. The masses, the commercial regime, America, kitsch. At this stage film and cinema are each other's natural enemies. Our belief in the pure, autonomous film, film as art and as future is useless if we do not take matters into our own hands.'

The last element was taken literally by Joris Ivens, for the next day, 16 May, Henrik Scholte writes in his diary: '... of greater artistic interest is the fact that Joris Ivens wants to execute plans to make a film based on a script by Hendrik Marsman... will this first truly artistic Dutch film experiment come to something?' Ivens made some screen tests of Scholte's present girl-friend, the actress Charlotte Köhler.[26] It did not evolve much beyond a wish, however, and the question remains which Marsman script Ivens had chosen to be filmed. In Marsman's 1923 prose poem 'The Flying Dutchman', published in 1927, there is no leading lady, but it might have offered a reason to film a friendly beauty.

In the following months, Ivens appears to have used scripts by various prose writers and friendly artists. Jef Last noted in the margin of an exercise book with the script of DIE STRASZE: 'partly filmed by G. Ivens'.[27] And of Erich Wichman (anarchist and fascist Bohemian artist, always after a riot and anticipating new trends) a script was found with the title THE SICK TOWN (1927), in which Joris Ivens has the leading part. [28] As with earlier Ivens films this somewhat surrealist script was set in an Amsterdam café. Some shots were taken and seen by viewers shortly after the founding of the Film League. The script prescribes remarkable automatic camera work and forms of pictorial rhyme: a hand turning the wheel of a barrel organ moves across the hand of the cameraman, Ivens. And Wichman and Ivens filming each other... One script version opens with a '*Vorspiel im Himmel*', 'A grey rainy sky. Rainsqualls. A quagmire, in which the rain is pelting down. A rainy street. People in rubber coats, their collars turned up, hurrying.'[29] Even some animation by an Amsterdam artist was to be filmed. Ivens's start was therefore not defined by the documentary film, but by the feature film. First and foremost, he was an avant-garde filmmaker who wanted to renew the film language of both fiction and non-fiction film.

From that first year – 16 May 1927 until the first performance of THE BRIDGE on 5 May 1928 – remarkably little data and film remains. It was not even clear to his closest friends what he was up to. It seems that in that first year Ivens spent his time training himself, paying attention to every aspect

Drawing by L.J. Jordaan for the first issue of the Filmliga magazine.

of film. He worked feverishly 'in the dark' and 'silently', both practically and theoretically. As technical advisor to the Film League he had the opportunity to see and analyse films. In this way, two-hundred kilometers of film must have gone through the CAPI projectors. 'Spelling' these films taught him the grammar, the laws, and the essence of cinematography. In the first issue of the Film League journal, he described, using the same words as Moholy-Nagy, that the essence of film technology is: 'the duration of the successive images; the direction and speed of movement in one image compared with its direction and speed in the next and finally the black and white division of the image compared with that division in the next image'. The visual and psychological laws of film resembled those of mathematics, which appealed to him especially in the absolute film, but 'making a film will not appear to be a summation. But what then?' he wondered. He tried to find answers in actual praxis.

From his house on the Damrak, across from the Stock Exchange, he went into town with Germaine Krull. Relations between Ivens and Krull were tense, because even as early as April 1927, at the time of their wedding – necessary for Krull to get a Dutch passport and a residence permit in Paris – the two had had affairs. It did not prevent them from collaborating intensely during visits to Paris and Amsterdam. They crossed the Damrak to the Zeedijk and Oude Zijdsvoorburgwal areas. Krull took pictures of the warehouses and the harbours, and Ivens filmed glimmering water, dangling legs, a street under construction, and a pumping station in what he appropriately called: KINOSKETCHBOOK (1927). A café in Mother Heyens' boardinghouse became the site for new film experiments. Its everyday characters appeared attractive to painter Charley Toorop who painted two paintings there, for Germaine Krull photographed the same characters, and to Ivens. Charley Toorop's painting *The Boardinghouse* illustrates the influence of film editing techniques. She painted the characters' heads without them being interrelated, and the three-dimensional effect and proportions do not correspond with the laws of perspective. She was to use this type of editing often in her work. Ivens called the ZEEDIJK FILM STUDY (1927), a sequence he spontaneously recorded and did not edit, his first film.

As technical advisor, Ivens regularly went abroad to view films that might be suitable for a Film League program and to meet and invite cinematographers to Amsterdam. In the first years he met, among others, Vsevolod Pudovkin, Dziga Vertov, Sergej Eisenstein, Germaine Dulac, and Alberto Cavalvanti. In the second week of October 1927, Ivens visited Hans Richter and Walter Ruttmann in Berlin and Dresden. Walter Ruttmann's studios really impressed him because Ruttmann's abstract films such as OPUS II, III, and IV appeared to be the result of simple craftsmanship with simple scale models, an old camera, and little technical skill. I can do that too,[30] Ivens must have thought. Ruttmann's film BERLIN, DIE SYMPHONIE DER GROSS-STADT (1927) especially influenced Ivens, because for the first time the laws of the *cinema pur*, were combined with documentary shots of a town; welded together to a dramatic unity without the sentimental connotation of a feature film.

Back in the Netherlands, Ivens received a scenario for a film about rain from Mannus Franken in his letterbox. A week later, Ivens answered the letter: 'Rain scenario, I am walking in the rain here, and look, look. These days I will film some of it.'[31] Some months later, the first takes were shown to a few people, but the subject appeared to be too poetic and nature appeared too capricious for an artist to manage. Moreover, he noticed a dilemma that was especially true for a documentary filmmaker, that no moment repeats itself. To capture unsuspecting reality at the most powerful moment is the real art. Playing it again is not done. Although he immediately found a subject to render town life in a new, objective way, it would take two years before he completed RAIN (1929), called 'Film of Moods' in the newspapers. Ivens was looking actively for an easier subject. At first, he found it in Paris, where, upon visiting Germaine Krull, he made a film about the movement of the bustling city traffic. Krull's photographs and Ivens's stills corresponded again: the pictures of Parisian roofs taken from Krull's flat, the Op-

Joris Ivens sketching and explaining his experiments with the subjective camera.

era, black Humble taxis and Bugattis. In ÉTUDES DES MOUVEMENTS (1928) the camera catches a car driving from left to right past the Tuileries until the camera spots a car approaching from the other side of the frame and follows it in opposite direction. Thus, the camera wanders about and becomes a study of movement.

In December 1927, Ivens and Hans van Meerten investigated the possibilities of I-FILM (1928), with which they attempted to make the viewer's eye not merely watch the picture statically from his chair, but to let him take part in the action itself. In the pub, the camera looks through a glass of beer, which, after having been emptied, reveals a picture of the café. Still more curious was the camera that Ivens designed to imitate the movements of the human eye. On a four-wheel cart, a tripod was mounted that imitated the turning, lowering and raising of the human eye. This subjective camera did not have the required effect however, because when Ivens saw the shots they suggested two possibilities: 'I am walking down the Kalverstraat, drunk, and: the Kalverstraat looks inundated and I am rowing to the Dam.'[32] The two experiments showed that Ivens was looking for new ways to confirm the authenticity of perception by using subjective camera work.

THE BRIDGE

After the experiments, the screen tests and the first attempts to film RAIN, Ivens began searching for a bigger issue to practice his newly acquired knowledge on. Railroad architect Sybold van Ravensteyn, like the architects Rietveld, Berlage, J.J. Oud and Van Eesteren, active in the Film League, directed him to the Railway bridge called 'De Hef' in Rotterdam. This steel colossus, which opened in October 1927, was a wonder of technology that, with its mechanical movements and horizontal and vertical lines, linked ideally with what Ivens considered the essence of film: movement in rhythm and direction.

The subject may also have been inspired by his father's efforts on behalf of the new Traffic Bridge in Nijmegen, to which Parliament had given the green light in 1927. Kees Ivens had stimulated the construction and discussed the latest technical developments with engineers for decades. Ultimately, it became a bridge with a steel arc and as his father stated proudly, the largest span in Europe at that time. In this way, the subject was useful for his father and highly suitable to convince his father that he could work on the film during working hours.

When Joris Ivens began filming in 1928, he felt anything but an artist and filmmaker. This becomes clear from a series of lectures he gave entitled 'Amateur cinematography and its possibilities',[33] both before and after completing THE BRIDGE. In the lectures, he paints a picture of the origin of the film medium, which, he explains 'at first became a curious side show and then attached itself to fairs.' Amateur cinematography will enrich professional cinematography, just as amateur photography has done for professional photography, he argued. His father had expressed the latter idea a year before, in an article on the history of photography. 'Amateur photographers felt freer about their subjects and unhindered by the public's bad taste. The photographer Atget could take pictures of empty street scenes in Paris around 1900 in which no human is present. Photography initially imitated painting without considering its own technical possibilities and laws but eventually it developed out of its cosmetic stage to become a historic document, thanks to amateur photography.' Joris Ivens drew a parallel with the genesis of film, which at first imitated, in this case, the theatre. But amateur cinematography could change that: 'The possibility to produce an art work using moving photography with its own laws, just as painting, photography and music, is now realized after years of 'Stage reproduction'. People began to learn to 'spell' after having 'read' for a long time.'

Photomontage made by S. van Ravesteyn: Joris Ivens filming THE BRIDGE, 1928.

This amateur approach which Ivens considered as essential to raising the art of film to a higher level, was strengthened by the Kinamo camera, a camera that was not generally used by professional filmmakers. Ivens knew this camera very well from his vocational training, and with it in hand became a pioneer of working 'from the shoulder'. Germaine Krull, who went to Rotterdam to take pictures of the bridge, used a similar unacademic approach with a comparable still camera, the Ikarette. The choice of subject itself may also have been inspired by her, because she had already taken pictures of metal structures before, in Amsterdam and in many other ports. In Paris, she befriended Robert Delaunay, who had produced a series of paintings of the Eiffel Tower, the same tower that had served as a model for the pictures Krull had published in her successful photo album *Métal* (1927). Ivens discovered the essence of film because Ivens used this Kinamo with only one lens of dubious quality, without a tripod, and without resorting to tricks and devices or being distracted by direction. 'Nobody remembers the laws of the seventh form of art, but these laws must be discovered. He who 'kinoes' should realize that movement is the governing element of film. In this way film returns to its essence. The laws of every form of art are based on their own character, the demands of the material and the technique from which they spring.'[34] The Film League theorists, foremost among them Menno ter Braak, also pursued this idea. Writing on the aesthetics of cinematography, he stated: 'the unity of the film opus is the unity of visual rhythm; in other words the outer rhythm of the pictures has to symbolize an inner rhythm, a dramatic continuum. Every mistake in composition damages the dramatic development; every picture does not only involve technical, but also psychological connections with the foregoing and the following.'[35] It is exactly this psychology of perception that Joris Ivens attempted to fathom while editing THE BRIDGE. He was assisted through conversations he had with a psychologist and a card organizational system, so that he did not lose sight of the internal connections.

In contrast to the many diagonals in the photographs Krull took from the bridge, Ivens limited himself to the horizontals and verticals. A comparison with Piet Mondrian, who also tried to balance the counterparts of contrasting movements and directions, is evident. At first, Ivens wanted to strengthen the abstract impact of the film by refusing to give the film a title, and with the final shot of the black square in a white field he approached the 'absolute films' of Eggeling and Ruttmann. Ivens was interested in abstract art, because in the same year, he designed a completely abstract and avant-garde stage set for light projections made of cones and prisms. With these intended light effects, a parallel can be drawn with the Licht-Raum Modulator of Moholy-Nagy dating from the same time. When shooting THE BRIDGE he worked on scientific films for Leiden University as well. The takes with the microcamera resulted in an almost abstract world of forms.

During the shooting and editing of THE BRIDGE Ivens was well aware that he was doing something special. It resulted in him losing the artless attitude of the amateur: 'At the moment of editing I found myself in such a state of creative tension that I dared not even use the scissors to cut the film. I worked every evening with the zeal and enthusiasm of a pioneer who has just discovered virgin territory.'[36]

He started THE BRIDGE as an amateur, but after the applause and hurrahs died down on the 5 May 1928 opening night, he was already being considered a pioneer and figurehead of Dutch film art. 'THE BRIDGE was made amidst a movement which rebelled against the murderous ennui of large-scale commercialized industry. It became both *cri-de-guerre* and credo. Furthermore it was made at his own risk and was not influenced by any assignment – in other words, it has the characteristics of the greatest economic limitations and at the same time that of total artistic freedom.'[37] Ivens's most aesthetic and formalistic film, in which hardly a human being is seen and containing no psychology and no message, was highly esteemed by those in Film League circles. That appreciation was to decline considerably after Ivens began to take his political stands.

With THE BRIDGE Ivens concluded a year of praxis, and although success was welcome, he still could not say goodbye to the photo shop. 'It is really awful that those CAPI peanuts have such a hold on me. All kinds of areas that I love and interest me lie ahead of me and I cannot reach them. Must change!'[38] The following years he moulded the business to his own will and he learned to take advantage of both situations. He admired the independence of the avant-garde filmmakers abroad and their lack of limitations imposed by commercial clients. In the first years, Ivens could only build up an independent career thanks to the CAPI photo shop. He used the cameras, projectors, and projection space, but also called in staff members - at first, for distribution, correspondence and translations, but gradually for film work as well. In this manner, his personal secretary Helen van Dongen developed into a talented editor and managed to make a good career out of it. She was to contribute greatly to many of Ivens's best films and ultimately assisted Flaherty in LOUISIANA STORY (1948). Joop Huisken rose to become one of the founders of the documentary film in the first decades of GDR cinema. When his father, on the advice of Joris Ivens's elder brother Wim, established a Film Organisation (F.O.) within CAPI, the father was saddened by how his son had distanced himself from the business. According to his father, Joris Ivens stole about one million Dutch guilders (in current terms) from CAPI for the film projects through his creative internal bookkeeping.

In his diaries, father Kees called him a deserter and blamed him for the bankrupcy of CAPI in the thirties. Feelings of guilt about this situation may have given rise to Joris Ivens using the name of CAPI (his father's initials) for his and Marceline Loridan's production company some decades later in the sixties. In this way, he became a worthy successor to the family business, only in a different form.

Everything is Present in the Seeds

The first year of practical self-education was followed by the recognition of his pioneering work in the years that followed, and he worked like a madman on what would become the basis on which he built his oeuvre. When later he described the documentary as a new form of art – as a new terrain of expression which spans the wide gap between feature films and newsreels – it became clear that, even according to his own definition, Ivens cannot only be judged in the genre of the documentary. Even in his early years he was already using every form and type of filmmaking including feature films and newsreel. Within four years, between 1927 and 1931, he had worked on: science films (microfilms at the university); home-movies (family films 'T ZONHUIS, THEA'S MAJORITY); feature films (trial runs of THE FLYING DUTCHMAN, trial runs of THE STREET, trial runs of THE SICK TOWN, BREAKERS, DONOGOO TONKA, some of which were somewhat surrealistic); newsreels (*VVVC-Journals*); social reportage (POOR DRENTHE); company films (PHILIPS RADIO, CREOSOTE) and many other commissioned films (WE ARE BUILDING and ZUIDERZEE); even animated films (THE SICK TOWN, diagrams); aesthetic form and movement studies (ÉTUDES DES MOUVEMENTS, THE BRIDGE); poetic nature recordings (RAIN, BREAKERS); subjective film (I-FILM); political pamphlets (BREAKING AND BUILDING); film sketches (KINOSKETCHBOOK); and abstract art (lighting and stage sets, final shot of THE BRIDGE, final shot of PHILIPS RADIO, many close-ups in the early films). He also worked on contrasting aspects: microshots as well as panoramic shots from an airplane; expressionist influences derived from vitalism as well as the abstract 'absolute' film; the feature film as well as the newsreel; assignments for a trade union or for umbrella organizations of the communist party, as well as assignments for large capitalist enterprises; subjective imagery as well as scientific imagery; formal aesthetics as well as social reportage; animation as well as news pictures. He boasted a many-sided and inspired start like nobody else. In essence, all of the elements of his later work were present at the start. As Ivens himself put it, 'in a way I am glad that I have been able to lay the foundation of technical and creative perfection before starting to work on other, more important subjects.'[39]

He who sees Ivens only as the maker of THE BRIDGE and RAIN in those initial years, and ignores the many screen tests and lost films, might overlook the fact that all the ingredients of his later films, were tested in those first years. He continued to pursue and attempted to make feature films, alternating anti-aesthetic films with political stands with more poetic films. In this way, his development of various film techniques, remained a cycle in which themes of nature, labour, politics, and culture define his films.

All of the early, more or less contrasting, elements of the first years were combined in KOMSOMOL for the first time. In this film, there are both news images and reconstructions utilizing elements of feature films, nature films as well as social reportage, animated movies, individuals as well as groups, and panoramic shots from airplanes as well as close-ups. Although KOMSOMOL does not satisfactorily integrate these elements mainly because of some troublesome clients in Moscow, its method provided a theoretic justification of his film work. Contrasts play an important role in the film: old farm labour in the country versus industrial labour in Magnitogorsk; work in the Soviet Union versus unemployment in the West, youth versus the older generation; the individual versus the collective. He worked without actors, with the workers themselves taking the leading roles. He writes: 'The method I will use in the Komsomol film is based on dialectical materialism, developed from my experience with old methods and from close personal contact with members of the Komsomol.'[40] This dialectical method is in keeping with Eisenstein's theory and shows significant parallels with the work of Brecht and Eisler of the same period.

Avant-garde and Illusions

From the moment in 1927 that Ivens joined the avant-garde, he had high expectations. According to Ivens, the documentary could only manage to secure a place of its own by reacting against the feature film. In 1927, the Film League supporters associated the cinema with 'the masses, the commercial regime, America, kitsch' and marked film and cinema as each other's natural enemies. Ivens concluded that: 'The film industry generally expresses itself in bad films that court the public by adapting to the public's bad taste.'[41] By going back to its essence, by letting the camera and the film be first, instead of real or enacted nature – film could emerge as a full-blown art form. 'Not an internal series of ideas, but the objects themselves require their sequence in time and place.'[42] Under the principle 'No false illusions,' Ivens pleaded for cinematographic sincerity which was the only way to change the cinematographic language in a revolutionary way. 'In today's state of affairs the documentary is the best means to find ways to true film. You do not run the risk of being reduced to theatre or music hall, in short, to everything that is not film.'[43] And 'The documentary is the only means left to the avant-garde filmmaker for taking a stand against the film industry.'[44] The avant-garde became, Ivens wrote, 'a cinematic stormtrooper' that fights deflation of art by the film industry. For Ivens, the documentary as art therefore became a normative notion. 'A documentary filmmaker cannot tell lies, cannot violate truth. The matter does not allow treason: the documentary demands the filmmaker's personality, for the artist's personality alone distinguishes him from vulgar topicality, from simple photography.'[45] This strong morality has always remained part of Ivens's work: maintaining one's independence, apart from commerce and the illusion that images of documentary films would be more 'real' and 'true' than those of feature films.

Later he came to the conclusion that the feature film and the documentary are much less opposed to each other, and have adopted elements from each other and influenced each other on several levels. In fact, the making of a feature film haunted him all his life. In various films, fictional elements do occur to a certain extent. While with UNE HISTOIRE DE VENT he and Marceline Loridan achieved an innovative integration of fiction and non-fiction. More documentarists, who referred to themselves as a 'movement', even a militant movement, fostered illusions about the normative character of the documentary. As late as 1974, Basil Wright wrote 'in a certain way the documentary is something essentially to do with democracy. It implies the right to disagree and the right to criticize. It cannot therefore flourish in a totalitarian atmosphere.'[46] Ivens's oeuvre is both confirmation and denial of this thesis. Two Dutch documentary filmmakers of a later generation have stated their views about the normative element of the documentary. Jan Vrijman once said in connection with Ivens: 'An artist must lie, must not tell the truth.' And Johan van der Keuken stressed that the only democracy a filmmaker has is the democracy of the images: 'The democracy in the film is the only concrete democracy an artist can realize because he has the final say in it. A democracy of forms, a democracy of material, but also of fiction which must ultimately remain symbolic, because it cannot have any actual power in the real world. This powerlessness was unacceptable for Ivens for the greater part of his life. One might say that he was committed to the degree in which he risked the democracy of forms (and even postponed it occasionally) to choose from the powers in the real world.'[47] The most striking thing is the shameless postponement in SONG OF THE RIVERS.

The Film League fell apart shortly after its founding in the early thirties. The students that started the movement found employment and lost interest. Cinemas screened other avant-garde films, while the advent of sound shifted the attention from formalism to representing reality while the the the Great Depression of 1929, and the rise of fascism forced artists to make political choices. Just when the avant-garde thought it had realized its goals in the early thirties and had absorbed its criticism of the cinema and the film industry, Ivens broadened his criticism. This signaled a break in his career. By going on two journeys to Russia and meeting Eisenstein, Vertov, and Pudovkin, his formalistic criticism was given political weight: 'The film in capitalist countries is a means for the ruling class to keep the masses from joining the class struggle and tempting them with false bourgeois values...'[48] The political avant-garde and the artistic avant-garde joined forces for a short time. There was the conviction that the documentary was better film which coincided with the notion that socialism was the better social system and the artist has to realize a prophetic social role and start social reform. 'The documentary must not only be a motive for emotion, a literary ecstasy for beauty, but it should also stimulate slumbering activities, evoke reactions.'[49] He criticized his earlier period as a filmmaker: 'I imagined that I was fighting the bourgeois ideology using a formal revolutionary work of art, but because of my apolitical attitude everything remained parochial.'[50] A work of art might gain a revolutionary content by 'transformation'. 'Transformation', 'redefining functioning', and 'process of remoulding' were notions that occurred very often to Ivens, Eisler, and Brecht. Their developments showed striking parallels. Not only were they born in 1898 into middle class families. They were also in Berlin when revolution and counter-revolution were the order of the day. Their artistic and political growth also nearly mirrored one another: they began as avant-garde formalists which they came to criticize as bourgeois after their association with the labour movement. Brecht: 'dialectical dramaturgy began mainly in the sign of formal experiments, not with respect to content. It operated without psychology, without individual... everything was kept, with respect to content, within the atmosphere of the middle class.'[51] The relation to Ivens's self-criticism is evident. Theoretically the views of Brecht, Eisler, and Ivens closely paralleled that of two famous essays by Walter Benjamin: 'The author as producer' (1934) and 'The work of art in the period of technical reproducibility' (1936), in which he used these three artists as examples for his ideas especially in response to Lukacs's Marxist theory of art (notion of realism) and Lenin's theory of reflection.

Ivens's political choices were also inspired by the impossibility of disassociating himself from his father and the photo shop. He had never learned to fight personal conflicts, so that he could only escape his father's dominance by aligning himself radically to an ideology and then by removing himself geographically, first to the Soviet Union and then to America. In spite of this, he kept promising his father that he would return to strengthen the business, and there was continued mention of him as vice-president in the annual reports.[52] The inability to negotiate personal conflicts was apparently compensated for by violent conflicts on the screen, in which Ivens distanced himself from the bourgeois. The French historian Francois Furet called opposing the bourgeois middle class against itself 'self hate' and one of the most important causes of totalitarian seduction.[53] But in other respects, Ivens's choice of communism was determined by his education. Communism concerns the axiom that it carries out unstoppable historical patterns in a seemingly scientific way, and that everybody plays an inevitable historic role in it. Living to the full, taking risks, pioneering, pursuing an ideal, taking initiatives, participating in change with new technologies and social welfare for everybody, making your mark on history, these are elements that Ivens recognized from his home life and he found his own historical role in this movement. As the universal heir of the French revolution, Marxism seemed to be a farther-reaching and higher form of democracy than the familiar liberalism because it included the workers on the basis of human equality, emancipation, and progress.

In the fundamental struggle against the 'false illusions' of the feature film, Ivens himself had begun to harbour a number of persistent illusions: the documentary as superior form of film, communism as a better social system, and the artist as the better visionary. It took him nearly his whole life to rid himself of these illusions. When by the end of the eighties he had succeeded in doing so, thanks to Marceline Loridan and a long therapeutic depression, the courageous unmasking immediately resulted in a masterpiece, in which imagination, religion, and mythology play a role once more. He returned to his paternal 'faith and science', embracing metaphysics and at the same time coming to the conclusion that communism was more a faith than he had ever thought before. He was inspired by Georges Méliès, as a result he entered a no man's land between the documentary and the feature film – an innovation with which he embraced the avantgarde again with a film that drew lines to the next century. A circular course in the avant-garde, although Ivens prefered to view it as a spiral. 'I see it more as a spiral. It does not return, but goes on to a higher level. Now I can make that film, because I have undergone the other disciplines.'[54] He became the Bohemian once more who, as before, detested materialism and consumer society, as is shown in the scenes from the film studio where a couple of newlyweds are filmed in a mildly critical way amidst all kinds of consumer goods. Ecological awareness also has a voice in the film, deforestation, dams, blast furnaces, power pylons, and factories that he once used as examples of progress become example of destruction. Meanwhile, only a ridiculous ventilator which is supposed to create high winds across a huge desert remains. This rudimentary example of technical progress which has to compete with the violence of nature, the magic of an old woman, and the imagination of the old filmmaker, has no chance. The theme is no longer man's victory over nature, but harmony between man and nature. The old woman and the old man can laugh again and the wind resumes its role as innovator, filter, changer, as it continues to sing the song of movement. The old man rises and is absorbed into the wind.

Convinced and at peace.

High-tech Avant-garde: PHILIPS RADIO

Karel Dibbets

PHILIPS RADIO, made in 1931, tries to combine two seemingly incompatible worlds: the film avant-garde of the 1920s and sound.[1] The film takes a crucial place in Joris Ivens's filmography as well as in film history for this reason. The avant-garde at that time was extremely dubious about the new sound engineering. Ivens and his composer, Lou Lichtveld, wanted to break with the fixation on the art of the silent film without giving up the ideals associated with it. They began an experiment in moving pictures and sounds when Philips Radio Company commissioned Ivens to make a film.[2] This article will first of all deal with the style and structure of PHILIPS RADIO and then with the origin and reception of the film. Emphasis is put on the dimension of sound and in particular on the sound effects to which the makers paid so much attention.

PHILIPS RADIO is an industrial film about the production of radios at the Philips Company in Eindhoven, the Netherlands. The film consists of three parts, each of which is split up into two sections. In this way, six 'chapters' have been made, with an introduction and an epilogue.[3] The first two chapters show the production of radio tubes: first, the receiver lamps, then the transmitter lamps. The third, short chapter is a visualization of radio communication. The fourth part shows the work at the office and in the laboratory. The final two chapters deal with the assemblage of radios and loudspeakers respectively. Intertitles inform the viewers which part of the production process is going to be shown. The complete film is thirty-six minutes long, the chapter about the production of receiver lamps is the longest (twelve minutes), and the one about radio communication the shortest (thirty-five seconds).[4]

In the hands of Joris Ivens, photography and editing were tools that produce a remarkable style. They were not, however, intended to gratify the connoisseur. His visual style had been geared to the most prominent function of the film: public relations. The film had to mould and promote the Philips image. Philips wanted the 'internationalization of name and product', Ivens said during filming.[5] 'The public must be fascinated by what they see, they must be impressed by the company, so that they get the impression: The product of a company organized like this must be good.' Ivens explicitly used the term 'montage of concepts' in this context; 'the intention is

Publicity poster made by Anneke van der Feer, 1931.

to work with notions such as: order, precision, scientific preparation, product control, etc., [...] In his subconscious the viewer must remember these notions together with the producer's name, so that when three days later the radio is mentioned, he specifically remembers these basic notions and that particular name brand.'

This power to surprise and convince through visual means became highly developed in film and photography during the twenties. The New Photography at that time applied itself to showing something ordinary in an extraordinary way. In the Netherlands, the typographer Piet Zwart has become the best-known exponent of this movement.[6] At the same time, the editing by Russian filmmakers such as Eisenstein and Vertov changed into an instrument for ideological propaganda: film should not portray reality, but reconstruct it by 'intellectual montage', according to Eisenstein. Both schools meet in Ivens's work.

The New Photography and the 'montage of concepts' have both been used in PHILIPS RADIO to give shape to Philips as a 'high-tech' company. This term did not exist at the time, but was unmistakably what Philips had in mind. 'High-tech' means notions such as advanced technology, innovation, scientific progress, automation, mass production, internationalization, etc. That was the world preferred by Philips, and PHILIPS RADIO is what radiates these notions. For this reason, the film was called 'Symphonie Industrielle' in France.

Philips also knew how to make combinations of concepts. By choosing Ivens for this assignment (and Hans Richter for another film) a connection was suggested between Philips and the avant-garde – a surplus value that would have fitted public relations policy. Althoug Joris Ivens was known as a talented filmmaker with modernist ideas at the time, his oeuvre was still small. Apart from some short experimental films such as THE BRIDGE (1928) and RAIN (1929, in co-operation with Mannus Franken) he had been assigned to make a long film, WE ARE BUILDING (1929). The avant-garde film movement had enthusiastically received these films both at home and abroad and was extremely keen on high-tech; the filmmakers and photographers of the New Objectivity were particularly inspired by it. Philips was probably trying to join this development. The question, however, is whether the image of Philips as a high-tech company was favourable to Philips itself. The answer to this question was to have a surprise in store at the first performance.

***

The sound track of PHILIPS RADIO is just as remarkable as the picture. Its four dimensions – music, sound effects, spoken word, and silence – will be discussed briefly. It is important to point out that sound was added to the film after completing the editing of the images. Originally PHILIPS RADIO was to be a silent film. Halfway through production it was decided to make it a sound film. This method put a stamp on the final result.

First, the music[7] was composed by Lou Lichtveld. The compositions were written for a small orchestra consisting of, in order of prominence: piano, violin, cello, and clarinet also trumpet, saxophone, and a little drum. These heterogeneous instruments produced a transparent sound. The music reveals the influences of modern composers such as Honegger, Milhaud and Poulenc. It has a strictly fragmentary character: not only do other sounds interrupt the music regularly, the music also interrupts itself repeatedly, especially during the intertitles. Moreover, the melodies are rarely allowed to finish. The result is that expectations are raised, but seldom realized. The music remains serene and clinical, and never becomes romantic. This clear, sober character fits the subject of the film: the cool realism of a high-tech company.

The music has a supporting role in PHILIPS RADIO. The composition and orchestration are such that the attention remains on the images undistracted by the music. 'The influence of the music on the action of the film is practically nothing. [...] In this film Ivens's camera plays the role of prima donna in an Italian opera. The orchestra is not allowed to fulfill an essential task anywhere.'[8] The modern combinations of sounds may sometimes attract attention, yet it is the camera that comes first, and the music that follows. The nuances exist in the music. First, it nestles in the pictures, then it moves away in a contrapuntal direction in order to be absorbed by the image all the more. 'The delicate, delicate sheen of thin glass tubes dissolves into the pearly discount arpeggios of a piano – the rapid, short jerks of a card puncher are supported by cello pizzicati.'[9] Only once does the music get a chance to contribute on its own behalf, and that happens at the end.

The end of the film is a true finale, an audio-visual coda. For once, the music appears as an independent entity and it overwhelmes the pictures. In the previous sections the film revealed how a radio is assembled. By the end of the film the radio is finished and now it must show that it also produces sound. This takes place in a 'loudspeaker ballet': big round loudspeakers revolve around in the image to the rhythm of the music – a stretto – ringing from their cones. Here the images dance to the music. This example of 'absolute filming' concludes PHILIPS RADIO.

Sound effects have been modestly applied in the film. They are completely absent in several scenes. For that reason, they are all the more noticeable when they are used. Then they are all too clearly present, especially when the music is silent: little moving carts rattle and squeak, a machine stamps and hisses, a generator buzzes, a shop floor is full of sounds of grinding, while glass blowers breathe heavily. The sounds create a suggestive image that complements the image, even if they are sometimes unsynchronized.

Yet the sound effects are not only present to illustrate the image, they are also present to be listened to. The film presents an intense fascination with everyday sounds which are just as important as the music. This use of everyday sounds creates a terra incognita or tabula rasa phenomenon: sound on film is being discovered, tested, and listened to for the first time. Just as with the New Photography, PHILIPS RADIO aims to make the most ordinary noises sound striking. They sound clear, articulate, and nearby; their timbre and rhythm beg for attention. In PHILIPS RADIO the sounds of the factory have been selected and arranged to give a characteristic tone. In this sense, the sound effects track contributes to the 'symphonie industrielle'.

Words are almost totally absent from PHILIPS RADIO. The film does not open with the usual titles and credits. Instead a voice says: 'And now the Philips film.' For the rest of the film the spoken word is as rare as words in a cemetary. In the lift, someone raises two fingers and says clearly, 'two'. That is the only moment where a word is synchronized with the sound and the image. In two other scenes a voice is audible, but the words only illustrate the action. For example letters are signed in various languages, while a voice drones: 'Very truly yours. *Agréez messieurs. Hoogachtend. Hochachtungsvoll.*'[10] Words like that do not need to be translated for an international audience. Remarkably the voices are always accompanied by music; this combination of words and music had only seldom occurred before 1931. Lichtveld treated both types of sound as equal elements in his composition.

The sparse use of spoken word contrasts sharply with the use of written words in the intertitles. The voices are part of the space before the camera while the titles are not; the intertitles seem to come from an external source and interrupt the action, a clear inheritance from silent films. Had the film been made a few years later, they would probably have been replaced by a voice-over.

Silence also had to be re-invented. The rare outdoor shots of the factory site are mostly shown without sound, as if they were filmed from inside through a glass window. Violent sound effects and music, alternated by sudden moments of silence, accompany the tests in the laboratory. Silence is to be synchronized and diegetic again and again – that is, the silence is part of the action shown. PHILIPS RADIO uses silence as a building block for the construction of the acoustic image, just as it uses the voices and sounds.

The film presupposes a great curiosity on the part of the spectator and a love of sound that is as passionate as Lou Lichtveld's. Lichtveld has treated music, voice, sound effects, and silence as completely equal elements. This does not make for easy listening. The soundtrack of the film is fragmentary and complex; the music has a heterogeneous character and the various sounds often seem to be autonomous. The visual argument of PHILIPS RA-DIO does not reveal a solid structure either. The loose structure of the sound-track has a special background, however. The film is an exploratory voyage in the world of sound. The factory sounds are performed and tested one by one. In this way, an ode to factory sounds is born. This fascination with sound is graphically represented in the scene that shows the testing of the loudspeakers. Here, listening is shown in images and made the subject of the film. A technician, hand to ear, checks the loudspeakers. He turns the volume knob, switches off the music, coughs the silence away, switches on the music again, etc. This is the method of the film: it is an exercise in listening.

***

How did the soundtrack of *Philips Radio* come into being? Originally PHILIPS RADIO was to be a silent film, so it was decided at a rather late stage, after most of the film had already been shot, to add sound. Two different contracts were drawn up, one for the image track and one for the soundtrack. The first contract was signed on 1 September 1930, when Ivens started shooting the film.[11] For the sound a new contract was drawn up in February of 1931, but was not signed until May.[12]

At first, Ivens had second thoughts about using sound, as so many of his colleagues had at the time. 'I am not an absolute supporter of the sound film,' he confessed, 'but with this radio film sound is laid on thick.'[13] Under no circumstances did he want to make a 'spoken film'. He did realize the value of sound montage. In December of 1930, Ivens began thinking of the possibility of sound for the first time. While filming in the Philips glassworks, he draws a reporter's attention to the wealth of sound in this space: 'Beautiful material for a sound film. Inhuman symphonies of tinkling glass combined in all kinds of strange, chime-like chords. Low, dull, explosive sounds like faraway timpanic beats, and in between, the voice of a warehouse manager, who bellows through the loudspeaker.'[14] These sounds were later heard in PHILIPS RADIO as well.

However, Ivens had had no experience with a sound film. He was assisted by the younger Lou Lichtveld, composer and 'musical advisor' of the Film League, more well known by his pseudonym, Albert Helman. Lichtveld did not have any experience with the production of sound films either, but at least he had thought about it. He was one of few – if not the only one – in the Netherlands who had a definite interest in the relation between pictures and sound. Lichtveld travelled to Berlin in January of 1931 on Ivens's advice. There, he visited not only the new sound film studios, but he also spoke with artists such as Oskar Fischinger, a filmmaker who made abstract films with music. Lichtveld stayed with his brother-in-law, Karel Mengelberg, a composer and conductor, who had just been appointed 'Tonmeister' at German radio and who was equally fascinated by the world of everyday sounds.[15]

While Lou Lichtveld was familiarizing himself with Berlin, Joris Ivens travelled to Paris to study sound engineering in the French Tobis studios. Ivens had a long talk with René Clair, at that time the most important director at Tobis. René Clair enjoyed great respect among critical film circles. In 1930 he made his first sound film, SOUS LES TOITS DE PARIS, and was now working on the next, LE MILLION (1931). 'We discussed his new film and mine at great length,' Ivens told after his return, 'and it did me a lot of good.'[16]

The sound of PHILIPS RADIO was recorded in the French studios of Films Sonores Tobis in Epinay, where René Clair was also working, from 18 to 22 May 1931. No recordings were made on location at Philips in the Netherlands. 'The big trouble was recording factory sounds,' Lichtveld wrote. 'Originally we thought we should record them in the factory at the same time as the film, but it was impossible to isolate the sounds we needed. We had been given every facility by Philips, but we were not allowed to interrupt anything to get the sound of one particular machine.'[17] Consequently, the factory sounds had to be imitated in the studio afterwards.

Dutch journalists arrived in Epinay and every large newspaper and many weeklies sent reporters to France to report on this story as if an event of national importance were at stake. This pre-publicity, satisfying to both client and filmmaker, also had its drawbacks: all attention was exclusively focused on the sound aspect of the film. This focus of the soundtrack did not at all match its subordinate function in the film. In this way, the impression arose that the creators were rather pretentious. It would be hard to compete with the overblown expectations later. The colourful reports in the press also contained a wealth of information about the post-synchronization process of PHILIPS RADIO.

The sound studio had been outfitted like a small film room. The walls were covered with heavy acoustic curtains. The orchestra, which had taken its place in the room, was conducted by Armand Bernard, a Frenchman who had written the music for René Clair's LE MILLION. A motley collection of tools lay ready to reconstruct the factory sounds, objects not usually found in a studio, such as a grinding stone, an oxygen cylinder, a saw, a windlass, roller skates and chains. Gramophone records were also made available containing the sounds of, for instance, a noisy shop floor. For the human voice, Eddie Startz who was well known for his command of languages and imitations was kept ready. Anyone familiar with the technique of post-synchronization as it was generally performed in the thirties and later, will recognize parallels with the way people worked on PHILIPS RADIO.

The German 'Tonmeister' Kretsch was in charge of technology. The French sound mixer Leblond, who followed the projection of the film through a large window, assisted him. 'In every studio [...] the central point is the cubicle of the mixer who controls the army of microphones spread out in the room and who checks the sounds the loudspeakers emit during the patient rehearsals [...].'[18] The mixer could only adjust the sound of the various microphones, for at that time, technology had not progressed to the point where different soundtracks made earlier could be mixed down to one sound. All sounds – music, voices, effects – had to be recorded at the same time and on one optical soundtrack.

Every recording was preceded by the necessary preparations. The film had been cut into parts of a few minutes and every part had to be recorded individually. First it was decided how the factory noises had to sound. Then the orchestra went through the music once more without watching the film, then with the film. The mixer, in the meantime, could adjust the various microphones from his cubicle. Finally, the recording took place. When the conductor, the 'noisemaker' or the speaker had not paid enough attention to the synchronization, the recording had to be started over again. The final result was only heard on the following day, after the film with the optical soundtrack had been developed in a laboratory. If the result was disappointing, they had to decide whether to do the recording over again:

> Most of the time and effort was required for the combined recordings, those in which the factory noises and the music had to sound simultaneous and complementary. The conductor looks somewhat nervous with all those hissing and stamping disturbers of the peace behind him, and he gazes a little reproachfully at the composer who approves of his music being disturbed by such a cacophony of noises. But the director smiles resignedly. The effect is better than expected, as the mixer knows how to balance the two types of accompaniment excellently.[19]

Lou Lichtveld paid a lot of attention to the reconstruction of the factory noises. At Philips, he had heard the strangest noises, and it became an enormous task to recreate those impressions and memories in a studio. 'We had been searching for the sound of a particular machine for a long time until one of the labourers suddenly found it by moving a piece of iron across a co-

conut mat.'[20] Leo Jordaan devoted a report to this obsessive search for the right sound in *De Groene Amsterdammer* of 30 May 1931:

> 'Woo... woo... woo... woo... – Psssst! Luah... Luah... Luah... Luah...! – Tjonk-bang... tjonk-bang... tjonk-bang...! – Ffffft-tsching!' '*Aber nein – hören Sie doch: es ist nicht* fu-u-u-u-t! *Aber vielmehr*: fuah – fuah – fuah!' '*C'est-ça, je comprends, mais c'est impossible de producer*... fu-u-u-ut! *Ça va – mais*: fuah – fuah – fuah... *pas possible*!' '*Maar meneer Ivens, als we het eens zó probeerden*...' [...] The light is switched off and on the screen is the image of a labourer, apparently a glassblower, vibrating strangely and unreal. In front of the equipment with which he labours on his brittle material is something like a Bunsen burner... the wide flame flickering slowly. And behold the question *brûlante* in a double sense. It is the sound we are looking for.

It is true that Lichtveld and Ivens went to a great deal of trouble to find the right sound, but they were not always after a realistic, anecdotal illustration of the image. Leo Jordaan describes this in the following scene that occurred when post-synchronizing the glassblowing:

> Mr. Startz, will you stand near the microphone? Attention – we will project the glassblowing one more time. When the picture of the blower is shown you start to breathe heavily – slowly and with difficulty, as if you are doing a heavy job. But do not forget – we are not concerned with a naturalistic clarification... we only want a strengthening of the sensation: laborious work. You absolutely need not breathe completely in synch with the labourer on the screen.

Synchronization was, different from what the quote assumes, a necessity. 'The word synchronous in those days was rife. For that is the greatest difficulty to be conquered: making sure that the various sounds coincide accurately with the places in the film where they are required.'[21] Lichtveld, who wrote these words, repeatedly had the orchestra begin over again when synchronization was not to his satisfaction. The orchestra appeared to have great difficulty with one particular scene: the loudspeaker ballet. Lichtveld had composed fugal music to accompany the swirling images:

> But the short duration of the visual image did not make things easy for the musicians. It appeared that the image ended sooner than the music. 'Quicker,' they called after the first trial. So once again. 'Still quicker,' was the result. 'Still too slow,' and several more times like this, till they finally succeeded to synchronize everything by playing the fugue at breakneck speed and both filmmaker and composer were able to realize their aims.[22]

Why those problems with the synchronization of the music? Post-synchronization is never easy, but here something else was going on as well. Joris Ivens had recorded PHILIPS RADIO as a silent film at a speed of eighteen to

Sound engineer Kretsch, Joris Ivens and sound mixer Leblond (right) working on the soundtrack for PHILIPS RADIO.

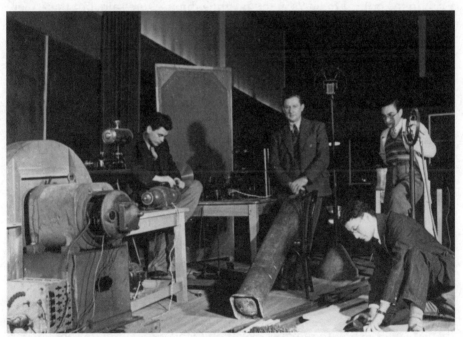

The sound studio in Epinay, France: Joris Ivens, Kretsch, Leblond and, kneeling Mark Kolthoff.

twenty frames per second. As a sound film, it had to be projected at a speed of twenty-four frames per second. This change of speed not only results in wooden movements, but also disturbs the editing rhythms. Most likely, Lichtveld wrote his compositions on the basis of the silent version. The tempo of the written music was consequently too slow to synchronize it with the sound version. This would explain why the orchestra had to play quicker and quicker, not only in the final scene, but in the other scenes as well. This discrepancy between recording and projection speed is characteristic of the hybrid nature of PHILIPS RADIO, a film on the border of two eras.

***

On 28 September 1931 PHILIPS RADIO and Hans Richter's EUROPA RADIO were screened in the Tuschinski Theatre in Amsterdam for the first time. The film got a rather bad reception in the press. The criticism was applied in a positive way, however. Judging by the many articles and large headlines – a large number of dailies and weeklies featured extensive reviews – the impression might be that the film received good reviews, but that is only a fantasy. The press was sympathetic towards Ivens and Lichtveld's first film. Even in the critical reviews many positive things were said, but there were objections, nonetheless.

The positive reviews often refered to the imagery and the music, although many critics admitted that they were not competent enough in the field of music. They appreciated the spectacular images in the glassworks, the testing of the loudspeakers, and the final loudspeaker ballet. The objections were directed at the structure of the film in the first place. The film is not a single unit, the *NRC* wrote; it is 'too long-winded, too fragmentary'.[23] Secondly, there were objections to the leading role of the machines. The film was 'blind to the people behind the machines', *Het Volk* concluded; it had become 'an ode to the machine', a 'document *inhumain*'.[24] Thirdly, the film was criticized for showing a lack of fantasy and playfulness. 'Frolicking movements, an uncomplicated representation that handles and combines the motives with grace, this is what we miss very much,' *De Tijd* wrote.[25] This last perceived shortcoming was all the more striking, because the much lighter and more humorous short film by Hans Richter, EUROPA RADIO had preceded PHILIPS RADIO at the screening. But what did the press think of the soundtrack?

Only a few critics gave their opinion about the film's sound. Most of them dismissed it with remarks like: 'Lou Lichtveld's sonorization is generally perfect. Only the natural sound effects that are, in our opinion, sometimes too arbitrarily used.'[26] The weeklies went into sounds aspects more extensively. Leo Jordaan praised the film profusely because it 'took into ac-

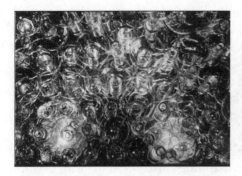

Stills from PHILIPS RADIO.

count the basic principles of sound film: independence of images and sound.'[27] His colleague at *De Haagsche Post* wrote the exact opposite: 'The music by the young Dutch composer is essentially simple accompaniment to a cinematographic movement. The camera comes first, the music follows.'[28] Whereas Jordaan was jubilant about examples of musical sound imitation (the short jerks of a cardpuncher are supported by cello pizzicati'), the *De Haagsche Post* reviewer disapproved, calling them old-fashioned examples of 'music-with-the-film', put in a modern context. Lou Lichtveld would have agreed with this latter view: he repeatedly made it known that his music played a subordinate, accompanying function in the film.[29] Modernization was not to be expected from him at this juncture.

The great obedience of the music was also criticized by Meyer Sluyser in the socialist newspaper, *Het Volk*, but for a different reason. Sluyser first poined out that the film was an ode to the machine, and then continued:

> Lou Lichtveld supported this tendency with his accompanying music. The furious tumult of the enormous machines has been worked into the accompaniment, but when the camera then wanders into the machine workshop, where the receivers are produced on the assembly line, the accompaniment becomes definitely romantic. Lichtveld did not see or hear anything of the hustle and bustle of the people, toiling against each other as the result of a cunning premium and group system. On a hook high, in the air, hangs the shining machine and the music sways in the same cadence as the machine. But the people below are absent, as they are absent in the whole film and only occasionally appear when it could not be avoided, as an incidental part of the space.[30]

In contrast, the communist newspaper, *De Tribune*, claimed to know why Ivens made the machines speak more than the people:

> Well, they spoke depressingly enough for our tastes. [...] This film clearly shows that there can be no job satisfaction in the modern company. [...] Joris Ivens will make something quite different, of course, when he goes to the Soviet Union later, where he [...] will be able to see machines as the labourers' comrades, who with their steel arms will help build a new society.

All reviewers did, however, agree that PHILIPS RADIO was an ode to the machine, a 'symphony industrielle'. Looked at it in this way, Joris Ivens achieved what he wanted: to give shape to the image of Philips as a 'high-tech' enterprise. Yet, it should be asked whether this high-tech image was favourable for Philips. Philips had its idea of its own image and that required that they not show any manual labour, preferring to focus on the machines. Reactions however, were the exact opposite of what Philips desired: too many machines, too few people. Every newspaper praised the fragment with the glassblowers who performed heavy, physical labour. This, ironically, is the fragment that troubled Philips the most and was the portion of the film they wanted to cut out afterwards.[31] In conclusion, Philips got from Ivens what they had asked for. The fact that the press and the audience reacted differently than expected was a miscalculation on Philips's part.[32] The company would learn its lesson: Philips turned to the production of puppet films and George Ivens was replaced by Georg Pal.

PHILIPS RADIO became the first industrial sound film. It is also the first sound film by a Dutch avant-garde filmmaker. The film avant-garde had been on the brink of disappearing in 1931, first, because the movement had exhausted itself, and second, because the new sound engineering was a serious obstacle to free development. PHILIPS RADIO borders on two worlds. The film may therefore be seen as a farewell to the avant-garde, the end of an era. Afterwards, there were some minor experiments in this direction, but PHILIPS RADIO is the turning point that also led to its end. Ivens and Lichtveld's film even bears evidence of this.

Adding sound made PHILIPS RADIO into a hybrid, a kind of amphibious film belonging to both the silent era and the new sound era. This amphibious nature can still be associated with this film because the images were recorded at a speed of eighteen frames per second while the sound was recorded at twenty-four frames per second. The consequence is that the film can never be shown correctly: either the images move too fast, or the sound moves too slowly. PHILIPS RADIO shares this defect with other avant-garde films that were provided with subsequent soundtracks.

Lou Lichtveld saw PHILIPS RADIO as an experiment, and in that sense the film certainly served its purpose. 'It was the necessary exploration of the whole dimension of sound in the documentary film,' he thought:

> The PHILIPS RADIO film [...] attempted to render the half-musical impressions of factory sounds in a complex audio world that moved from absolute music to the purely documentary noises of nature. In this film every intermediate stage can be found: such as the movement of the machine interpreted by the music, the noises of the machine dominating the musical background, the music itself is the documentary, and those scenes where the pure sound of the machine goes solo.[33]

PHILIPS RADIO links up closely with MELODIE DER WELT, the documentary sound film that Walter Ruttmann made in 1929 and which was shown in Dutch cinemas in 1930.[34] In it, Ruttmann experimented with the relation between image and sound. He edited the soundtrack of MELODIE DER WELT to a collage of music, voices, sounds, and moments of silence. 'In this way MELODIE DER WELT became the first important sound documentary, the first in which musical and unmusical sounds were composed into a single unit and in which image and sound are controlled by one and the same impulse,' Lou Lichtveld wrote.[35] He was undoubtedly inspired by Ruttmann's film. It is not accurate to portray Lichtveld as an epigone of Ruttmann: both artists were much more kindred spirits who shared an interest in the new art of sound of their time. Lichtveld tried to translate factory noises into a refined form of charivari, a 'composition of common and uncommon sounds – a melody of the machines'.[36] Through his efforts the soundtrack of PHILIPS RA-DIO has become a resounding monument to the New Objectivity, a true partner to Ivens's images.

Between Two Letters

Five years and Half a Life: Joris Ivens and the DEFA

Günter Jordan

The relations between the DEFA and Joris Ivens have a long history. In June 1948 a letter from Prague to Berlin: 'It is a great task for the cinema to be a part of making Germany a habitable country again, democratic and at peace with all its neighbours. If you want me to help you, make the board of the DEFA write me a letter now and then. Then I can come to Berlin for a few days to speak to you.' The last letter arrived from Paris to Leipzig on November 25, 1988: 'All over the world the documentary film is gaining more and more influence. This movement encourages documentarists to attempt more ambitious themes for their films, whereas their realization further stimulates their imagination. [...] Unfortunately my bad health does not allow me to be with you. I wish you a succesful festival. Best regards...' Between these two letters lies half of Joris Ivens's life and almost the entire history of the DEFA and the GDR. What a horizon! What is Joris Ivens's place in it, what are the conditions like, and what traces does he leave behind?

Ivens worked for five years for the DEFA and made five films in East Germany (GDR). He not only is one of the founders of the International Documentary Filmweek Leipzig – without him this festival would not have existed, or at least not existed in this form – but is also the link between Leipzig and the filmmakers of the world. The festival became a film school and a window to the world. He celebrated his birthdays in Leipzig, had two small and one large retrospective of his films there, and took part in debates held by the *Freien Tribune*. In the GDR the first films about him were made (DFF/Machalz; DEFA/Hadaschik; 1963), the monograph by Hans Wegner was published (1965), as was Ivens's autobiography *The Camera and I* (1969). Here, he was awarded for the The Star of the Friendship of Peoples, receives an honorary doctorate at Karl Marx University in Leipzig, and a 'corresponding member' of the Academy of Arts. After Ivens criticized the 1968 invasion of Prague however, all contact was abruptly severed. For the second time, Ivens became *persona non grata*. This however, did not stop his DEFA colleagues from visiting him, when a 'view of the world' brought them to Paris; his academy colleagues kept in touch with him and per-formed a two-day homage to him in 1983; the director and the committee head of the Leipzig Festival contacted him, while filmmakers and authors often referred to him. The eighties were a time of revitalization of contacts, as the eighty-something Ivens strove to finish his film plans. The wound healed a little, but it remained a wound – for both sides. The last years of his life saw a substantial and rekindling of interest and friendships.

When Karl Hans Bergmann, co-founder of the DEFA and member of the board, contacted Joris Ivens in Prague in June 1948, he knew that Ivens was 'the most important documentary filmmaker and a man who sympathized with our view of the world.' A man like Ivens could be very useful to the DEFA in helping them to create a new German documentary film. In the postwar years the East German documentary - both in practical and theoret-ical terms – was not worth mentioning. It would require a new start from the beginning. Even left-over memories could not simply be recycled, because the situation demanded a new attitude, a new way of working – with reality and the strategies of documentary filmmaking. On 20 July 1948, the DEFA board decided to invite Ivens to Berlin. Ivens never came. We can only imagine what might have come out of this collaboration.

After the reconstruction and settlement films, the election and instruc-tion films, the retraining and the *Assistence for life* films of the early years, the first conceptional programme was instituted in 1949. With the support of the first economy plans of the SED (Socialist Unity Party), the 'two-year plan', Ivens produced the film series TWO YEARS THAT WILL CHANGE THE COUNTRY. In comparison with the average productions of the time, these two-year film plans were an advance in both content and image. Arguments regarding factuality, as well as theory arose.

In the early fifties, two directors defined the DEFA style. Andrew Thorndike returned to Germany in 1948 from Russian captivity. In a period of a year and a half he made a career from out of political documentary filmmaking. Joop Huisken, who had worked with Ivens on RAIN and ZUIDERZEE, was sent to Germany after the occupation of Holland where he did forced labour, became a DEFA cameraman after the war and stayed in Germany. They were opposites.

Thorndike's attitude toward the spectator was that of a propagandist. 'The documentary film has to instruct, and the instructor can be the socially-committed author, who represents the progressive strength of society, the working class and its guiding light.' He did not concern himself with reality; he worked in a deductive way. For him, the purpose, the argument, the means – the 'orchestration' – was sacred.

Thorndike wanted to show a general, broad, valid image of the period, without concerns about perception, discovery, or analysis in advance. Thorndike did not shy away. He did not illustrate texts with images or vice versa, but instead created illustrative editing sequences. The editing did not reveal the meaning of the images, rather the images were meaning itself because they had been shot as symbols. This working method made the argumentation both stronger and weaker, because of changing rhetoric into affirmation, in having 'no necessity of intellect' despite the necessary screen.

Huisken preferred the construction of precise images of human acts that revealed a certain attitude. Watching them, the spectator could appreciate them while learning from the stories - or not. Huisken was interested in the people he was involved with. They remained themselves, and were not prostituted for a purpose. Huisken knew that labourers do not instruct, they debate and discuss among themselves. His intention was to share his experience, using the narrative power of a situation.

As for the image of people – Thorndike showed it by arranging an overall image, while Huisken preferred telling a story and providing an inside view: two different concepts, two different methods. The DEFA used both. Founded in 1946 by people who we would nowadays call 'reform-communists', the DEFA was subsequently taken over by the SED in 1947 who placed it under the party's authority. In 1948, after the change of course from 'the special German socialism' to the Soviet concept, everything in East Germany became tailored to the 'New Style Party' which meant the *Stalinisierung* of the SED and the GDR. Film became a device used to proclaim the new doctrine – propagandize political views, popularize desirable standards, mobilize the spectator – and was presented in a way that preferred pedagogy to experience, guardianship to knowledge, propaganda to analysis. Consequently, Thorndike's method – aesthetics transformed into politics - was favoured which meant that workers in these films became the voice of a will from above. Delivering films on assignment with no film experience was called the bond of the standard of art with the supposed goal. An alternative journalistic and artistic method as self-confirmation and illustration was therefore hard to find. The images were considered in a way that justified their presence in the films – for their value as testimony. They became the decor of a text, whose formulations turned into formulas and persuaded, instead of provoking the audience.

When Joris Ivens finally came to Berlin in June 1951, he was already a different man than he was three years before. After his work in Warsaw and Prague, he was considered to be a man of the 'people's democracy' and, after INDONESIA CALLING, a fighter with a camera. By hiring Ivens the DEFA was able to inflate its own reputation.

The film about Third World Youth and the Student Festival that he was supposed to make with Ivan Pyrjev – fiction film director and winner of the Stalin Prize – would mean political prestige, being directly commissioned by the party's offices in Moscow and Berlin. The two prestigious directors are themselves the perfect men for the job. Over twenty film crews with cameramen, directors, assistant directors, producers, stage designers, lighting engineers, sound engineers, editors, film printers, interpreters, drivers - all together six-hundred people were involved, and almost the entire recording and copying capacity of the DEFA was reserved for their production. In the Berlin studios, twenty-five to thirty offices were cleared, seventeen cars, five trucks and a bus were made available, a medical base was prepared, and the DEFA sanatorium was placed at the disposal of their Soviet comrades. By the end, more than one-hundred kilometres of Agfa colour film were used and taken to Moscow for editing.

FREUNDSCHAFT SIEGT (1952) is a triumph of logistics over art, an unappetizing banquet of largesse in image, music, and text. The decor of the film is not simply 'bites too big, swallowed the wrong way by the directors' because they just can't seem to get enough but they are merely exhibiting the aesthetics of their era.

Marches, banners, presidential staffs, war metaphors, unity, and society – and the shooting of all this – changes the real world into simulacrum. This process of returning over and over again to the same structures of image and text manages to emblemize them. Film is, first of all, the messenger of these distorted realities, but it also facilitates its own emblemizing, making film mere ornament. It is not presented as a decorating supplement, but as the subject itself, which explains the use of the represented societal regularizations instead of testing its functioning. The control over the new society becomes mere image. The fetishistic promise of fullfilment starves and transforms the organs while waiting for it - including the documentary film, put into service as 'agitator, propagandist and organizer'.

Ivens eventually recognizes these contradictions in the following years. 'For me making films is a creative process, in which things should be deepened and not presented as window-dressing. There is a danger in that. I don't care about ornaments, not in the least. And whenever they showed up in my work, I always edited them out, I think.' (1963). Where FREUNDSCHAFT SIEGT is concerned, he got rid of the window-dressing – in his memories at least – and retained the deeper things. Deeper things such as the meeting of a young English woman whose brother died in the Korean War with a young Korean man on a Berlin street. When she cries, the Korean touches

Even before Joris Ivens came to the DEFA he had filmed huge crowds: here a still from PEACE WILL WIN, 1951; just before Ivens was invited by the DEFA.

Joris Ivens and Joop Huisken (right) during the shooting of FREUNDSCHAFT SIEGT.

her gently with compassion; her face brightens, she smiles. Once, but only once, the camera stays with these two people who are speaking, and he recognizes a scene in it. What Ivens remembers best is the escape from the prison of rituals and the violation of rules. The fact that he focused on this scene proved that he had not lost his filmmaking standards. This proved that it was not lack of talent on the part of the filmmakers, but rather the circumstances of the period which tempted them to a kind of aesthetics that sneered at the creation of generalizations.

In 1952, the reorganization of filmmaking in East Germany continued on a large scale. The DEFA was divided into several studios, which in 1953 gain the legal status as *Volkseigener Betrieb*, 'peoples companies'. The film commission was quietly passed over to the State Committee for Film. The centralization of the Party descended upon the state.

This state of affairs affected even Joop Huisken. With 1952 – THE DECISIVE YEAR he and his scriptwriter Karl Gass not only produced a cinematic report of the building of the coke factory Lauchhammer (the first factory in the world to process brown coal into coke) but also an ode to the second SED Party Conference, where the systematic build-up of socialism is documented. The subject is important, but the commentary ignores it, astonishing music kills it, and when the workers momentarily are allowed to speak for a short moment on the original soundtrack, a happy message is put into their mouths. At the State Film Committee screening the words of the foreman were ridiculed, but at the same time permitted, 'because these scenes were shot in reality and reality can't be changed'. This is the way documentary films should be created. As if this is not enough, the final cut was put into the hands of writers, painters, and composers 'in order to develop a sense that they created art'.

With all due respect to Joop Huisken, a year later he was to make a film that still today shows how art is created. This film served as the starting point for all DEFA documentarists: TURBINE 1 (1953), is a reportage about the emergency repair of a power station turbine. All the right conditions are there: unity of place, time, and action; a surveyable group of people, among whom two central figures, an objective and a subjective conflict, the real indistinctness, the way they are solved, a theme of great importance, a camera that participates in the same three-layered way as the labourers in the race against time, and the film crew that sleeps with the labourers in the turbine-hall and experiences the subject from 'inside'. The camera follows the workers from a distance as well as close up. It also captures the daily manners and social behaviour, registers hope and depression, doubt and courage, tension and happiness – and the crates of beer at the end. The editing creates a rhythm that respects the work and propels the story of the film. The action makes itself independent of everything else, the image says something about the subject but it is not an illustration.

Just like the woman who in 1930 confessed to Joris Ivens that, after seeing one of his films, she finally understood her husband and his work, so the initiator of *fast repair* takes his film reels under his arms, travels from power station to power station, and convinces his colleagues of this new method, for the very reason that film is not about agitation, but, for the sake of the people, and about reflecting their interests in its themes. Huisken has returned to his roots. 'Recording the tangibility of a situation is the essence of what I learned from Ivens. When we made the film about the Zuiderzee we started with the psychology of people in action, so we moved from people to actions, not the other way round [...] I think this is the nature of the documentary: starting from people and their psychology, their character and the way this translates into actions.'

On 2 June 1953, a telegram was sent from Vienna to Berlin's DEFA Documentary Film Studio: 'Trade-union federation plans film about struggles and successes among international united labourers. Director: Joris Ivens. Had telephone conversation with him yesterday. Please discuss prossibility of the project with Ivens and send telegraphic confirmation'. The DEFA only needed half a day to agree to the project and wired back to Vienna: 'Agree to production of your film, on condition that you bear all expenses.' It is, of course, insane to believe in these times of burgeoning bureaucracy that two offices could make such an effortless deal. There is no evidence to explain why, of all Ivens's connections – Moscow, Warsaw, Prague, and Berlin – Berlin was chosen, or who was responsible for this choice. Ivens had fond memories of the DEFA and this time, the conditions were even better than before; the supervising office was in Vienna and the DEFA provided all that was necessary for production, meanwhile Ivens was independent and unburdened. Internal GDR affairs did not need to concern him.

This time around however, he only had two rooms, a telephone, and a car at his disposal. Hans Wegner, one of the few 'educated' assistants the studio could offer, became Ivens's production head – a stroke of good fortune because, through their intimate working relationship, he later became Ivens's first German biographer. With a team of writers, the 'Ivens Group' embarked on a worldwide project as never seen before: SONG OF THE RIVERS (1953-1954). Ivens knew a lot of people in Berlin back from the period of the Spanish War and his time in Paris. Two were to become his close friends: Kurt Hager – in 1953 department head of the Central Committee of the SED, in 1954 elected as a member of the same committee, and a year later ideology secretary of the Party – and Alexander Abusch, secretary of the Culture

Union, and in 1954 Assistant Minister of Culture. To his travel routes between Vienna and Prague and Berlin Ivens added another: between Vienna
and Warsaw, where Ivens's third wife, Ewa Fiszer, lived and where he has
his second home (in 1951 half his honorarium was paid out in zlotys). His
travels across borders were arranged and guaranteed by government ac-
quaintances and during his trips to Poland and Czechoslovakia his safe passage is guaranteed by Hans Wegner. He travelled freely, no stamp smudged
his passports; a small official letter was enough for his safe passage.

The production of the film has been thoroughly described by Ivens and
Pozner. Again, enormous amounts of film material had to be processed.
This time, Ivens made the film, created the sequences, and combined all the
elements. But time took him by the hand. The images drum an unending
staccato, the subject exhausts itself into a construction. People operated it,
Ivens used it. Remarkably, the film is of importance in exactly that part
where the tone is general and he shows the state of affairs of the planet. With
his images of work, from the depths of the social area, he created the film's
message: 'Nothing is more beautiful than the labour of the people and the
spiritual strength it offers... We create all the riches in the world. With our
yellow, white, and black hands, we change the face of the earth and humanity every day.' This is the lesson offered by Vladimir Pozner's commentary,
which questions – or rather, makes it possible to question – the images in an
abstract and rhetorical new way, because it offers variants that allow the
spectator to create his own narrative. Pozner's commentary registers the
swings, connections, and meanings of the images and sequences, and develops a new concept for the combining of image with text. Unfortunately, as
the film goes on, the images offer him less and less reason to work with. The
motive for the film and its progressive credentials are outdated. Ivens's
achievements are to present the view of a coherent world, and to command
a successful worldwide film project as well as discovering Pozner as a film
author. His weakest points are oversimplification of the world and using
the method of essay and reportage, story and documentation, analysis and
action.

By the time the film opened in September 1954, the character of East German film had changed once again. In January, the Ministry of Culture declared the *hauptverwaltung Film* Department as one of its main policies. This
is a reaction to 17 June 1953 and the demand for more openness, democratic
participation, and transparant decisions. And it is the release of films into
normal state society.

New films appeared on the screen. Stephan Hermlin and Max Jaap's film,
LUDWIG VAN BEETHOVEN (1954), was the most outstanding.The German

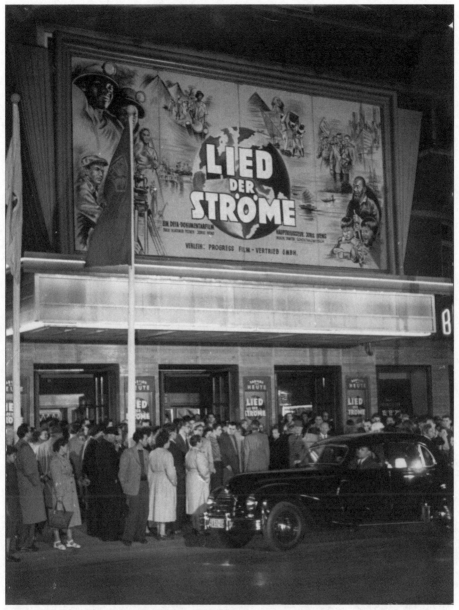

The premiere of LIED DER STRÖME (SONG OF THE RIVERS) in Berlin at the
Babylon Filmtheater, September 17, 1954.

theme popped up in EIN STROM FLIESST DURCH DEUTSCHLAND (Kunert, 1954) and DIE SIEBEN VON RHEIN (Thorndike, 1954), while during the same year, under Ivens's supervision, Thorndike's people began work on the historical epic, KRIEG ODER FRIEDEN. Renamed DU UND MANCHER KAMERAD (1956), it touched people like few films ever had before. The work assignment was given to Ivens and Thorndike, as they maintain in the scenario foreword, 'by the leader of HV Film, Hernn Ackermann, in the presence of Herrn Pronin, Joris Ivens, and studio-director Günter Klein'.

What started out as a picture book of German history – not unlike Thorndike's WILHELM PIECK (1952) – through an intensive immersion into the material, evolved into an active film that comes alive from inside out. Thorndike's protégés discovered the internal force of archive material. The fact that they did not expose it and did not let it guide them, is the fault of the stiff image of history and its immanent method; just ten years later it found its master in Romm and DER GEWÖNLICHE FASCHISMUS (1965). But they ignored the arguments of co-author Von Schnitzler. The commentary, written by author Günther Rücker, revolves around the images, works with them, thinks about them. For the first time in a political DEFA film, the commentary builds a bridge of words and sentences adapted to the audience. The audience swallowed it: it went to the cinema on its own free will to see a so-called feature length documentary film, which is actually a political one.

By the mid-fifties, DEFA films were presenting the world in a totally new way, almost with 'cleansed eyes'. In 1954, Karl Gass captained a fishing trawler VOM ALEX ZUM EISMEER to deliver four films from Greece: HELLAS OHNE GÖTTER, INSEL DER ROSEN, ZWISCHEN HIMMEL UND ERDE, and AN DER VIA EGNATIA. Jochen Hadaschik, Ivens's assistant director during SONG OF THE RIVERS, went to Indonesia and brought back the reportages THAI UND MEO and VIETNAM (1955); Peter Ulbrich shot IN DEN BERGEN NORDVIETNAMS (1957) and DIE FISCHER VON VINH-MOC (1957); Heinz Müller, Huisken's former assistant director, showed MORGENRÖTE ÜBER DEN INSELN (1957); Alfons Machalz, together with Pozner, used international film material for MEIN KIND (1955) and went to Poland with WANDERUNGEN MIT HANKA (1956); and finally, Joop Huisken, together with author Bodo Uhse, succeeded in making the great film, CHINA – LAND ZWISCHEN GESTERN UND MORGEN (1957).

It is hard to determine which films, what intentions, which documents Ivens had a hand in. Most of it happened indirectly. Even a film like MEIN KIND, which originated in Ivens's direct surroundings is impossible to overlook because it did not imitate any film before it and thus emerged as a totally independent work of art, in fact, the most poetic film in the history of the DEFA documentary film. A moving commentary that is able to organize the manner of reading the images, music that continues to be Beethoven – with its own message that originates in the music, and is able to make the image stronger. Editing that develops the thoughts on the growth of humanity out of the gestures of the images. The film unfolds as a panorama of the Family of Man, that, first of all, is able to handle the rejection the World Press Photo Exhibition (1955-1956) of the same name is confronted with in the bureaucratic GDR because of class indifferences and convergence. It serves as an unparallelled awakening, especially for the young, up and coming directors, whose own films are more than evidence of their talent, and who want to follow their own paths without being labelled as an Ivens- or Huisken-protégé.

One unheralded, perhaps unfashionable theme remained however: the life and work of the people in the homeland. One film, Hugo Hermann's STAHL UND MENSCHEN (1957) does manage to approach the working people like no film before it, including Huisken's TURBINE 1. For the first time, a machine shop becomes a tangible place of beauty and horror, the severe working conditions are not ignored, and the workers are taken seriously in what they do, say, and think. In a craftily and dramaturgical sense, the use of the original soundtrack and atmospheres is very new. Hermann, invited to the DEFA by Ivens, distanced himself with this and other works from the political montage film, which he had developed at the same time as Ivens through his Viennese films KAMPF UM DEN FRIEDEN and SCHATTEN ÜBER DER WELT, and returned to the beginning, as he had known it in the early period with Ivens. Hermann became a predecessor of those films that became the reference-marks of the next film generation, which regarded his – and Huisken's – work as their starting capital.

In discussions that emerged in the second half of the 1950s, the schematic agitation- and survey films came in for a lot of criticism. The films were regarded as particularly irritating, because the same questions were always answered in the same way, in other words, 'The audience has been satiated by this kind of film.' The screen adaptations of unfilmable themes, their schematic nature, the increasing differences between the best films and the rest were discussed. The missing pieces as far as dramaturgy, text, and camera work goes were immense. An adjustment in the production conditions in the studio was demanded. 'When film artists are tempted to play it safe, then increased mediocrity is inevitable.' An artistic atmosphere that guaranteed the freedom of artistic creativity for all artists was demanded. But only on the condition that 'church-tower perspectives and film governors' were renounced, the dogma of 'spooky representations of the ordinary and the conflicts within the documentary film' were settled because it led to misconceptions regarding publicity which further led to 'constructed fables, schematic text composition, even to the violation of the very nature of the documentary'. Real life, the starting point for documentaries, came to be regarded as the only place where changes could be enacted, because 'life is a great author'.

The discussion continued on half-heartedly, because it was the DEFA documentary film that, after the twentieth Convention of the KPdSU (Communist Party of the Soviet Union), could not come up with a manifesto concerning the principles of society and film, how they worked in feature films, and how this could be expressed in director Maetzig's catalogue of 'Time is Right' demands which included the end of guardianship; the thematic and economic independence of film production; smaller structured units; support offered to various film schools; the total responsibility of the artist for his own film; democratic transparency of institutional decision-making; and the separation of power of the state and Party in discussions. No trace of this was at that time found in the documentary film. This immediately hit home: the political leaders, the studio heads and the plotted to discipline the entire studio system. They got their way to make the studios more accountable, and Austrian DEFA director Hugo Hermann (the most innovative man in the studio) had to leave the studio.

The creative discussion however, was for naught. Nothing changes, the studios preferred footage of film to art. Nepotism and unsuccesful international cooperations were their fatal blows. 'What possibilities do we have left?' Joop Huisken asked himself, 'only the ones that contain their attempt to make art, or documentary film art will succeed again. Art must be an experience for the people which offers them strength [...]. We must therefore concern ourselves with human problems.'

Huisken finished the year with his film, DASS EIN GUTES DEUTSCHLAND BLÜHE (1959-1960), which investigated what the GDR meant to him. He preferred, he discovered, staying with the workers with their self-confident production levels. The same relaxed self-confidence which radiates through the film. Nothing recalls the zealous 'way up'. The shots are beautiful, almost too beautiful, but not overly polished. Poetry is not an addition, but the organic subject matter itself. The film presents information in passing, which consists mainly of a montage of emotions – or better yet, *for* emotions. Huisken does not create sensibility, but stimulates the activated mind of the spectators by employing a passage that penetrates the image without interpreting it, measures the meaning of an image but does not touch it, evokes with a single word the impulse of a scene which the spectators can finish for themselves. Stephan Hermlin's language creates a point of reflection between the images, which keeps the film tense. He juxtapositions himself with the spectators, who become interested, and begin to participate; their involvement emerges out of emotion, not commotion. Pozner's lesson in SONG OF THE RIVERS, led to the progress of this fruitful method treading on old and yet, at the same time, new terrain. DASS EIN GUTES DEUTSCHLAND BLÜHE is the lone highlight, maybe even the last of the DEFA documentary films, which started with the survey film and was able to drive them to a subjective reflection of social life. Subsequent films do not have the same energy; they are weaker films. This film is, in its cautious, quiet thoughtfulness, a true Huisken film. Its cinematic genius is unimaginable however, without the preparatory work of the Ivens film. It is like a greeting card sent by Huisken to his friend.

What nobody thought possible happened: The film was rejected by the Politbüro, and a new script was demanded. The author of this new script was head commentator Karl Eduard von Schnitzler. Huisken was not consulted. The film, released in 1960, regresses back to 1950. All copies of the original film were ordered destroyed, but, through some miracle, the archive copy was saved and to this day, remains the only copy. Anyone who wants to know why East German documentaries lagged a decade behind the other arts, need only look at this version of the film.

When Ivens returned from Warsaw to Berlin with the World Peace Award in May 1955, his DEFA colleagues welcomed him back by lining the streets. The atmosphere was not quite festive, but at least it was cheerful. They know each other, like each other, sit through the official part, because the unofficial part is right. The camera saw and shot it.

Ivens went in and out of the studios, just like the others. He was a colleague of his colleagues. They had enough work on their plates and took it for granted that, after Huisken, a second Dutchman was in the studio, and even one of the same caliber as their house-owner. Ivens not only shared the dreams of other filmmakers, but also the fate of so many filmmakers: SONG OF THE RIVERS would not find distribution after its premiere. When the same thing happened again two years later with the artistical and political CHINA – LAND ZWISCHEN GESTERN UND MORGEN, the Academy of Arts appealed against the decision to not distribute Ivens's films. The press said 'it is the most humiliating incident in our documentary film history. This lack of appreciation for Joris Ivens's SONG OF THE RIVERS, one of the most important works in the history of the international documentary film.'

Meanwhile instead of SONG OF THE RIVERS, viewers could now see Joris Ivens's earlier films such as RAIN, BORINAGE, NEW EARTH, SPANISH EARTH, INDONESIA CALLING, THE FIRST YEARS at the afore mentioned second International Documentary Filmweek in Leipzig in 1956. One year earlier, the screening of THE FIRST YEARS in the Club of Berlin film-makers, it garnered only a tepid response from his peers. Ivens did not present himself as a great master and he did not concern himself with the history of this society and they did not call on him for thinking about the documentary film. Renowned colleagues proved to be equal partners, and the younger directors did not want to concern themselves with films like SONG OF THE RIVERS. They were impatient for their own careers. So again, the prophet obtained no respect in his own country. The next generation however, did not fail to discover him in 1960s in Leipzig.

Ivens and his DEFA crew had finished work on DIE WINDROSE, a commission he had received from the International Women's Federation, located in Berlin. Again, he was his own lord and master. And again the DEFA organized a worldwide film production from its two small rooms. Maybe Ivens was possessed by the devil and perhaps he overestimated himself (after all it was feature film directors, not Ivens himself, who produced the staged episodes of DIE WINDROSE), or maybe he wanted to help Gérard Philipe in directing his first feature film. The fact is that in 1956 Joris Ivens commited himself to being co-director of the screen adaptation of De Coster's *Till Ulenspiegel* (in his autobiography he modestly referred to himself as 'adviser'). Perhaps he also saw a chance to obtain his French work permit from the contract and so he not only signed with the DEFA, but also with its French production partner, Films Ariane. He saw the chance to obtain a French passport, because his passport had been withdrawn by the Dutch authorities after INDONESIA CALLING. In any case, this is how the break-up was programmed.

In 1957 Ivens took revenge in Paris with his declaration of love called LA SEINE A RENCONTRÉ PARIS. When he returned to Leipzig in 1960 with this film, he presented the opening shot for initiating discussions about the image of the militant documentary film in the reorganized Film Forum. His DEFA colleagues, of all people, did not understand him. Andrew Thorndike immediately placed Ivens on the other side of the barricades: 'The poetry is beautiful, but nowadays the political and historical moment are in the foreground. And that does not happen in *La Seine...*' Günter Klein, former studio-director and president of the festival, plays the different 'Ivenses' off one another: 'SONG OF THE RIVERS is profound, and LA SEINE... is just a babbling brook according to so many people; it is very beautiful, but it is no river.' Karl Gass asked, simply: 'Where is the fist, Joris?' The German censors withdrew this classic pugnacious film. Three years later, Gass explained his behaviour at the time: 'For me documentary film is a weapon and that is how I got to know it with Joris. It did surprise me and many others, that film could mean something else to him as well: poetry.' Nobody understood that it might have been very simple: after ten years of exile from his homeland and his beloved Paris, Joris just unleashed his heart.

In the decade in which Joris Ivens spent five years at the DEFA, important preparatory work for the modern documentary film was also done.

On the one hand, there were functionaries for whom film was just an 'informative, educational and didactic' apparatus; on the other hand, there were filmmakers who had to deal with political demands and who had to adapt their aesthetics accordingly. The first person to describe the term 'artistic documentary film' was Eva Fritzsche (DIE BRÜCKE VON CAPUTH, 1949); and from then on it was used to describe films from the DEFA. 'I refer to Bert Brecht's definition of audience entertainment in the sense of activating sensory experiences, in which he sees the only opportunity to have a long lasting influence on the cultivation of a social-conciousness.' Fritzsche concluded, 'This contains the dramatic and epic and also its glossy elements. It will actively come forward.' With this impulse, a new, modern aesthetic understanding of the documentary film was initiated, of which the practical consequences were endless, and which was meant to counter ignorance. But another question arose, and it took more than ten years to answer it – re-enactments in documentary film, which were used in practically every film. The prototypes of it can be found in 1946. The reconstruction of an event is seen in Huisken's POTSDAM BAUT AUF when he introduces the town-councillors. Only a year had gone by between the real event (1945) and the filming (1946), but the gravity of the situation was still on their faces: the staging was believable. FREIES LAND by Milo Harbich was a cultural film that had been linked to the land reform and developed an appropiate historical commentary. Occurrences during pre-production led to the introduction of acted scenes, with actors and agricultural workers. This is the way the first German semi-documentary feature film came about – not without justification, it was compared with neo-realism by contemporaries. That same year, Richard Brandt took a concentration camp supervisor along with some Soviet army investigators to the tribunal in the Sachsenhausen concentration camp. Scenes and cameras were arranged, and the line of questioning and the responses were decided by the Soviets, who also subjected themselves to the film's regulations. Everyone who works in film production knows that a lot of things can happen during live sound recordings. The prisoner, for instance, who lets his tongue run away with himself, and does this, for obvious reasons, at least five times and to his and our shame, comes across as totally believable. In 1949, when Eva Fritzsche shot the building for BRÜCKE VON CAPUTH, the 'hole of the needle' of the north-south railway to the southwest of Berlin, the action – here in the shape of the students of the railway repair shops who took voluntary extra shifts to make the nails for the bridge – was almost over, and the inspectors of the employment office hid themselves behind thick walls and closed doors. Eva Fritzsche could not abandon it, but did not want to report it in dull commentary either, for her film was not about explanation, but action ('activation of the mental experience'). So, once again, and with the same enthusiasm, the young people replayed their scenes and foremen and employment office councillors were replaced by actors to uncover certain internal issues. When Werner Bergmann showed us a war victim with an amputated leg who has to ask himself how his life will be with only one leg, he physically and psychologically asked too much of the people involved. The part was played by an actor, which was difficult enough, but not an impossible job, because the one-armed Bergmann himself was behind the camera (ZURÜCK INS LEBEN, 1948). Dahle and Thorndike rearranged complete passages of their films in their studios to fully expose the enemy of the working class. Complete shifts were stopped until enough workers filled the workshop. Man was centre stage, so that the camera could see him better. This was the way it went on, from the actors who carried the film like pillars, via the scenic arrangement of reality like in a feature film, to the re-enactment of scenes, that were inserted as historical scenes in FREUNDSCHAFT SIEGT or DU UND MANCHER KAMERAD. Strangely enough CHINA – LAND ZWISCHEN GESTERN UND MORGEN (Huisken, 1956), a totally re-enacted film, is so pure and beautiful in its storytelling and artistry that you step over the seamless editing and the perfectly matching scenes in surprise. Measured against these other films, DIE WINDROSE (Ivens, 1957) is from the beginning an actor's film, in which only such elements as the commentary text point at its documentary background.

This procedure did not discredit itself on its own and has to be accepted as a transitional phase in the self-discovery of the genre. Important exponents of the English documentary film of the 1930s rely on agreements and re-enactments, and Ivens's postwar epic THE FIRST YEARS (screened for the first time in the GDR in 1955) was shot in the same way. Behind all this was a dilemma of which the contemporaries were aware – documentary truth and a sense of reality versus cinematic film in their representations of conflict. The documentary film had not yet found another method to solve this dilemma with fiction. Feature films that were presented as documentary feature films (Rossellini, Käutner, Staudte, Tschiaureli, Sawtschenko), but achieved exactly the desired effect of documentary films – 'not the bare report of things, but the reality behind things' – invigorated this. The DEFA short-film direction reacted in a way typical of the GDR, and immediately forbade the use of actors in documentary films. But that did not resolve the problem. Only in the 1960s, with its new views of documentary film, new dramaturgical methods and new techniques, was this dilemma pushed into the background. It has not been taken up since.

The third aspect of the preparatory work for modern documentary films concerned the changes in influential aesthetics, especially in textuality and receptional advantage. The basis was rhetorical. On the one hand, there was a knowledgable person, on the other hand an ignorant one who, in the most ideal situation, wanted to acquire knowledge. Out of this pedagogical relationship information, education, and explanation followed; in the politicized versions, assertion, persuasion, and appeal were added. The spectator was the object of the author above him, and accepted his work (images, thoughts, and ideologies). The difference was assumed and stressed. Not only the earlier defined communicative relationship, but also the choice of themes and subjects, their dramaturgy and the application of filmic methods evolved out of it. It was obvious that this model had been based on a traditional cultural-historical mould, but also on a notion of author-spectator relationship, that was connected with views of society anyway. Changing the one could not be done without changing the other. The alternative was an anti-pedagogical concept, making the author/filmmaker and the spectator partners. Both are competent, the first takes the second on an exploration of reality in his consciousness, which the latter already is aware of, so he does not have to be convinced of anything. What both parties want to get out of it is something that has never been seen or thought of before. The relationship is one of dialogue (which does not mean that the aesthetic, or in our case textual, form must be a dialogue). It is free from external, non-filmic – therefore political – instructions, objectives, servitude, role models or codes of conduct. The spectator is taken seriously in his life and artistic experiences. This makes him the subject in the relationship that establishes itself in the film theatre. The text is developed in his head.

1954, 1957, and 1959 were 'leap years' as far as the quality and functional development of film language. LUDWIG VON BEETHOVEN (Jaap/Hermlin, 1954) and LIED DER STRÖME (Ivens/Pozner, 1954) marked the break up of the rhetorical model. The new elements had been studied thoroughly by colleagues. It was visible in the text reworkings of CHINA – LAND ZWISCHEN GESTERN UND MORGEN (Huisken, 1956) by Bodo Uhse, DU UND MANCHER KAMERAD (Thorndike, 1956) by Günther Rücker, DASS EIN GUTES DEUTSCHLAND BLÜHE (Huisken, 1959) by Stephan Hermlins. The modern impulse of the anti-rhetorical model only occured once and it did not reach the spectator and thus was abandoned. What the audience wanted to see was realism, nothing but realism, and this was being produced by only one filmmaker,

Hugo Hermann (TRÄUMT VON MORGEN, STAHL UND MENSCHEN, 1956-1957). He let people talk in their own language, he put the sounds of machine shops on the screen, and he did justice to the original soundtrack in idea, dramaturgy and appearance. These films had no followers however, because they dealt with a dogma, although they almost broke this restriction: the original soundtrack is capable of illustrating, but does not pass an action and does not sense a dramaturgical function, therefore is just able to hear 'declarative key sentences instead of realistically observed human expositions'. Hermann's films were related to earlier films like STAHL (1949) and TURBINE 1 (1953), and extrapolated them in an unusual way. They were the reason for the upgrading of the Huisken line in the studio, and with their method took away the procedures that should have brought the DEFA, in the hands of the next generation, closer to the public and international success.

The fourth result of the work was the expansion of the number of genres and the increase in genre awareness. This was first of all asserted in travel films, as they have developed since 1954. Karl Gass especially elevated the social questions to include image and text, without taking away the spectator's pleasure of seeing the world. The split between satirical elevation and readability in the serials and their tendentious development or deception was worth a separate analysis. Because the continuing gazing at behinds and breasts in FENSTERPUTZERSERENADE (Schnabel, 1961) remains deceptive with which the company of men saved itself when they were afraid to focus on the important issues. The DEFA developed its own exclusive genre with its modern history films. Despite an explanation of the historical problem, DU UND MANCHER KAMERAD (Thorndike, 1956) was the first exploration by means of dramaturgy, editing, and speech of German history in this century. It was a test case of how film material can be regarded as an historical source and showed how advanced knowledge can, or indeed has to, increase the actual analysis of a filmic contemplation. This was quite frankly the weaker part of the exercise, caused by a still narrow-minded understanding of narrative endings and their power. The genre found profundity and extension in the film series ARCHIVE SAGEN AUS.

Fifthly, the way was paved for a new concept of man in the documentary film. Making individual human beings the object, or even the subject, had political, dramaturgical, and technical consequences, and the solution of their representation was not easy to find. It had been generally accepted to present people in large sociological groups, in mass-events, marches, manifestations, as the inventory of plants, industrial regions, streets, as the image of an over-image. That was one of the characteristics of everyday Stalinism, but also of the British school of sociology – or rather its misunderstanding.

The documentary filmmakers were raised with political and aesthetic dogmas. 'Our films are still too neutral, too descriptive and dry, too encyclopaedic,' Ivens declared in 1955. 'We were too strict and too dogmatic when we defined the nature of documentary film. We were told that man – the hero – belongs to the feature film and not to the documentary film. But man does have his place in the documentary film!' The ruling abstract image of real people had to be questioned anyway, which, in a political context, meant destalinization, and in an aesthetic context, de-dogmatization. In the steaming hodgeepodge year 1953, Huisken made his mark first with TurBINE 1, which could not be denunciated politically and aesthetically had an open front.

In the compilation of this new concept of man, in which the audience, according to Ivens, 'not only wants to see an image of man, but also living people', the reportage film (STAHL UND MENSCHEN), the discursive (SONG OF THE RIVERS), the poetic (MEIN KIND, FRITZ CREMER) and the historical film (DU UND MANCHER KAMERAD) all played their part. The head of dramaturgy of the DEFA documentary studio, Gustav Wilhelm Lehmbruck, had a far from negligible part in this phase of the development. 'The political themes only become active in the documentary film when they are connected with a human problem... The current Marxism-Leninism is a human matter, and showing it is a human task for artists.' In 1960 Huisken took up an Ivens-programme from 1955, titled *Man in Documentary Film* ('connect human experience with artistic representation'), because the mid-fifties swallows did not make a summer: documentary film was and remained an agitation and propaganda device. In the way documentary film was used by the country's political leaders, it only needed to deliver the confirmation of the superiority of the socialist society. There was no room for real people, their experiences, and the protests against the growing complexity of real life, and even less room for the introduction of the concept of 'activating sensory experiences' as the only opportunity 'to have long term influence on cultivation of a societal conciousness'. The head of dramaturgy, who understood film and society quite well, was replaced by a politician; Machalz's MEIN KIND was not distributed, and Huisken's DAS EIN GUTES DEUTSCHLAND BLÜHE was robbed of its soul. Coming to the artistic documentary film became the job of the next generation of DEFA directors - Böttcher, Junge, Mundt, Cohn-Vossen, Tetzlaff, Nickel - who in the 1960s elevated the term 'DEFA-documentary film'.

The first one to concern himself with this job was Jürgen Böttcher with his film DREI VON VIELEN (1961). The subject of his film was three young workers whose passions, compository and plastic productivity, are linked with one another (and with Böttcher); as well as their everyday lives, their

ideas about life, and the town they live in. A totally new subject, a completely new development of the theme, a seemingly evident ease of life.
Böttcher showed the influence of Flaherty, Ivens, Huisken, and Hermann.
His storylines, however, were totally developed from the stories of the three
men, who, formulated reductively, just wanted to be 'what they are: three
out of many'. The enthusiasm at the studio was immense. Here it was, the
scenario for a new documentary film completely narrated by emancipated
people, no longer needing political back-up, and, therefore, not willing to
take it anymore. This was seen by the authorities as the reintroduction of
spontaneity, as subjectivism, as an attack on their explanatory powers.
Their answer was – we were living, after all, in enlightened times – that the
film limited the capacities of the DEFA documentary filmmakers. So, the
end they ate humble pie with everyone except for three people. They must
be mentioned because they were not included in the honors: Willi Zahlbaum, studio director, who had participated in the opening of the DEFA
documentary film studio and who had kept his word; Renate Wekwerth,
substitute chief editor of DEFA's AUGENZEUGEN, who came to the DEFA at
the same time as Böttcher, and had not been prepared to play a part in this
absurd theater; and Alfons Machalz, for whom a film dream had been realized. Zahlbaum was fired. Wekwerth was allowed to stay and brought
AUGENZEUGEN, together with her colleagues Hartmann, Loewenberg,
Cohn-Vossen and others, to the highest level. Machalz turned his back on
the studio and developed the portrait series MENSCHEN AM PULSSCHLAG DER
ZEIT for German television, which commenced with Joris Ivens and pro-
ceeded with Vertov, Cavalcanti, and Karmen. Böttcher's film was banned
for decades. Nevertheless, the ball had been set in motion, both in reality
and film, and it could no longer be stopped.

    At the end of his eulogy 'The Secrets of Art and the Films of Joris Ivens'
(1955) Bodo Uhse refers to Goethe's words when he sealed the manuscript
of FAUST II: 'In the world as well as in the history of mankind the last solved
problem always contains a new one that has to be solved,' and applies this
to Ivens's film, SONG OF THE RIVERS, by saying that he added the 'new problem that has to be solved to his solution and in this way puts insights in our
heads, that make new demands upon us.'

MEIN KIND – As if it Were Ivens's Child

Alfons Machalz

Is it, or is it not, his? My starting point is that it was both his and not his. To-day, the term *artificial fertilization* would probably be used, or *artistic fertilization*. The history of MEIN KIND from beginning to end is a curiosity. That is not surprising, but it does have some similarities with the history of its spiritual father, Joris Ivens. Ivens was well-known and respected throughout the world, but in his own country he was not everybody's favourite. How do you get to Ivens? How do you work without Ivens, with Ivens, or for Ivens? These questions sound somewhat complicated, but can be answered very logically. They explain a small part of a now non-existent film praxis.

In 1952, my friend Hans Wegner, who later became the producer of the Ivens films and his German biographer, told me someone like me was needed in the DEFA Studio for Documentary Film. My objection that I knew nothing about making documentaries, he laid aside with the argument that was then typical for our country, that 'a communist should be able to do anything'. Fighting my scruples with happy self-assertion and remarkable semi-knowledge, I started in January 1953 at the *Weekly News* as science editor – what else? After all, I came from a large company. Apart from a few light technicians, sound technicians, and film editors, maybe fifteen people in all – for the larger part former camera-assistants who became cameramen – had worked in film companies before 1945. The others came from all kinds of professions and tried their utmost to penetrate the secrets of the film medium. And that was not easy at all. There was no literature available, there was no film academy, and the old and new 'experienced film people' were hesitant to share their knowledge, for all kinds of reasons. So you had to steal with your eyes and ears and learn from your own pitifully laughed-at mistakes. Anyone who knows situations like being in the cutting room and finding out the rushes are missing or the cuts are wrong, will know what I am talking about.

Luckily, there was a light in the darkness – our 'Pietje'. This man would almost blossom when he could share his knowledge with others; he would discuss things with you all night long in the cafeteria or a bar, and drag you into the cutting room or to a screening to explain the big and small ideas behind cinematography. And I need to say that he never denied his socialist views where big ideas were concerned. His credo – which could be understood in two ways – 'The point of view defines the perspective', influenced more than two generations of young DEFA directors and cameramen. I am talking about a Dutchman who had already worked with Joris Ivens in the 1920s. The fascists made him a forced labourer in Germany, where he went into hiding just before the end of the war. After that, he made himself available for the DEFA. I am speaking of Joop Huisken. It is from his lips that I first heard the name Joris Ivens. He spoke of his films, of their work together and the way Ivens explained the difference between painting and film. Joris used the paintings of Pieter Breughel, who tells his stories next to each other, whereas in film we have to tell them one after the other. By the way, many years later, in the biographical documentary film I made about him for GDR television (MENSCHEN AM PULSSCHLAG DER ZEIT), Joris explained this example in a most profound manner. One day Joop Huisken said to me: *'Der Alte* (the old one; that is what used to call Joris) wrote to me that he wants to make a film here. If you like, I will suggest to him that you will be his assistant.' That is how it went and an exciting time began. Ivens brought along his films, among them films of Buñuel and Paul Strand that were unknown here, which we analyzed and discussed. We exploited him according to all the rules of art. The conversations we had at Wegner's home lasted for hours. They have been recorded on tape and give an extensive view of Ivens's life and work. My knowledge of Ivens's work is a result of these conversations, which were an irreplaceable basis for my work on MEIN KIND and my Ivens documentary. This period was for me and many of my colleagues the beginning of an academy, that later developed into the Leipziger Dokumentarfilmwochen, that was initiated and created by Ivens.

This was the atmosphere in which I was allowed to assist on the pre-production of the film LIED DER STRÖME (SONG OF THE RIVERS). I am not a man of many words, but when you realize that between the first concept and the world premiere of this film there was just a period of one year, it is justified to speak of a brilliant mental-artistic and organizational achievement. This achievement is usually associated with Ivens, Pozner, Brecht, Shostakovitsch, and Paul Robeson; and that would be correct. But, to round off this theme, I quote Vladimir Pozner: 'The meetings and conversations, the notes and letters – they troubled Joris a lot and caused many sleepless nights – had not been for nothing. In the four corners of the world people heard about a film about the 'world of labour' that was being produced, and to play a part in it many had risked prison and even their lives. Among them were world famous film people, others, just amateurs, and there were even people that on this special occasion held a camera for the very first time.' Every metre of this film has its own story, that, back then, could not be told because it had been written by someone whose name could not be told either.

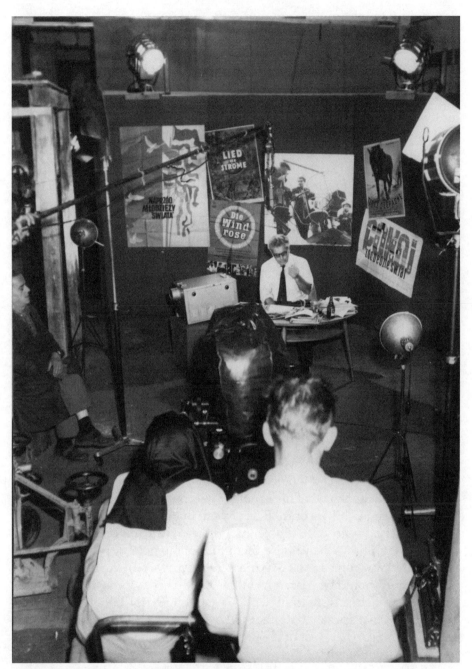

Joris Ivens being filmed for the biographical documentary MENSCHEN AM PULSSCHLAG DER ZEIT made by Alfons Machalz for East German television, 1963.

Everything was organized by six people with one telephone in two rooms in the heart of Berlin, in a state that should not have existed, that called itself East Germany and whose stamp would never be found in Joris Ivens's passport. It is a matter of common knowledge that we were living in the Cold War back then. My job was to take care of the archive materials. After this task had ended, I quit the staff for a few months to take a course at the Humboldt University. I did not really have time for it, but Joris thought it was an opportunity for me to increase my theoretical knowledge and he insisted on me taking it. Upon my return, the preparations of DIE WINDROSE had just started. In this film, which was produced with the support of the International Democratic Women's Federation, the subject would be the problems of the lives of women. Ivens at first thought of a few separate episodes made in different countries, that could be connected and generalized by sequences of archive material. He handed over these documentary sequences to me, while he temporarily entrusted his old friend Alberto Cavalcanti with the general direction of the project. Anyone who knows Joris and his life a bit, knows that this was not new to him. This time, too, he had a well-founded reason, that he, being a Dutchman, could, or would not withdraw from. It was his secret love, his favourite child, *Till Ulenspiegel* which took shape and began to eat away at Ivens with impatience. Beforehand at meetings however, including ones with the authors and directors of the national episodes, we expressed our objections to the documentary part. We feared the possibility that it would be too pedantic. But Joris did not let go of this documentary section. A few days before he had to leave – I had just been in a meeting with Hans Wegner – Joris came in and said: 'We should make two films, without any extra costs. DIE WINDROSE and a documentary film about mothers and children.' It would be a film that spoke to mothers all over the world. Then he took one of his usual scrawls out of his pocket and read his idea out loud: 'A child is born. Everywhere in the world children are born. They are raised with difficulty and sacrifices. Their mothers protect them from pain and danger and raise them to become honest, peaceful people. But one day war comes and takes their children away. In the future, women and children should be spared from this fate.' These words, written on the back of a menu of a restaurant, was our shooting script until the end of the film. 'A film that speaks to mothers all over the world.' This line became a useful warning for the rest of the production. Pozner and I were, according to Joris, the right team for this job. After the approval of our management, I travelled to the film archives of some socialist countries and looked for material and Pozner did the same in Paris.

Then the problems began. Ivens left, the material arrived, Pozner came back from Paris, and the irritation started. I had chosen the material with

Joris Ivens at the DEFA Studios, after being awarded the Kunstpreis in 1961: from left to right: Willie Saalberg, Willie Müller, Hans Wegner, Alfons Machalz, Jochen Hadaschick, Joris Ivens.

clear, even musical, ideas behind it. Volodja Pozner saw it from an unprejudiced angle and had other ideas. We soon agreed on a lot of passages, with other ones it sometimes took days to come to an agreement. So, whenever our ideas clashed, we tried to work using the principle 'what decision would Joris make in this case?' Because we could not contact him, we used examples that he left us in his films. And when even that did not help, we went outside to shoot; because for some passages we did not have the right follow-up shots. We needed, for example, some different close-up shots of women, the face of a woman during childbirth, a child saying 'mummy', a school playground, someone coming back after a war, climbing over debris, and a lot more.

These interruptions were definitely very important for our co-operation. We did not disagree merely out of a petty game of 'who knows better', but because everybody wanted the best solution for a good cause that Joris had entrusted us with. Our problem was how to make our ideas clear to mothers from different regions, different cultures with different views of the world, different religions; to young and old, educated and uneducated mothers. So we had to communicate elementary, simple, clear and general thoughts;

thoughts that appealed to the mind and to the feelings of women. Volodja had already formulated the clear, almost spartan ideas for the text during the cutting which was invaluable to us. That is how the film, the text, and eventually the book also evolved. A book, because an author eventually has to live from his fee and the bookseller obviously needs a book as his proof. The hoarse voice of Helene Weigel gave the slick text a moving warmth and logic. This was the way we wanted the adaptations in other languages to be.

During work on the score our opposite intentions again collided. Together with the head of our music department, Pozner had prepared a variant that was based on Mozart and Bach compositions. I did not agree with this at all, because it neither supported the images nor the text. It killed the film. We stopped sound editing and, together with a totally desperate assistant – who now had to cut the work of her boss – replaced Mozart with the second part of Beethoven's fifth piano concerto. We made the dramaturgically necessary contrasts between war and peace more noticeable in the music by adding parts of Bach's *Air*. However, Pozner remained loyal to his ideas, so we showed the film to composer Hanns Eisler. After seeing it, he said, 'Dear Volodja, please recognize that Beethoven is the better film composer.' He gave in, and then completed our child profile with a French children's song that he played with one finger on the piano, and edited it into a scene of a small Mongolian child. That led me to provide a piece of barrel-organ music to a backstreet. The film was soon ready, but Ivens had not seen a metre of it. We phoned him in Paris. It was a very long, very expensive conversation. Eventually, after a lot of doubts, he agreed to let us add 'artistic direction Joris Ivens' to the credits.

The distribution of the film was in the hands of the staff of the secretariat of the International Democratic Women's Federation. After the first screening there was silence for some minutes. Finally, an African woman said something Joris Ivens would have wished to hear, 'every mother in the world will understand this film'. All of the women present were very impressed which gave the green light to this version and supported its distribution in many countries of the world.

In December 1955, Joris Ivens finally came to Berlin. In his biography, Hans Wegner writes, 'He saw the film and was very impressed. On the one hand by the film itself, on the other hand because colleagues and friends had showed how highly they regarded him by making the film in a way not very different from the way he would have made it.' Thanks to the support of well-known artists with the adaptation into many languages, the film reached a worldwide audience. In the GDR the film could be seen at closed screenings and arthouses.

No-one who had worked on the production of MEIN KIND was part of the delegation my country sent with the film to international film festivals. Although the film won first prizes in Montevideo and Mannheim, it was denied the National Film award in the GDR on numerous occasions and for obscure reasons. The reason: the film was too pacifistic, according to some cultural officials. They demanded changes in the text and the images, which Pozner and I refused to make. But enough has been said about the similarities of the stories mentioned in the beginning. To anyone who still asks whether MEIN KIND was Ivens's child or not, I would like to say that we just honoured a good old Dutch tradition – we regarded ourselves co-workers in the school of a great master.

LA SEINE A RENCONTRÉ PARIS and the Documentary in France in the Fifties

Michèle Lagny

At first glance, LA SEINE A RENCONTRÉ PARIS seems to be a very strange work compared with the other French documentaries from the fifties. Very different from most of the numerous films serially produced by little specialized firms, often commissioned by institutions or enterprises, in fact it could remind me of the productions of the 'Groupe des Trente' who, since 1953, had been trying to invent a new aesthetic for the realist cinema. Between 1947 and 1957, I have found 160 titles about Paris, sixteen a year, and ten for 1957 (of which the two most interesting are NOTRE-DAME DE PARIS by Franju and NOVEMBRE À PARIS by Reichenbach, with Resnais as editor, nine minutes about autumn in Paris, for a series called ENCYCLOPÉDIE DE PARIS). Most of them are documentary tourist films, generally showing the monuments or the curiosities of the city. Ivens's work, on the other hand, looks rather like a Deleuzian 'film-balade' or almost like a 'river-movie'.

Ivens on the Seine

LA SEINE A RENCONTRÉ PARIS had been a great success with both the critics and the audience. With its numerous awards (Golden Palm for Shorts in Cannes in 1958, Golden Gate in San Francisco, and also an award at the Oberhausen festival), in its own time it was seen as an exemplary work.[1] For instance, in 1965, Robert Grelier wrote: 'LA SEINE A RENCONTRÉ PARIS is one of the more accomplished films of Joris Ivens, indeed, maybe even one of the greatest documentary films of contemporary cinema.'[2] Nevertheless, it is generally considered a minor film by most of the books about Ivens, and it was strongly criticized by one of the best connoisseurs of the French documentary, François Porcile: 'disorganized, confusing, it strings the images one after the other, without any conducting line, amassing the repetitions, taking the déjà-vu for unusual. No rhythm to the editing, to organize that gathering of ill-assorted pictures, while Prévert was using his language tricks which had already been worn out for a long time over and over again.'³ Actually, the worst criticism was saved for Prévert, but Ivens was not spared either! As a matter of fact, the film was produced not by Ivens alone, but by a kind of team. Georges Sadoul, then a very well-known critic and cinema historian and Ivens's friend, offered the initial idea for the film. The commentary text was written, after the shooting and the editing of the film, by Jacques Prévert, who was very much influenced by the poetic realism of the thirties and the fourties. The producer was a small new company, 'Garance', of which the name is a reference to a fiction film (LES ENFANTS DU PARADIS), and whose directors are three actors, Betsy Blair, Serge Reggiani and Roger Pigaut – Serge Reggiani being the voice-over narrating Prévert's text in the film.

A long paper written by Sadoul about their collaboration, served as the preface to Zalzman's book about Joris Ivens released by Seghers in 1963.⁴ In the book he explains how, having followed a photographic reportage with Henri Cartier-Bresson, Ivens wondered how to make a film in the same way. Ivens said after THE SONG OF THE RIVERS in 1954 that 'the present and the past, everyday life and the history of a country, following the course of a river'. And before his brief stay in Paris, in 1957 (between a stay in the GDR and another in China, Ivens told him he was interested in the project he would realize in the following year. So it's Sadoul's idea, from an idea of Ivens's, in which Ivens was interested, and about which Prévert wrote a poem afterwards.

Sadoul explains that there was no shooting schedule, only some ideas, photographs and notes he had taken like a 'Kinok-éclaireur', to imitate Vertov's way of speaking and to make a 'little guide of the stroller on the two edges', speaking in the manner of Baudelaire or Walter Benjamin. Actually, there is a handwritten text in the BIFI, from the Cinemathèque Française archives, with numerous funny spelling mistakes, entitled 'first version, april 1957'.⁵ It is an account of the trip of the river Seine going to the sea, and running through the course of a day from east to west. During her trip, the Seine encounters Paris, and the narrative is divided into four parts. Part one: 'In the countryside', where 'The Seine, quiet and happy, runs to the sea through the fields and orchards... The Seine is feeling well, she does not know what is awaiting her.'⁶ Part two: 'Entering Paris': 'The day is still young. Before entering Paris, the Seine receives the Marne on her right, widening generously. On her left, high black cranes are incessantly unloading the coal barges. The light she reflects is strange; Paris is showing itself...'⁷ After a long description of the encounters of the river (the cars and the metro near Austerlitz, the noise, the rubbish, but also the children and the busy boat men), it seems that the Seine is delaying its course. Running, she bows to the people who are living their life along the Seine.'⁸ Parts three and four:

'Paris's heart' and the 'Beaux-Quartiers', where the life is happier and idler, with a lot of fishermen, children, artists, lovers and tramps, between Notre-Dame and the Grenelle Bridge. After a last encounter with the Renault factories, in Billancourt Island, the Finale: 'Running into the sea, the Seine... again finds the countryside.' So there is a real program, conceived in a strolling way, in the course of a beautiful sunny day, with just a little rain.

The project was very clear: Ivens wanted to show, in the course of a day, the brief encounters between the Seine and the people of Paris, along the edges of the river, from the industrial areas to its centre – les 'beaux quartiers'. Seeing the film, we can observe how the plan was followed and despite some minor changes, Ivens concentrated on human lives along the river's edge, and the structure of the film is discernible for every spectator.

François Porcile's criticism can be explained perhaps by the contrast between the project, the editing of the images, and Prévert's text. The text pursues another sense than the synopsis: the poem-commentary is given in Zalzman, and the titles of its eight parts insist on some clichés. There is an introduction (part I), a riddle answered by a little boy, like Oedipus in front of Thebes, then 'a worker' (II), 'a lover' (III), 'a pilot' (IV), 'a gentleman' (V), 'the Seine' (VI), 'a lord' (VII) and an allusion to 'le grand Palace des Allongés' (the cemetery, or rather, near the Austerlitz bridge, the morgue (VIIa)); and for the finale 'It was time on the Seine, it was a time in a life'. The text heavily stressed the commonplace relations between love and death, life and a flowing river, and the anthropomorphic character of the Seine in the film, which weakens Ivens's purpose.

I think it is the weakest part of the film, even if, in my opinion, Ivens (or maybe Sadoul) remains a prisoner of some stereotypes, from Notre-Dame to the Tour Eiffel, from the lovers and the 'midinettes' to the tramps, from the traffic jams to the fireworks and the night shots of the City of Light and the film gives too much importance to stereotyped figures, focuses too long on sparrows, children, lovers and tramps, the traditional figures of Paris of Poulbot, Doisneau and poetic realism. Sometimes Ivens can't resist using a cliché (for instance, the two nuns on the Saint-Michel bridge, ironically filmed from underneath); but there are also some unusual images, such as the shot of three athletes with glasses, or the one of a male couple (maybe gay?). But, even if this film is, as Zalzman noted, *'une permission de détente entre deux batailles sociales'* ('a relaxing break between two social struggles'), the journey is also a method for revealing differences. Before the center of the town, he portrays the working people on barges, carrying and unloading life's necessities, coal and food (wine and corn between Charenton and the Grands Moulins de Paris), sorting and crushing the rubbish, washing and drying the linen, and so on. Dealing with the opposition between the

outskirts and the centre, dirty and clean areas, working people and the relaxing possibilities of the banks, poor and rich, men and women, old and
young, loneliness and happiness, Ivens simultaneously creates a sentimental and a social landscape of Paris.

Nevertheless, LA SEINE A RENCONTRÉ PARIS remains very ambiguous. In
his preface to the Zalzman book in 1963, Sadoul called Ivens 'a master of the
cinéma-vérité', underlining the fact that in 1956-57, Ivens's references were
to Vertov, and not to that new idea. Actually, the similarities between many
of the images with those of the realist poetic films I emphazized, as well as
the anthropomorphic character of the Seine, which was greatly emphasized
by Prévert's poem, gives the film a strong fictional ambience. This
anthropormophic character is partly produced by the fact that we do not
leave the river, except for some shots of the metro and some traffic jams near
the Sarah Bernhardt Theater. More important is the choice of the point of
view, which places the spectator's eye in the eye of the gaze of the Seine herself, creating a subjective effect. Apart from some high angles, especially in
the countryside or on the crowded Deligny swimming pool, Ivens and his
cameraman (André Dumaître) filmed long travelling shots, sometimes from
a low-angle point of view, framing the river herself or the banks. They shot
from two boats lent to them by some firemen; in the script, a sequence with
firemen doing exercises was scripted, but this seems not to have happened
in the film version.

The organization of the shots is not always the same, often, its seems that
there is no structure, and that we are only flowing downstream, idly watching the landscape and the people on the river bank pass, like when we arrive
near Pointe de l'Ile Saint-Louis. Actually, there are many very organized
shots, especially those of the first cranes unloading the barges, and the
bridges with the cars moving across them. The editing is faster and contrast
greater when the film begins to show the working world (especially the man
unloading the corn). Even if we seem to follow the topographical course of
the river, from the first to the last bridge, we know that the contrasts proposed by the real world cannot be seen without the filmmaker's eye and
thoughts. For instance, between two shots of a painter, Ivens sucessively ed-
its in two women, one hanging out her wash and another reading her newspaper, as well as a young white girl and a black boy; some children and an
old man with a white beard. In the same manner, he contrasts some young
fresh girls with their picnic, an elegant restaurant on a Bateau-Mouche with
dishes and servants, and after the reflection of the Eiffel Tower in the water,
a high-angle shot of a tramp spreading butter on bread on an old newspaper, thereby constructing simultaneously the opposition between rich and
poor, young and old, friendly party and lonely lunch. So we are not allowed

forget that the town is organized not really by the course of the river and of the day so much, as revealed by the narrative, but rather by the artist's gaze, which is shown at least three times: when the young Fine Arts students are drawing along the river bank, when the camera frames a painter (before and after the contrasted shots I have just indicated) then, later, a photographer, filming the Seine.

Ivens combines several modes of filmmaking, using reconstructed scenes as well as an observational mode, with the editing playing a leading part. Among the reconstructed scenes is the sequence where some models are posing in Balmain dresses. Others are purely fictional, such as the arrival of two young lawyers in a 4 CV Renault near the Palais de Justice, quai des Orfèvres (a bad idea which Sadoul regretted). The sequence of the tramp giving bread to sparrows, with his bottle next to him, who was surprized by the camera's long gaze, was genuine according to Sadoul. Most certainly, a lot of images came straight from life; but they are always used in a tightly edited framework simultaneously providing the impression of a stroll on the banks along the river and its dialectic opposition, the populated sections of the city.

Between fictional details, demonstrative thought, and *balade*-form, we come to question the actual nature of the film. I think that both its success and the Porcile reaction are linked to its ambiguous turn, and, incidentally, to the fact that it is simultaneously different and yet very close to numerous French documentaries from the fifties. So we need to observe the film in a French context.

The Documentary Landscape During the French Fifties

The film was produced in 1957, during the war between the 'Syndicat de Hubsch' (Union of Producers of Educational Films, Shorts and Documentaries) and the new Association of Independent Producers and Directors of Shorts, established in 1954 by Louis Cuny. The fight began when the CNC changed the rules concerning aid for the production and distribution of shorts films. Since 1940 a short had to be screened as 'the first part of a program' before the feature film and, since the law of 1948 (loi d'aide, Assistance Law), it automatically received three percent of the receipts. The new 1953 law gave aid to eighty quality films each year, but it suppressed a large part of the receipts (leaving only one percent) and put an end to the law requiring that a short film had to be shown before the feature film. The Cuny Association fought to keep the old order, while the Syndicat de Hubsch claimed to represent 'quality films', but wanted to keep the shorts in the first part of the program. So the fight was between two lobbies, but one of them was supported by an intellectual and aesthetic approach to the documentary which it was conducted by the 'Groupe des trente' (who actually numbered forty-three), established in 1953 to promote shorts and to organize not only their own group, but all producers and directors. As portrayed by Roger Odin in *L'Âge d'or du documentaire, Europe: années cinquante*[9], several filmmakers, some of whom are now considered very important (such as Resnais, Marker, or Franju), supported the group, not only by making important works, but also through their discussions and declarations such as their declaration of December 1953 and their programme of 1956 as presented by Marcel Ichac. So it was a period of impassioned statements about the function and the role of the shorts, especially documentary shorts. The documentary was considered 'a matchless instrument for culture, an essential means of teaching and knowledge'.

Actually, the documentary seemed to be going through a very sunny period, in fact, the fifties are often considered the golden age of documentaries. First, because the production was very important: about three thousand films were produced between 1950 and 1959, according to the database we have been working with for six years. The majority of these documentary films were commissioned by national administrations and enterprises, who were putting up the money. In general, they were made for ministries (such as the Foreign office who sent cultural films to foreign countries, the Reconstruction and Development Ministry, or the Ministries of Agriculture and Education). A lot of them were made for nationalized enterprises, especially the SNCF (French Railways), EDF (French Electricity), Charbonnages de France (for coal extraction), or Renault (for cars). Some private, and even foreign industries, made their own films (such as Shell for tractors and farm equipment). Many of the films were made to promote tourism and were sponsored by towns or regions. Three of my research students have worked in the Agriculture, SNCF and Charbonnages de France archives and have explained how and why those films were shot.[10] They found many documents, especially in the archives of ministries and of some large enterprises, which show how these films were produced and made, and for what audiences.

The SNCF set a pattern for enterprise films: since 1945, the SNCF has had a Cinematograpy Department, which produced its own films. The team was directed by filmmaker, André Périé, who shot two of the three films produced during the fifties and the sixties (things changed in the seventies). They were working at the SNCF, for the SNCF, which had its own distribution system, lending the films to its own workers'cine-clubs, in every regional section.

The second form of organization, the institution, was the most common exploiter of the film medium. They suggested a film idea to a production company or to a filmmaker, most likely working for that institution (but sometimes they used freelancers). The institution exerted much control over the film by checking the synopsis, the scenario, and after shooting, the editing. This is the case for the Charbonnages de France, which had no cinematography department, and often preferred a small producer namely 'Son et Lumière', whose best filmmaker was Henri Fabiani. As a matter of fact, Charbonnages de France used a collective of directors among whom the syndicalists (mainly the CGT) were well represented, until the big strikes of 1948. This might explain why they first chose Fabiani, who was rather leftist.

A third method was the one-half in-house and one-half sponsored production which was used by the Ministry of Agriculture. After 1947, they had their own production team, directed by Armand Chartier. But, more often, they commisioned films from small production companies, like JE VOIS TOUT directed by Paul de Roubaix, or from 'Coopagrifilms'. In such cases, private companies would also put up some money as secondary sponsors. For instance, in a film like ALPAGES, a firm producing electric wire fences for cattle in the mountains partly sponsored the film.

This was the major method of production which is interesting because it gives an official social image to the country: most of these films, during the postwar decade, were dedicated to the reconstruction and modernization of the country; they tried to explain and popularize the politics of modernization in farming as well as in industry. Their greatest hero was the man who worked with the new machines, and the big emphasis given to rural workers can be explained by the revolution that the ministry encouraged using in the old mode of French small farmer exploitation, which was not paying enough. The ideas developed were however, more a project than a realistic reflection. It does allow us to understand how, in those films, much of the social representation is not reality, but a dream of that reality, a dream of the people who wanted to offer to France a dynamic and modern society.

However, one must stress the weakness of the self-portraits of these workers. Some of them were produced by the working class organizations, especially the Communist Party in France (PCF), as well as the CGT trade union, which was a close ally of the PCF. Nevertheless, it seems that the syndicalists and leftist parties were not really interested in filmmaking and in using cinema to inform its people. Maybe they just did not find the films serious enough. Another reason could be that the shooting of a film is very

Stills from LA SEINE A RENCONTRÉ PARIS.

expensive as well as the part played by censorship. For instance, one of the most interesting films made for the Syndicate of the Underground Workers by syndicalists of the Cinema Union, LA GRANDE GRÈVE DES MINEURS, had obviously been censored, because it concerned the big strike of 1948. Another point must also be stressed: the dominance of males in the union. Women are only filmed as housekeepers (especially in educational housekeeping films), except in films that showed the countryside, where they are often shown working with their husbands. Children are shown in films about health education, and sometimes at school.

Many of the French documentaries of the fifties also deal with colonization, because, despite the decolonization struggles (in Indochina, between 1947 and 1954, and in Algeria after November 1954), France made large economic investments, especially in North Africa.

Another very important production category concerned tourist information, as well as culture (especially spectacles, painting, literature, and sometimes, history). Most of this work was done by the 'Groupe des Trente' filmmakers. They made numerous films between 1953 and 1959.

It is not easy to know precisely how these films were received. In general, they ran with more amusing films about sport, fishing or tourism, or with cartoons, produced by the SNCF or the Agriculture Ministry, and were shown in local organization halls or in farm schools (we have found some surprising numbers: 2.5 million rural spectators in 1950-1951; 7.5 million in 1954-1955). They were also showns in cine-clubs – which were very important in the fifties. Some of them were released in commercial theatres, before feature films – at least until the mid-fifties. This was the case for films sponsored by the Foreign office, the Ministry of Education or the army. Even though several excellent productions received numerous awards during the fifties, they were more often judged 'boring' by the spectators, who were anxious to see the feature film. Perhaps that is because the good films as well as the bad ones all wanted to show and explain the world, and how to improve it. They had an instructive and idealistic disposition, and perhaps people did not want to be educated when they went to see a movie.

Both its independent production method and its subjective viewpoint helped explain the originality of the Joris Ivens film, and its success. But from a cinematographic point of view, despite its wandering structure, it is not so different from many other documentaries from the fifties. In LA SEINE A RENCONTRÉ PARIS, we observed two interesting points: the large influence of fiction film on the documentary representation, at least at the beginning of this decade, and the difference of editing and filming between rural films and industrial films.

For instance, when the cinematographic section of the SNCF shot its first film, it was in order 'to show the real work of the real conductor of the real locomotives'. But the first sequence of the first SNCF film in 1945, PILOTES DU RAIL, is so close to LA BÊTE HUMAINE of Jean Renoir that it stands out as an image from the previous decade. And if we studied the film, we would also recognize THE WHEEL by Abel Gance, (during the twenties) and LA BATAILLE DU RAIL by René Clément, a reconstruction of the resistance movement's use of the railways during the war, also released in 1945. It is as if the 'representation of the real' was following fictional realism, treading the boundary between fiction and non-fiction. Besides, it could have been a voluntary choice, such as that of Resnais, Marker and Heinrich in 1957 who made LE MYSTÈRE DE L'ATELIER 15, which looks like a detective story in order to tell the story of the investigations about the illness of a worker in a factory, in a narrative but also in a fictional way, as Roger Odin explains very well.[11]

For my second point I will provide the example of EN PASSANT PAR LA LORRAINE ('Going through the Lorraine', also the title of an old popular song). In 1950, a documentary film was commissioned by the industrial association of the Lorraine to present the question of regional modernization, of a big industrial area with coal and iron mines, and large iron and steel works. During the fifties, an important modernization program was launched, and the area was presented as the 'Far-West', or rather the 'Far-East' for France. But at the same time, farming remained very important, and most of the factory workers still farmed a little, at least gardens for vegetables and some cattle. The factories themselves were built in the countryside (for instance, more often in the Fentsch and Orne Valleys than around cities such as Metz or Nancy).

The production company used was 'Forces et voix de France', and the filmmaker was Franju, who always tried to shoot his films in a traditional manner, even if, by some accounts, he had an *'esthétique de la déstabilisation'*, that is to say an aesthetic which is critical of the stereotyped mode of representation, as he did in his first documentary, in 1948, THE BLOOD OF THE BEASTS (LE SANG DES BÊTES), about the Paris slaughterhouse, la Villette.[12]

There is a big editing and ambience difference between the countryside and industrial factories. The countryside called for smooth grey colour, long shots with a moving camera, long pans and quiet music; for the factory, short cuts, black and white contrast, loud sound – generally influenced by the image of modernity proposed by German or Soviet films from the twenties. During the fifties, they became 'stereotyped images', the traditional mode of filming and editing we find in the majority of documentary films of the decade. Nevertheless, by the end, we're not sure whether country and factory are so complementary as the film should have revealed, because

Franju shot some frames which offered us some critical propositions. For instance, high angles on large white clouds of steam coming from the chimneys, and presenting images of pollution (people were not aware of this problem in the fifties, when the main concern was to produce more, more quickly). Another example is the beautiful ballet of the workers making steel in long and dangerous ribbons of glowing molten steel. This is a reminder of how dangerous this work is and how dependent the workers are on their wits and abilities. With or without modernization, steel mill work remains dangerous and tiring.

In this context, LA SEINE A RENCONTRÉ PARIS is closer than we think to the dominant mode of representation which was prevalent in France during the fifties and it seems to me that it is less critical of stereotypes deriving from both poetic realism and the modernity of the twenties than films by the best directors at Groupe des Trente. Maybe this is due to the influence of Sadoul or Prévert. Maybe, as Zalzman intimated, Ivens was 'on leave' for some weeks!

Joris Ivens and Documentary in Italy

Virgilio Tosi

In the fifties, cinema was the most popular form of public entertainment. In Italy, average attendance at the cinema was very high: statistically, about twelve times per person per year, which means that each adult went to the cinema two or three times per month.

Italian feature-film production was important and still enjoyed the artistic legacy of neo-realism. But the state of documentaries was very bad, at least in terms of quality. Italy, throughout the century-long history of cinema, had had no relevant tradition in this field which could be favorably compared to, for instance, Grierson's British School.

After the Second World War, to encourage the reconstruction of an industry and to protect the national character of film expression, certain laws were adopted, as also occurred in France. By this means, documentaries (and newsreel magazines) were aided in a variety of ways: they became a virtually compulsory accompaniment to any screening of feature films, as a 'cultural' addition to the entertainment; they were allocated a fixed percentage of the income, exhibitors were granted tax relief, and money-based 'quality awards' were offered to the producers. This situation quickly degenerated, favouring speculation, mass low-quality production, and the emergence of an unwritten but strict rule: documentaries should never exceed ten or eleven minutes in length (the minimum laid down by law) in order not to interfere with the daily schedule of the exhibitors, who were anxious to save space for advertisements and at the same time, to maximize the number of screenings of the feature film programmed.

I myself can attest to the absurdity and the excesses of this situation, since my professional career as a documentarist dates from that period. Michèle Lagny quotes the number of about three thousand documentaries produced in France between 1950 and 1959.[1] In Italy, in the year 1955 alone, production reached 1132 documentaries.[2]

Ivens and the Italian Film Clubs

Very early in the fifties I had the opportunity, in my capacity then as General Secretary of the Italian Federation of Film Societies, to invite Joris Ivens to come to Italy to present about half a dozen of his documentaries personally. For him, it should have been a very good occasion to visit and get to know the country; his only previous trip to Italy had been a very short one to Perugia in 1949, in order to take part in and speak at an international meeting of filmmakers.[3] Ivens's name was legendary among film enthusiasts, hardly any of whom had seen even one of his films. Ivens accepted the invitation and adventurously arranged for five or six of his films to be brought to Italy, one of which was the sole copy available at that time. Over a three-week period in the spring of 1951, we travelled through Italy, visiting a number of film clubs: his presentations were a great success, despite a number of bans imposed by the police, which we were able to get round by one means or another.

His screened films included THE BRIDGE, BREAKERS, BORINAGE and NEW EARTH. Ivens also had some friendly meetings with outstanding Italian film directors and screenwriters. He was very satisfied with this engaging though tiring tour, often repeating 'I am a son of the film clubs', with reference to his role in the Film Liga of the twenties. This Italian tour remained strongly impressed upon his memory; Ivens recalls episodes of this trip in several pages of his second autobiography. I only quote a few short excerpts:

> During my years of isolation behind the Iron Curtain, a first three-week trip had opened the doors of Italy for me. [...] Italy, and Italian cinema, were a revelation to me. The neorealism, so close to my own work, brought me close to the Italian directors. [...] About BORINAGE or SPANISH EARTH they said: 'your films are a basis'. To me, those people of postwar Italy gave *me* a lesson in cinema. [...] From my first day in Italy, the relations came easy, and I felt very close to the people, in a natural way. Warm, direct, the Italians accepted me as I was [...] In Italy I discovered the lightness, the art of living, the spontaneity, the immediate friendships, so many things of which my character had always kept me away. Here I built up solid relations and long lasting friendships. [...] And Virgilio Tosi! Another friend forever. Responsible for the ciné-clubs, he had dragged on that crazy tour through Italy, fifteen presentations in Rome, Florence, Trieste, Venice, Parma, Livorno... The ciné-clubs movement was very popular in Italy, very close to the cultural associations of the Communist Party, and this trip had an enormous impact. The press had given it a big echo, and, very soon, my work was known to 'cinéphiles' and others.[4]

Leaving Italy in 1951, he feared that, owing to the existing international 'cold war', some of his films might disappear or be buried in a cinémathèque; he then officially authorized the Italian Federation of Film Clubs to make a copy of some of his documentaries to ensure that they could be distributed in the future. A collection was organized by some Italian film directors and members of the cinéclubs for the purpose of quickly raising the substantial sum needed to pay for the 35mm dupe negatives, so that the selected films could be copied before the positive prints were sent back.[5]

Nowadays, an interesting topic of research would be to study the possible influence of that early impact of Joris Ivens's work on the young Italian filmmakers of the time. Traces of that influence can be observed in some documentaries of that period, as well as in the Italian official and unofficial contribution to some Ivens compilation films of the fifties (POKÓJ ZWYCIEZY SWIAT, DAS LIED DER STRÖME), and in the Italian episode by Gillo Pontecorvo in DIE WINDROSE).

Ivens and Italian Television

The late fifties saw another important interaction between Joris Ivens and Italian documentary film and television. The Italian state trust for petroleum, ENI, was then led by Enrico Mattei, on whom the Italian film director Francesco Rosi based an important 'engaged' fiction film entitled IL CASO MATTEI (1972) after Mattei's mysterious death in an air crash in 1962. In 1959, the director of ENI had invited Joris Ivens to make a series of three documentary films about Italy and the successful discoveries of petroleum and natural gas. The films were to be broadcast by RAI, the Italian State Television. Ivens hesitated for a while before accepting the proposal. Then, having agreed to it, he devoted himself wholeheartedly to the production, having obtained guarantees of expressive freedom as the author. The team of four young Italian filmmakers drafted in to help him prepare the script and to assist him during the filming and the editing included some documentarists. Later on, they all became fiction film directors: they were Tinto Brass, Valentino Orsini and Paolo and Vittorio Taviani.

Ivens was very interested in this absorbing project for two fundamental, though different, reasons. On the one hand the subject matter of the three films was a controversial confrontation of the policy of the big international oil producing and distributing trusts (the so-called Seven Sisters). At the same time, the project provided an opportunity offered to document the social and economic situation of Italy, a country full of contradictions, with large areas of great poverty, but also making a serious effort to create modern industries capable of bringing the country into the fold of the industrialized nations. On the other hand, Ivens was attracted by the new professional challenge he would have to face, with quite large production resources at his disposal, allowing him to experiment with the new television language.

It is not possible here and now to describe in detail the long development of the production of L'ITALIA NON È UN PAESE POVERO, except for the dramatic ending, when the leader of ENI was no longer in a political position to force the Italian state television company to broadcast the three films in the version prepared by Ivens. The television company agreed only to programme an extensively censored and manipulated version. Censorship (either that carried out by the official censor's office for films and documentaries, or the internal censorship of TV programmes) was very strict and draconian at that time. The case of Joris Ivens was not an isolated one.[6] Through lawyers, Ivens ensured that these broadcasts were described as 'fragments from a film by Joris Ivens'. They were broadcast in July 1960, late at night.

For many years, we in Italy thought that the complete version of L'ITALIA NON È UN PAESE POVERO had been lost. During my courses at the National Film School in Rome, I used to screen for students a shortened English version of Joris Ivens's film as manipulated and circulated by RAI Television for sale abroad, until one of the students as part of his studies decided to prepare a documentary film reconstructing the eventful story of the Ivens Italian films. The research work of Stefano Missio (the student in question) revealed that one of Ivens's assistants had secretly sent (in a French Embassy diplomatic bag) a copy of the original and complete version of the Ivens films to the Cinémathèque Française.[7] Now, as part of the courses on the History of the Documentary Film, we were able to screen this complete version and I personally, when viewing it for the first time, was surprised to discover that in one of the end sequences compiled with stock footage from scientific images, Ivens had included scenes from one of my documentaries on nuclear physics.

Within the vast and highly varied filmography produced by Joris Ivens, the Italian production L'ITALIA NON È UN PAESE POVERO represents an interesting case: the film was made under commission, but the sponsor did not interfere with the freedom of expression requested by the author. Neither Mattei, the president of ENI, nor the management of the petroleum trust succeeded in having certain sequences they did not like (e.g., the science fic-

Paolo Taviani and Joris Ivens during the shooting of L'ITALIA NON È UN PAESE
POVERO.

Still from L'ITALIA NON È UN PAESE POVERO.

tion episode with the child sleeping and dreaming of being able to fly) cut or altered.

Ivens freely decided to experiment, formally and thematically, with a potpourri of different expressive styles: imitating a 'live TV broadcast', using animations in a scientific sense but also as a humorous satire, and including fictional short stories reconstructed with non-professional actors mixed with purely documentarist sequences. He did not remain within the boundaries of a commissioned film which was to be about the discovery in Italy of petroleum and natural gas, but extended his scope to an analysis of the devoloping socio-economic situation, and hoped to send a message to future generations. In this sense, unfortunately, the film now seems dated and strictly committed to a firm belief which was widespread thirty or forty years ago: the lack of environmental awareness concerning the trend towards massive industrialization (see the sequences concerned with the siting very near to Venice of large, highly polluting industrial plants); the naive belief in the future of science helping mankind (see the sequences with the ballad singer identifying war and nuclear weapons as the devil, but pointing to a happy future with the help of peaceful applications of nuclear energy).

Further analysis of this Ivens film throws light on the contribution made by his Italian assistants (particularly in the case of the Taviani brothers), which seems important in certain parts of the film. There was, in this instance, a profound mutual interaction between Ivens and the Tavianis: Ivens accepted their creative help which led very nearly to fiction, whilst they came to realize, through Ivens's influence, that they should abandon their work as documentarists and move for good into fiction film.

The recent centenary of Ivens's birth provided opportunities for special screenings of the original uncut version of L'ITALIA NON È UN PAESE POVERO, in Nijmegen and in Italy (Rome, Torino, Pitigliano, and Florence). The impact of these three films, which until now have remained almost unknown even to the scholars of Ivens's work, is nowadays very forceful, although some parts strike the viewer as obsolete. The quality of the expressive form is very interesting and the construction of the thematic narration presents the dialectic evolution of Ivens's ideology when compared with previous works made in the early fifties in Eastern Europe.

The original TV language used demonstrates Ivens's great interest in it as he used it for the first time. The length of the three episodes (nearly two hours) enables various styles of filming to be combined, including the repeated use of stock footage from the most varied sources.

The eventful production and post-production story of Ivens's Italian films certainly deserves to be studied in greater depth, starting with a comparison between the uncut version produced by the author, the mutilated extracts broadcast in Italy, the version he was preparing but never completed for screenings in cinemas, and the manipulated version sold by Italian Television in many foreign countries, misleadingly using Ivens's name. Important and still unpublished documents concerning the events relating to L'ITALIA NON È UN PAESE POVERO are available in the archives of the European Foundation Joris Ivens, whilst others have certainly yet to come to light. The work begun with the documentary film QUANDO L'ITALIA NON ERA UN PAESE POVERO[8] is only in its early stages.

I quote here from a long letter written in Rome on 17 December 1959 by Mr. Valli, head of the PROA Film Co. in charge of the production of the ENI films, and sent to the hotel very near to Rome where Ivens was working with his Italian co-workers. He wanted to inform him immediately that the previous evening, Italian TV had broadcast a documentary about the first findings of petrol in Sicily by the Gulf Oil Co. Excusing himself for his faults in French, he adds some comments on the significance of the programme:

> ..that is, the American monopoly: that is one of the main aspects of the polemic with Mattei and his 'socialist' and Italian ideas. The film was horrible, and the commentary heavy and false. But they said so many things on the importance of the political and economic aspects of the battle Mattei is leading. It is clear that the projection has been done those days, because the films of the ENI were not ready yet, and it is clear too that this answers to a polemic you, being political next to being a poet and an artist, can not ignore. We have to think that Mattei has to say and show everything that is possible. And *not because he pays, but also because he can not have other evenings on television*, for – we must not forget – television is the monopoly of his enemies.[9]

Another interesting document is a cable sent on 14 April 1961 (also by Valli) to Peking (Central Studio Newsreel & Documentary) where Ivens was working (having unhappily concluded his Italian production), in order to respond to the protests repeatedly made by Joris Ivens for the unauthorized use of his name in the manipulated TV version of L'ITALIA NON È UN PAESE POVERO, and the fact that Ivens had not yet received the requested copy of the full editing.

> Your name and prestige safeguarded by us because Hollywood version much nearer your original than to television version stop Titles indicates telefilms extracted from film by Joris Ivens stop. Original version has not obtained Italian censorship nor export license this is the reason your copy still Rome stop Best wishes friendly regards – VALLI[10]

It is worth concluding these short quotations with a passage from one draft (of the at least two existing, hand-written drafts) of a letter from Ivens to

Valli which was prepared between the end of July and the beginning of September 1961:

> Dear friend, how are you? It's been a while since I've heard from you. During more than a year we only had some telegrams from different corners of the world. The life of our film L'ITALIA NON È UN PAESE POVERO has been quite stirring; if I understand well at the Venice Festival 1960, and elsewhere. After I made the film in three parts (each about 45 minutes), they forced us to cut and maltreat the film, which has damaged its contents and its form of expression. Those cuts were demanded by reactionary authorities, and by people with a lack of artistic understanding. I'm insulted and at the same time unhappy that they destroyed my work, made with a pure concept, correct, honnest, accepted by everyone from the start. I'm proud of the complete film I made with your help and with your production company.

Yukong and Italian Television

In the sixties and seventies, Ivens came to Italy on many different occasions. On one occasion, as in a mythological nemesis, the same RAI television company responsible for the attempt to destroy the film L'ITALIA NON È UN PAESE POVERO decided to buy and broadcast in full the twelve-hour series of *Yukong* films. The political situation in Italy had changed. In 1976, the Italian Communist Party led by Enrico Berlinguer, with its policy of independence towards the so-called socialist countries of Eastern Europe, became very strong and ran the councils of all the major Italian cities. The state television company had also changed: not only was it willing to obtain and programme the YUKONG films, but it accepted a contractual clause to invite Joris Ivens and Marceline Loridan to Rome to supervise the preparation of the Italian version. In a country as highly developed in the technical field of dubbing as Italy was, the fact that a foreign documentarist had been asked to select the voices and decide the mixing levels between the original soundtracks and the Italian one was absolutely extraordinary. Even for the dubbing of Hollywood films which had been awarded many Oscars and for the big market of the cinema-theatres, such a procedure has always been very rare.

It happened in 1977 for the dubbing of YUKONG films, but, nevertheless, we need to remember that during the sixties, during one of his visits to Italy to discuss plans for films or for presenting documentaries at festivals, Ivens was declared *persona non grata* and asked to leave the country immediately. This occurred at the end of 1965 in Florence:

Virgilio Tosi and Joris Ivens during the documentary film seminar in Rome, 1977.

We arrived at the last moment, with the film [LE CIEL, LA TERRE] in our luggage. The Festival dei Popoli had been very keen to get hold of the film. It was during the Vietnam War. Unexpectedly the police knew that the film was in Florence [without any official import license – noted by V.T.]. They intended to expel me from the country, then the decision was withdrawn. Nenni intervened personally. Italian filmmakers, among them Fellini and Antonioni, expressed their solidarity, declaring that my being held for questioning was idiotic. In the end I received an official apology.[12]

Then, in 1985, the Italian President conferred on Joris Ivens the decoration of Grande Ufficiale dell'ordine al merito della Repubblica Italiana.

Professor Ivens

When he came to Rome in the autumn of 1977 to supervise the Italian version of YUKONG, Ivens was seventy-nine years old, but in very good shape. At that time, I had already started to lecture on the documentary at the Centro Sperimentale di Cinematografia in Rome, now called Scuola

Nazionale di Cinema, the second oldest film school in the world. Taking advantage of our long-standing friendship, I dared to ask Joris if he would agree to come to the school for a three-hour seminar. He accepted with enthusiasm.

The seminar was very successful. Some students recorded it with the then-available non-standard half-inch videotape. In 1998, to mark the centenary of Ivens's birth, it was decided that an attempt would be made to restore the old original videotape by transferring it onto more modern technology. The restoration work is not yet complete, mainly because of the poor state of the soundtrack, but one of the students has produced a forty-minute digest.[13] Having taken part in the seminar in order to introduce Ivens to the students and to translate questions and answers, I found it a moving experience to relive the events of the past through the old black-and-white images – after more than twenty years - and to present part of this as a yet unpublished audiovisual document during the celebration of the Ivens centenary, first in Italy (Pitigliano, Tuscany, November 1998) and then in Nijmegen during the International Symposium, December 1998.

Ivens and the 'Florence' project

To complete this short overview of the relationship between Ivens and documentary in Italy, I should like to draw attention to the fact that, in 1979, two Italian towns (Modena and Florence) held a comprehensive retrospective and an exhibition, organized in association with with the Nederlands Film Museum, to celebrate fifty years of filmmaking by Joris Ivens. Those events provided an opportunity for the publication of the Italian version of his first autobiography.[14] Furthermore, the Florentine city authorities and the Tuscan regional government invited Ivens to prepare a project for a documentary film about Florence. Subsequently, the project also included the Italian state television company.

Joris Ivens and Marceline Loridan spent several weeks in Florence and Tuscan, with a staff at their disposal, and they finally prepared a script about forty pages of which was acquired by the Tuscan regional government. Unfortunately, owing to bureaucratic and political complications, the project fell victim to a case of reciprocal 'buck-passing'. It was accepted in principle but never came to fruition.

Recently, on the occasion of the Centenary, a round table was organized in Florence to discuss the events surrounding the project. The text of the script, dated spring 1981, was studied and analyzed. Many very interesting observations and comments were discussed, in particular that the idea of the film was based on a highly original mixture of cinematographic and television languages and that the basic intention was not to produce a documentary on Florence. At the end of his second autobiography (1982), Ivens writes:

> When, tomorrow, I leave for Florence to make a new film, this will be another stage. Maybe the last? [..] I imagined that this film treats about the encounter of an old documentarist and a city, which also has experienced a lot. Each his own story, its museum, its richness, and their memory. It's a mirror game, and a two-fold interogation: that of a man who wants to grasp the city in its reality; that of a city questioning about the man that comes to film it. It's a duel, and I'm impatient to start. But when will it start? [..] Ultimately, nothing is sure for a filmmaker![15]

Ivens wrote these words full of youthful enthusiasm at the age of eighty-three. In the Florentine script, he even recalled with the same enthusiasm his first encounter with the city, in 1951, on the occasion of the screening of his films at the local ciné-clubs, for which he had fought so hard.

Joris Ivens and Marceline Loridan: A Fruitful Encounter

Jean-Pierre Sergent

Is there, on the cinematographic level, a Joris Ivens 'before' and a Joris Ivens 'after' his meeting with Marceline Loridan, as has been stated more than once? Marceline became his wife and close collaborator for more than thirty years. When one compares the style of the films he made just before their collaboration, such as CARNET DE VIAJE, ...A VALPARAISO or POUR LE MISTRAL, with that of the films they made together, LE 17ÈME PARALLÈLE, LE PEUPLE ET SES FUSILS, COMMENT YUKONG DEPLAÇA LES MONTAGNES (HOW YUKONG MOVED THE MOUNTAINS), one is forced to see a major change. This change moved the great documentary filmmaker from a purely visual cinematography, of which the narration is based on a symphony of images organized by very elaborate montage rythms, towards a cinema of which the sequences shot with synchronous sound constitute the strong and meaningful moments of oeuvre. On the one hand, cinema for the eye, on the other, cinema for the ear? Left brain (emotion, intuition) against right brain (reflection, logic)?

Because nothing is ever quite simple, let us turn to the source for a better view. It is on a cinema screen that Joris Ivens first got to know Marceline Loridan. Not just an ordinary film either! In his autobiography *Mémoire d'un regard*,[1] he tells of how he was very upset by the appearance of that young woman on the deserted Place de la Concorde during a summer afternoon, evoking in a long murmured monologue the death of her father, deported with her to Birkenau in CHRONIQUE D'UN ÉTÉ (CHRONICLE OF A SUMMER), the founding film of the 'cinéma-vérité', by Jean Rouch and Edgar Morin. The camera was held by Michel Brault, and the sound was recorded by Marceline herself that day, managing a tie-microphone and the twelve kilos of the Nagra on a strap with the potentiometer put on automatic recording...

Joris did not know it then, but this long take of several minutes, shot with synchronous sound, camera in hand (which was far from normal in 1960), would change his life and his way of filming. (Regarding Marceline, when she met the great documentarist of the silent film for the first time, she could not imagine the many hours of sync sound recording, microphone rod in hand and the Nagra on the shoulder, that she would do with him later...)

This encounter has something symbolic about it - two generations, two technologies, two filmmaking methods. Ivens never hid his fascination, mixed with irritation, for the way documentarists started to use the synchronous sound technique systematically. He, who had learned filmmaking shooting with a silent camera (compelled to, after all it was 1927-1928), of which the spring mechanism did not allow shots of more than fifteen or twenty seconds. He who had edited his first films by sketching the shots on cards with indications of movement, combining them and recombining them to build the sequences, imposing all the variations in rhythm and tempo he had in mind. He thought it was rather easy - and rather poor - to have recourse to such long takes, only driven by dialogue.

In an article which appeared in the early sixties in *Les lettres françaises*, a weekly on literature and arts conducted by Aragon, he expressed his interest and his mistrust regarding this instrument, and also his fear that young filmmakers would be carried away by its ease of handling and, in the process, 'forgetting to think'. Although he was convinced of the intellectual honesty of the directors of CHRONIQUE D'UN ÉTÉ, he remained suspicious towards the films of a Richard Leacock, whose virtuosity appeared to him a little suspect: 'I love his films up to the point of jealousy, but at the same time I'm afraid. Maybe I feel outdated? However, I don't think that's the real reason for my unease. The richness of those new techniques seemed to me announcing the facility of a superficial approach of reality, under the eyes of clever manipulators'.[2]

This mistrust did not prevent him, when he left for a second trip to Vietnam, with Marceline and on her advice, decides to film in 16mm with synchronous sound. They had the same need to commit themselves, the same vision of the struggle. But she had a new approach to propose on a cinematographic level. 'With LE CIEL, LA TERRE,' she said, 'Joris had made a filmmanifesto, very visual and beautiful, which waved like a banner in the wind. When we concieved LE 17ÈME PARALLÈLE, we wanted to show how the Vietnamese lived and fought under the stress of the bombings. We didn't want to show the public in the West icons, but real people, who we had let speak. I was a cinéma-vérité girl; I had made some documentaries for television for which I used my experience as a fieldworker to make people speak. This certainly played a role in our decision to use the technique of direct sound. But after all, this was the main tendency in documentary filmmaking at that moment.'[3]

In LE 17ÈME PARALLÈLE Ivens's characters, for the first time, talked extensively, spoke about themselves, individualized themselves. This change would be more manifest in the next project, the enormous (in every sense with twelve hours of edited film, and extraordinary testimony from China during the Cultural Revolution) HOW YUKONG MOVED THE MOUNTAINS, filmed in China in 1972-73. In this film, for the first time, we see and hear many Chinese people talking about their daily life and their efforts to participate in the transformation of their society. 'For LE 17ÈME PARALLÈLE,' Marceline recalls, 'we were limited by an intermediate technique, a blimped camera, on a tripod, which was impossible to move. For YUKONG we had much more modern equipment including a Coutant camera, a quartz driven Nagra IV. We could really work.'

True to his old custom, Ivens decided to film with a Chinese crew, at the same time teaching them how to make a film. But it was impossible to make the chief operator understand what was expected of him. Irreproachable regarding lighting and framing, he did not understand anything about the rules of direct cinema. A sync long take? He only understood what this was when Marceline, after two months of unfruitful shooting and a return trip to Paris to develop the rushes, came back to China with some sync sound films, made by young French filmmakers, of which one contained a ten-minute-long take with synchronous sound. 'The screening left our operator stupefied, and to convince him that one could really film like that we had to verify the copy that there were no jumps that would reveal the editing of different shots!' After this educational experience, the shooting posed no more problems than as if the crew had had a consummate practice in this way of filming. 'In fact, Joris was as new as the Chinese in this field, tells Marceline. But he was an innovator, always in movement, always facing the future, and he had an extraordinary facility to adapt himself to all kinds of situations and to all possibilities offered by the new techniques.'

It is interesting, in this respect, to remind us how Joris Ivens started to make his first, unfortunately now lost, film experiments, fifteen years after THE WIGWAM, his childhood film, and a few months before THE BRIDGE, which made him immediately one of the leading avant-garde artists. With his camera in hand, 'this magnificent Kinamo of Professor Goldberg's' he enters an Amsterdam bar where a few people are discussing and drinking. 'I focused on following the gestures and attitudes of the men in the bar, trying not to disturb the ambiance, but to film it as I felt it and as I saw it through the viewfinder of my camera. When I screened the copy of this experiment for myself, I was surprised by the quality of the images. I had attained a photography that reminded me of the lighting you can find in Dutch paintings. But there was something even better, with the camera in hand, I had liberated myself in a natural way from the rigidity of the tripod, and I had given a movement to that what normally would have been a sequence of fixed shots. Without knowing, filming supple and continuously, I had realized a long take.'[4]

Daily life and war: still from LE 17ÈME PARALLÈLE.

Joris Ivens (right) and Marceline Loridan (with microphone) during the shooting
of YUKONG.

All his life, Joris Ivens had moved from one form of cinema to another, with an astonishing lightness and facility, going from abstraction to lyricism and the epic, singing the beauty of the natural elements, or being touched by the efforts of people, sensible to the details of daily life as much as to the inspiration of the revolution and the interior song of the artist... Every time he found a form that matched his aims, he used it without abandoning the distinguishing marks of his style. Sometimes sound failed him, because, after all, his first films were made in the silent era. When he started using it, he knew how to make use of it in a convincing way. Here the twelve hours of YUKONG have not stopped to interest us as an example of what cinematographic research can attain, if led by the clear point of view of the authors. And I am convinced that people will find more and more interest and pleasure in seeing these films again in the coming years.

All his life, filming silent, with sound, or with synchronous sound, Joris Ivens remained true to his way of conceiving his films on a formal level, as dynamic compositions of moving images. 'When he had enough of the synchronous long takes, which broke the cinematographic tempo he so adored,' recalls Marceline (but wasn't that the price to pay to enter the time of others?), 'fatiguing him, he decided to film 'beauty shots'. Just to have a rest and enjoy himself.'

He was right; it is through the beauty of the images, which he knew how to capture with his lens, and by the consummate art of editing, that one recognizes his look and his mark – in every film since THE BRIDGE, as it is, in fact, well demonstrated in his last work, UNE HISTOIRE DE VENT. A work in which he does not hesitate, even at ninety, and with the desire to question himself at an artistic and a philosphical level, to imagine with Marceline a new form of cinema, crossing the traditional borders that separate the documentary film from the fiction film.

Reflection

The Documentary and the Turn from Modernism

Bill Nichols

When we look at the mature Suprematist work of Kazimir Malevich, with its extraordinary move beyond objects and beyond reason, we enter, Malevich hoped, into a transformed state of mind.[1] In this objectless world, Malevich insisted on the rule of law but not the rule of reason or realism, not the rule of cubism, futurism, surrealism or the other stylistic halfway houses en route to an objectless world: 'In transforming the world I await my own transformation; perhaps in the final day of my transfiguration I shall assume a new form, leaving my present image behind in the dying green animal world.'[2]

Inciting our movement toward the heightened level of awareness that could only exist beyond the world of objects and object relations, beyond everyday politics and representational art, clearly obsessed Malevich. Even after the pressures of a repressive political climate required him to retreat from the absolutism of his radical style, key elements, what he called 'supplements', persisted. His 'theory of the supplement', akin to Shklovsky's theory of 'ostranenie', isolated those vital elements whose appearance in a style produce dramatic change. Like bacilli, they were the active agents of aesthetic infection within Malevich's elaborate medical metaphor for art.[3] Providing a palimpsest of figurative coating to the supplement might disguise its appearance but its potency remains intact. Heightened awareness is possible in his later, more realist work, because Malevich infects us with what was of most value from the heights of his Suprematist achievements.

I want to ask if a similar form of persistence occurs across the gap between an early modernist impulse and a later realist style in the work of Joris Ivens. Was modernism something that fell by the wayside because of its own infirmity, its failure to reach the masses or arouse the passions appropriately, its ultimate decadence – or did a modernist element persist and in its persistence give greater, more complex figuration to the realist sensibility that replaced it?

Ivens's films of 1928-29 (THE BRIDGE, RAIN, WE ARE BUILDING, HEIEN, et al.) provide the testing ground for this question. What persists from these films? What 'supplementary element' does it contribute to the more fully re-

Kazimir Malevich, *Football Match* (Stedelijk Museum Amsterdam).

alist work that follows? What do these questions imply about our understanding not only of Ivens's career, but also of the history of documentary filmmaking and the shifts of styles and modes that characterize it?

The last question can be re-posed through a comparison with two models for the history of linguistic change.[4] The *Stammbaum* or family tree model dates back to 1861, and August Schleicher's *Compendium* in which he adapted many of Darwin's ideas about the survival of species to the survival of languages where the evidence for common ancestors such as Latin was obvious compared to the intense doubt about a common ancestor for man and ape. The movement from the supporting base of language-families up through the sturdy boughs of languages proper and on into the limbs of various dialects before terminating in the slender branches of idiolects, paralleled the connections of genera to species to varieties (or races) and individuals. The latest and most distinct variants display overlapping characteristics because they share a common ancestry. The strongest linguistic or animal species are those endowed with characteristics best suited to survival. Like primates or algae, languages are complex living systems that establish hierarchies of superiority and dominance over time, but stem from a single stock.

Such a theory, of course, smacks of formalism – an intrinsic movement toward progressively more advanced forms or structures – coupled to a virulent social Darwinism in which the survival of English at the expense of Manx or Welsh presumably demonstrates both the inherent superiority of the English language and a natural evolutionary progression that rewards the fittest.

Though problematic, variants of such a theory often crop up in relation to the tale of aesthetic struggle between the hearty language of what we now call 'classic Hollywood cinema' and those less well-endowed variants, or mutations, such as the modernist avant-garde, the European art cinema, or the great, but failed, experiments in Soviet montage theory. The strong survive and drive out the weak.

Addressing the question of how languages change, but abandoning the Darwinian *Stammbaum* model, Johannes Schmidt proposed, in 1872, an alternative view: 'Schmidt's wave theory.' This theory strikes me as a suggestive alternative approach to questions of how stylistic or structural elements persist, creating complex, syncretic or hybrid results. Waves overlap and intermingle, often in surprising and unpredictable ways. Their current shape is not wholly predetermined by their pedigree but subject to a variety of contextual factors. Put differently, we could explain common traits in different styles without recourse to the model of the family tree '[by] seeing the process of linguistic change in terms of *innovations* originating at *different* geographic points and spreading outward over *arbitrary* areas of territory, so that the resulting languages show a pattern of *overlapping* rather than hierarchically organized relationships'[5] [my italics].

What such a wave theory suggests is that the relations between modernism and realism, between formalism and Socialist Realism, between Hollywood movies and Soviet cinema, between a European avant-garde and Soviet constructivism, between Joris Ivens the lyric poet and Joris Ivens the social advocate are not necessarily binary, strictly chronological or hierarchical.[6] Similarly, the various modes of documentary representation that I have sketched out elsewhere should not be understood as an evolutionary progression favouring the strongest, most adaptable techniques of representation at the expense of their weaker, less adaptable counterparts.[7] The patterns of overlap are not necessarily accidental any more than genetic. Their characteristics must be determined in each specific instance as we examine the local conditions and contextual factors that contribute to a specific configuration.

How, then, might we retroactively understand the moves made by Malevich or Ivens to adapt and retain elements of an earlier mode when external pressures rendered that mode no longer in favour? Might we see THE BRIDGE, HEIEN and the other films of 1928-29 as symptomatic of what would persist despite the dramatic shifts in Ivens's direction as well as of what this shift toward a populist, rhetorical mode would foreclose?

For Malevich modernism ignited the possibility of an entirely new way of regarding the material world. Fragmentation, collage, subjectivism, relativity, anti-illusionism, stream of consciousness all speak not of a flight from the world but of a critique of 'an ideology of realism' designed to 'foster a belief in the existence of some such commonsense, everyday, ordinary, shared, secular reality'.[8] In the midst of upheaval, when, as the Russian revolution seemed to confirm, 'the bourgeoisie begins to decay as a class, in a world of social anomie and fragmentation, then that active and conquering mode of the representation of reality which is realism is no longer appropriate'.[9] For whom is it no longer appropriate? At the very least, for those who, like Malevich, now 'saw things' in a radically new way.

Suprematism, in this sense, springs from Malevich's desire to see the world anew, not to escape into abstraction for its own sake. His art and writings possess a messianic edge, a purposefulness as great as any orator's, even if it also prefigures a far less messianic abstract expressionism yet to come. For Malevich, a certain clairvoyance obtains. It permits a view into and through the opacity of objects to grasp what Italian futurist Umberto Boccioni, speaking in a tone that could have been Dziga Vertov's, called 'a psychic force that empowers the senses to perceive what has never been perceived before'.[10] The viewer's experience of Suprematism's supplementary elements raises his consciousness into the new realm that expectantly awaits him.[11] As one of Malevich's sympathetic critics, Nikolai Punin, aptly explained,

> If Tatlin's work is a pure experiment in the depths of painting-reality, then Malevich
> is a missile the human spirit has sent into non-existence, into the pure void of intu-
> ition, where the only realities are connections and ties... the 'reign of painting' ends
> here.[12]

Malevich takes the notion of an objectless world not only beyond reason but
beyond art as previously defined, at least within the terms of a mimetic tradition, and yet claims allegiance to its fundamental goal of re-presenting
what we routinely fail to see in the world of material existence. With this
gesture, he departs from the path toward transcendent realms that requires
not only objects, but also the careful reconfiguration of objects, into distinctly new patterns indicative of the new social relations of an industrialized and alienated world.

What Suprematism found in color, texture, volume, and paint itself, the
modernism that attracted Joris Ivens found in the machine. Machinery, but
not any machinery. Machinery in motion, in the juxtaposition and combination of its parts, in the orchestration of parts by the whole, in the display of
power and will, in the shimmering opacity of surfaces, in the synchronization of movements, in the suspenseful delays and anticipated conclusions of
starting and completion, climaxes and denouements – the machine proclaims the birth of man in the age of mechanical reproduction. HEIEN, like
the other early works of Ivens, gives testimony to the appeal of this metaphor, here in the figure of the pile-driver to which the camera becomes literally bound in one shot and in the representation of the overall process as one
governed by the rhythms of the tools and machines that enable it. The appeal of modernism lies in its acknowledgement of a transformed world, but
a world whose most vital qualities remain available to perception in their
everyday appearance.

Each of Ivens's early films represents a mini-event. The raising of a
bridge, the passing of a rain shower, or the driving of timber piles takes narrative shape – although it is more the embryonic narrative of an event than
of a fully developed story. Time and space function within the frame of a
formal pattern that dictates duration and composition without erasing the
recognizable event taken up within this pattern. The unfolding of this event
parallels the unfolding of a cinematic 'event'. The film gives representation
to the workings of another machine: *motion pictures* that transform reality.
Just as the dynamic dramas of bridges and pile-drivers yield tangible results
possessing use-value, the film's dynamic dramatization of events possesses
use-value of its own: a new account of the world and its potential for
change. The middle of each of Ivens's early films details the process by
which change occurs; this cinematic assembly of detail, with its displays of

elegance and tropes of suspense, *is* the change experienced by the viewer. 'Man' gets taken up by this cinematic machinery; he becomes one of the parts of an embryonic narrative event. The outcome or resolution brings the event to a close and man to a 'finish'. The event is the product of the external rhythms of an unspecified social order and of the internal dynamics of a cinematic machine.

If the product of the labour process is as Marx described it 'a piece of natural material adapted to human needs by means of a change in its form',[13] the product of the filmmaking process is an 'adaptation' of reality to the needs of a new historical era in which the machine reigns supreme. Futurism celebrates this change, others decry it. Ivens clearly welcomes it, but, unlike Malevich, never chooses to push his modernist sensibility beyond the object world of men and machines.

The hazard here is clearly a reverence for the machine, or for cinema, as an end in itself. Its power and elegance, the glistening of its parts, the variations in speed and new found mobility became the clarion call of futurism:

> We will sing of great crowds excited by work, by pleasure, and by riot; we will sing of the multicoloured, polyphonic tides of revolution in the modern capitals; we will sing of the vibrant nightly fervor of arsenals and shipyards blazing with violent electric moons; greedy railway stations that devour smoke-plumed serpents; factories hung on clouds by the crooked lines of their smoke; bridges that stride the rivers like giant gymnasts, flashing in the sun with a glitter of knives...[14]

HEIEN seems far more down to earth, as it were, than the delirious Marinetti proclaims, plastered in 'good factory muck' and 'celestial soot'[15] after surviving the nocturnal car wreck with which his Manifesto begins. (Could this be the only artistic manifesto ever inaugurated by an automobile accident?[16]) HEIEN is a much more sober-minded study of labour and the transformations it achieves. The larger story of urban change and the underlying question of whether these workers control the means of production or have their labour expropriated, however, remains off-screen.

For Carlos Böker the structuring absence of power relations remains so removed that it escapes materialist analysis altogether. The individual worker stands heroically on screen in his historical specificity, but confronts the invisible force of an 'abstraction' (corporate man). 'The forces of evil here are unseen, inhuman; they come ultimately from outside the group of men who have, through work, made the world what it should be.'[17] Ivens may not have had such a mythic battle against the gods in mind, but the absence of any indication of the actual face of exploitation not only licenses unreflective adulation of the worker, but also those flights of fancy that would see evil as an eternal enemy rather than an all too human product. It is presumably the state and its management of public works that mediates the in-cipient tension between labour and owner for Ivens, although this, too, remains off-screen.

Ironically, it is Ivens's first sound film, PHILIPS RADIO (1931), that identi-fies the capitalist who stands against the worker. It does so, however, with-out actually naming the capitalist or capitalism as such. Instead, it is the factory assembly line that materializes and externalizes capitalism's power to control the worker. Those industrial or urban rhythms to which ordinary people find themselves moving in the earlier films now clearly impose a de-termining cadence that expropriates individual effort to a collective but alienated outcome. To a large extent, Ivens makes use of sound to lend an acoustic body to this appropriating act acoustically through the tonality of Lichtveld's music, rather than through any more direct means.

The assembly line stands in synecdochic relation to capitalism and, per-haps less advertently, to cinematic 'assembly', or film form. The fullness of the event – commodity production – vanishes from the individual worker's view; his actions succumb to 'an external rhythm'.[18] Ivens's counter-assem-bly restores the event to view as an act of alienation. He reinforces the point obliquely – not by clarifying Marx's distinction between production for use-value, where money serves merely as a vehicle for the exchange of one com-modity for another, and production for exchange-value, where money con-verts to capital through the accumulation of surplus-value by he who controls the means of production – but by contrasting the assembly line rhythm with the artisanal rhythms of the quasi-autonomous glass blowers.

The work of the glass blowers exudes perfection whereas Marx notes that 'it is by their imperfections that the means of production in any process bring to our attention their character...'[19] The glass blowers are men who work to their own rhythm while, in vivid contrast, the assembly line falls prey to imperfection and disorder as its rhythms suddenly go awry. Ivens, here, clearly questions technology, the machine and its imposing power even if the film finally treats imperfection as precisely that, a flaw in need of retuning, the amusing intrusion of a false note. The basic character of the in-dustrial process remains unscathed even if now fully known to Ivens.

Having seen the potential wreckage of industrial imperfection though, Ivens takes the opposite road from the one proclaimed by Marinetti: he will step forward not to praise 'deep-chested locomotives whose wheels paw the tracks like the hooves of enormous steel horses bridled by tubing...'[20] but to rediscover the depth and complexity evacuated from man when he is re-duced to a component of industrial machinery or cinematic assembly.

To see industrial production (and the isolated event) anew calls for the added dimension of heightened consciousness. Such consciousness consti-

Joris Ivens filming HEIEN.

tutes an affective doubling, taking the consciousness necessary to grasp the discreet event, and folding it over into an awareness of the larger process to which it belongs. Malevich sought such doubling in the phenomenal but objectless world of heightened perception brought on by form and paint itself. Ivens sought this doubling in the material world of actually existing practices whose representation brought on a renewed awareness of what might be toward which his films gesture.

Ivens's choice moves him away from the machine as emblem. It moves him away from Malevich and his drive to push modernism to an extreme, but also away from Eisenstein and Vertov, the avant-garde and Brecht. It moves him toward realism, typification, and the modes of class consciousness described by Lukacs. Such a choice pushed Ivens toward the doubled temporality and space of narrative (the experiential time of representation and the historical time represented), the voice, its grain, and the embodied presence of man as well as those processes of identification, transference and persuasion made available through realist representation.[21]

Whereas Ivens lashed his camera to a pile driver in HEIEN, he threw himself into alliance with actual workers in ZUIDERZEE (1930), KOMSOMOL (1932), BORINAGE (1934), and, in an apotheosis of the construction of that man whom Ivens desires to bring into being, the untrained Parkinson family actors of THE POWER AND THE LAND (1941).

What happened? Was this the 'natural' dominance of realism flexing its genetic muscles; was it the internal rhythm of a film form which, having 'exhausted' the possibilities of modernism now turned to the invention of a distinctly documentary mode of representation? Or was this a product of different waves of influence coming together in a historically contingent pattern? If the wave theory is of use to us here, it suggests that inner rhythms and successions of form are inadequate concepts. Among other things, we would have to recognize the significance of external social factors. Of these, the mounting pressure for modes of representation that begin to appear in the mid-1920s and that congeal into Socialist Realism by 1932, and for types of narrative that further the cause of a popular front politics deserve, close consideration.

A full account of these broad phenomena lies beyond the scope of this essay. We should note, though, that by the time of Ivens's first visit to the Soviet Union in 1929, and vividly by the time of his second visit in 1932, constructivism and formalist innovation were widely discredited. The prevailing critique of 'bourgeois' cinema by the Soviet intelligentsia as fundamentally decadent was one the European avant-garde could readily share, but the opposition to formalism as a symptom of artistic elitism and alienation from the masses had a less familiar ring. With Eisenstein living abroad

Kazimir Malevich, *On the Boulevard*
(Stedelijk Museum Amsterdam).

Kazimir Malevich, *Peasan Woman with*
Buckets (Stedelijk Museum Amsterdam).

Kazimir Malevich, *Taking in the Rye*
(Stedelijk Museum Amsterdam).

Kazimir Malevich, *The Woodcutter*
(Stedelijk Museum Amsterdam).

from 1929 to 1932, with the advent of sound championed as the road back to character development and audience identification, with most actors and screenwriters favoring a realist style that gave more priority to their own contributions, and with zealous critics urging art in the service of the state it would be hard to imagine that Ivens's visit to Russia did not add incentive and legitimization to his move away from modernism.[22]

1928-1932 were also the years of Kazimir Malevich's return to painting after a hiatus where he turned to writing, travelling, and teaching as the head of his own studio at the Vitebsk School of Art in 1919, and then at the Museum of Artistic Culture in Petrograd which he transformed into GINKhUK, the Petrograd Institute of Artistic Culture. His Suprematist work had come under attack as early as 1923. His last one-man show took place in 1929. In 1926, GINKhUK's annual showing of new work provoked a scathing critique.

> A monastery has taken shelter under the name of a state institution. It is inhabited by several holy crackpots who, perhaps unconsciously, are engaged in open counter-revolutionary sermonizing, and making fools of our Soviet scientific establishment... The Control Commission and the Workers and Peasants Inspection should investigate this squandering of the people's money on the state support of a monastery.[23]

The Main Science Administration sided with the proponents of realism in the service of the revolution. It had Malevich replaced as Deputy Director by Vladimir Tatlin, while Malevich quickly arranged another trip to Germany.

When Malevich resumed painting in 1927-28, he returned to the themes of his earliest work, rendering 'impressionist portraits and primitivist peasant scenes', but as filtered through the lens of his mature Supremativist style.[24] His decision to back-date the paintings to the period from 1903 to 1910 undoubtedly fooled few. As Charlotte Douglas notes, 'The procedure of supplying himself with a new past shifted the center of gravity of Malevich's oeuvre from Suprematism to earlier subjects and styles more apt to find critical approval in the Russia of the late 1920s, while ingeniously avoiding overt capitulation to the insistent demands of realism.'[25]

Ivens had less reason to disguise his turn toward realism: he was not the apostle of a radically new but imperilled style, nor was he subject to state administrative control. His continuing involvement in films that sprang from a direct engagement with the conditions and consequences of industrial production and social transformation no doubt stimulated his search for a style that would not only represent but also address his worker-subjects clearly and directly. The fascinations of the machine, the metaphor of man as machine, and the parallel of cinema with machine remained in tension with cinema as a subjective, surrogate body. If the abstract domain of modernist representation suggested the product of a film machine, the historical domain of realist representation invokes the engaged body of the filmmaker on the scene, but out of frame. Making film was Ivens's way of putting himself on the spot with those who made what a new industrial order demanded.

Ivens's involvement also clearly parallels the political policies of the different Communist Parties in Europe and the US, given over to championing the great Soviet experiment, defending workers in their struggle against capitalism, and, with the rise of the Popular Front, contributing to the war against fascism. His films conform to the broad outlines of the New Revolutionary Period and Popular Front policies: they support the goals of the first Five Year Plan (KOMOSOL, 1932); celebrate the social advances made possible by industry and technology (ZUIDERZEE, 1930), while also demonstrating the degree to which capitalist development fetters the emergent forces of production (NEW EARTH, 1934); defend the rights of workers to the fruits of their labour (BORINAGE, 1934); and support the efforts of ordinary people to free themselves from oppressive, reactionary dictatorships (SPANISH EARTH, 1937). From modernism, toward realism meant a greater dependence on narrative to tell a larger story than the partial tale of isolated mini-events.

This, at least, appears to be the thinking that favors the techniques of resolution over the techniques of exploration.[26] Exploration involves the open-ended, ambiguous 'play' of modernist techniques that did less to address or resolve real issues than bracket their very terms of existence, proposing alternative ways of seeing and thinking about the nature of reality. The Cubist portrait denies the 'fact' of depth, presenting it as a surface illusion, and confounds our sense of the integral bond between appearance and essence. It is precisely this rejection of the object world and object relations that Malevich made into a messianic theology.

Techniques of resolution, on the other hand, direct empathetic involvement, itself heightened by the representational techniques of realism, toward possible solutions to actual problems, be it sympathy and support for striking workers (BORINAGE), for the achievements of the new Soviet Republics and the first Five Year Plan (KOMSOMOL); for the toil of thousands and hopes of a nation compromised by a stock market and a bank-induced Depression (NEW EARTH); or for the Republican loyalists struggling to defend their country and build a better society (SPANISH EARTH).

Further, sympathy and support call for another kind of depth: the depth of understanding that derives from an increased level of consciousness. This raised level of consciousness, pivoting on identification with realist situations and characters, becomes the core of Ivens's documentary commitment.

'Just seeing things' would not do, be it *zaum*-like transport to an objectless world or the beautified naturalism of *das neue Sachlichkeit*.[27] Understanding hinges on empathetic involvement. Involvement depends on the representation of a world of familiar events and recognizable characters. Familiarity and recognition require narrative realism. The pay-off comes with a transference of exemplary qualities and heightened consciousness from typified film characters to actual audience members. As Ivens himself put it during his stay in the United States from 1938-1945, 'The documentary must not remain a grounds for emotional or literary excitement at the beauty of matter; it must draw reactions and provoke latent activities.'[28]

The move from modernism involves at least four shifts of emphasis and direction:

1 A doubling over of time and space. The time of formal duration, the time necessary for a pattern to play itself out, folds over onto the historical time of social representation. The cinematic event acquires a clear sense of a social referent. A film may expand, contract, or replicate historical, experiential time, but an awareness of this dual temporality and spatiality now enters into the dynamics of viewing. The event, construed in realist terms, regains a sense of familiarity as narrative time takes up the burden of representing historical time. The elusive but felt present of a meaningful temporal-spatial, socio-political referent outside the formal pattern of signifiers takes on perceptible significance.

2 The filmmaker adopts the voice of the orator. No longer the elusive artist who speaks through (modernist) form, the filmmaker now speaks with a cinematic body of sounds and images, attesting to situated experience and conditional knowledge of the historical world. He forgoes the beauty of formal pattern, so dear to poetry, or the clarity of logic, so precious to science, or the metaphor of the machine, so central to futurism and constructivism, to acknowledge the indeterminacy of historical truth and the crucial centrality of a consciousness of design, effort, and consequence – a determining subjectivity *responsible* for history making itself. 'Spontaneous', or observational filming affirms this sense of physical presence and of the camera as surrogate body or corporeal prosthetic. The 'indirect narrative mode is replaced by a discourse employing direct address and embodying structurally in itself a challenge to the system that had made the former discourse impossible', Waugh writes of the rhetorical, even polemical shifts between ZUIDERZEE (1930) and NEW EARTH (1934).[29] Direct address invites response to a specific historical

situation and concrete set of social issues. After 1929, such a response is central to Ivens's work.

3 Documentary realism invokes a distinct form of audience subjectivity. The audience finds itself confronted with an more of an existential than a formal challenge. The rhetorical mode of the orator downplays the poetic pleasures of form and subordinates the logical processes of reason to emphasize the persuasive power of speech or film. To persuade is to predispose the audience to a course of action based on a particular understanding of a situation or event. Disinterestedness and its modalities of identification and empathy spill over into involvement and the potential for partisan, participatory action. Style or form, inasmuch as it acts as more than a trace or index of the filmmaker's presence on the scene, serves to win consent, to move the audience toward a specific form of latent activity.

4 The *documentary* and the heroic portrait of the documentary filmmaker emerge in clear contradistinction to a newly reconstructed avant-garde. The *fusion* of an active participation in the social construction of reality and the aesthetic construction of art that distinguished the Soviet constructivists's contribution to modernism divides into the two materialisms of formal, aesthetic, and sometimes reflexive-political work on the signifier, on the one hand, and social, political-realist work on the signified, tied to a familiar referent, on the other hand.[30] If Malevich provides us with a portrait of the artist as visionary, Ivens provides us with a portrait of the artist as documentarian. In Ivens's case we have the portrait of the documentarian who immerses himself in a situation, discovers a socialist or progressive plot line in need of vivification, and then addresses his finished work to a broader constituency.[31] The documentarian, committed to 'being there', has arrived.

Having characterized the move from modernism in terms of these four qualities, I need to step back to place greater perspective on this shift and what it does and does not accomplish. What seems most obviously problematic, in retrospect, is the unrelenting masculinism of the participants and their practices. Often couched as the idealist masculinism of those who 'stand for' all of us rather than the overt sexism of those who defend male privilege, the result remains a set of documentary practices that treat men as the exemplars of 'man'. This is the man whose 'invention' Foucault describes as relatively recent and whom Zizek convincingly presents as the site of paradox: the 'man' of democratic and socialist ideals is a transcendental fiction.

Such men share in social equality only insofar as they correspond, in flesh and blood, to the distinguishing characteristics of 'exemplary man', only, that is, insofar as they are white, male heterosexual, and, in bourgeois-democracies, middle-class or better, in communist states, working-class.[32] 'Man' extends beyond these boundaries hesitantly. We find little in the progressive rhetoric of this period to suggest a consciousness of the ingrained contradictions bound up in the realist practices that came to replace the modernist moment.[33]

Shall we speak of Ivens's work in the 1930s, in Thomas Waugh's words, as a 'Socialist Realist aesthetic of personalized didacticism', or a 'Popular Front strategy of group affiliation'?[34] Has Ivens left his avant-garde beginnings entirely behind? Has he, like the proverbial chameleon, altered his style to fit the moment and does this demonstrate the abandonment of modernism as the more virile genetic stock of realism gains dominance?

In the case of Kazimir Malevich, the complex pressures conducive to the syncretism of a wave theory of expressive combination are reasonably apparent: his later work retains a Suprematist 'dominant' in form and feel.

The primitivist and realist overlay does not disguise the emphasis on form and pattern that subsumes individuals and continues to point us toward the utopian domain of a heightened consciousness, freed from its attachment to people, places, and things. Painting resolves itself into a self-transforming act strongly guided by techniques of exploration. Denuded of nouns, it becomes strictly a verb, a 'middle voice' verb that alters the very state of those caught up in it.[35] What Johannes Schmidt termed 'patterns of overlapping relationships' converge in an unstable, contingent manner that defines no 'natural' (genetic) hierarchy of styles and their evolution, but rather a series of innovations responsive to a specific historical context and the forms of contestation permissible within it. The administrative guardians could find in late Malevich the realist elements that would grant him some reprieve, but Malevich simultaneously continues to pursue old convictions in a new form.

In the case of Joris Ivens, the persistence of a supplemental element is a bit more complex. His transition from modernism could be read as the 'natural' victory of a dominant mode of representation since realism prevails, but a wave theory of assimilationist syncretism allows us to see how the fuzzy category of documentary itself emerges from the interstices of realism and rhetoric, narrative and social representation. Narrative fiction does not triumph; a new mode of representation, documentary, takes shape precisely from the innovations at different geographic points that combine elements of modernism and realism, narrative and rhetoric. What, then,

Kazimir Malevich, *Suprematist Painting* (Red cross on black circle), (Stedelijk Museum Amsterdam).

Kazimir Malevich, *Suprematist Painting* (Stedelijk Museum Amsterdam).

persists of modernism, or at least from Joris Ivens's limited engagement with it?

Through modernism, Ivens confronts the machine and all its ramifications for man, cinema, and artistic production. Unlike Vertov, who never abandons modernism; unlike Grierson and the British documentary, which only flirts with modernism and never *confronts* the machine; and unlike Flaherty who confronts neither modernism nor the machine, Ivens moves into the 1930s on a distinct path.

A supplemental element persists that we may identify as a determination to see anew and recast the ordinary and everyday, especially action and effort, in terms of an increasingly complex, politically comprehensive perspective. The impulse toward a radical transformation joins Malevich and Ivens, but, for Ivens, movement and the event, machines and their rhythms gradually precipitate into the question of labour, including film *work*, and its power to transform the world it encounters.

Malevich and Ivens share in a desire to effect a radical transformation. Malevich's path passes *through* form, but resists taking up residence *in* the form of the familiar. Ivens, too, finds a path – a way toward objects and things, people, places, and the efforts they expend. His path also passes through form, but he also takes up residence *in* the concrete materiality of everyday life. Ivens finds a way toward a level of consciousness attainable *through* the form of a familiar perspectivism on the efforts of people as recast by the effort and purpose of his own innovative labour. Ivens aligns his creative efforts with the efforts of others, and with the latent activity of those who understand such efforts through the form of his representations.[36] Realism consolidates a politics of subjectivity and corporeal investment. Such a politics depends on a transformation of formal duration into a signifier of historical, narrative time; of formal composition into geopolitical space; of artistic vision into oratorical speech; of spectatorial challenge into audience engagement; and of modernist exploration into documentary representation.

To transform puts questions of desire in the air. And desire always demands an object. Whether, as Marx puts it, this object satisfied the needs of the stomach or the imagination makes no difference. And while, for Malevich, they are of the imagination, once freed from the stomach, they are, for Ivens, relentlessly of the stomach, but coupled to the imagination.

WE ARE BUILDING, HEIEN, PHILIPS RADIO and other early works provide that supplemental element of dignity to the individual worker that persists throughout Ivens's later work. These films issue a clear rejoinder to Brian Winston's polemic against the 'tradition of the victim' in documentary.[37] The potential for historical change resides, most pointedly, *in the hands of men*. The images in these films also exhibit a distinction between the respect accorded the individual worker and the critique addressed to the labour process: specific shots depict specific workers in well-lit, medium-framing that does not fragment or abstract the individual whereas the montage of assembly line workers relies on fragmentation, isolation, and repetition to underscore the alienating quality of the work itself. Unlike André Bazin, Joris Ivens puts his faith in *both* the image and in montage, depending on his goal.

It is this persistence of a desire – so different from Malevich's in the means designed to realize it, but so similar in its intensity, clarity, and transcendental element – that locates Ivens, from our retrospective vantage point, in a position of centrality within the documentary tradition.[38] These men – from the glass blowers to the Parkinson family, and from the Dutch pile-drivers of HEIEN to the Chinese peasant farmers of BEFORE SPRING – represent, through the iconography of dignity, the abstract transcendental figures of a great family of man. This universalist ideal indicates the presence of a certain *mythic* (and masculinist) as well as materialist desire. As a particular form of representation, it draws us away from the fully situated, the full historical, and toward the mythical and ideological. Ivens, of course, was not alone in such a move.

The rhetorical dimensions to documentary representation never fully extricate themselves from the principles of formalist abstraction and modernist collage, nor from the methods of narrative realism to which they are historically related. When tempered by a rhetorical subjectivity, documentary itself takes on an identity it can call its own precisely through its persistent relationship to those other modalities that are not entirely its own.

Kazimir Malevich died of illness in 1935. His cremated remains were buried in a field near the Moscow suburb of Nemchinovka. A cement cube, with a Suprematist black square on one side, marked the grave. As Charlotte Douglas reports, 'Malevich's work was carefully put away by his heirs; not until the 1960s would any of it be seen publicly again. World War II erased all traces of his grave.'

'Honest, Straightforward Re-enactment': The Staging of Reality

Brian Winston

In this essay I want to deal with just one aspect of how the documentary filmmaker interacts with external reality – that is, interacts with what takes place before the lens – and to question how far documentarists can intervene before all claims on the real become too suspect to sustain. This text will not therefore deal with questions of representation and distortions arising from the editing and reception processes. It will be concerned with filming, and preparations for filming only.

It was thought that, with the coming of the 16mm synch sound camera nearly forty years ago, these questions of authenticity would be finally laid to rest. The equipment was supposed to allow the filmmaker to work directly without the need of any intervention, much less reconstruction or re-enactment, at all. What this naiveté disguised was that while intervention and reconstruction were no longer as necessary as they had been, especially when shooting synch sound, they were, nevertheless, still possible. Moreover, such intervention and reconstruction was now even more hidden than it had been. It lurked, lurks, behind the observational, hand-held, available-light, long-take style of Direct Cinema where it was, and is, more or less invisible. The new approach might have made it more possible than ever to capture, as Rouch and Morin said, 'a type of cinema truth'; but it also was as easy as ever to lie, or, more often, distort. It is no wonder then that the documentary remains engulfed by scandal and controversy as its claims of non-intervention and non-reconstruction are periodically revealed to be more or less fraudulent. What I want to examine here, though, is the extent to which the camera's ability to capture, shall we say, data-rich, iconic information about the world can be used to preserve the documentary's essential claim on the real against these scandals and controversies.

When a blacklisted miner in BORINAGE cannot pay his rent the company sends a sheriff to remove and sell the miner's furniture. As soon as the miners hear about this, they all rush to the victim's house and sit down on all his furniture – on the table, stove, bed, as well as chairs. As the sheriff's orders are to move the furniture but not people, all the miners have to do is sit pa-

Filming the eviction scene for BORINAGE, with two miners dressed as police-men.

Still from BORINAGE: sitting on the furniture, re-enacted for the film.

tiently for hours and hours until the sheriff, afraid of a scandal in a heavy-laden atmosphere in the narrow street, finally leaves.[1]

As you know, the strike in the Borinage coal field had occurred in 1932 while Ivens was away. It lasted about a month and, as with Britain's 1926 General Strike, it was called off by reformist union leaders leaving the miners unemployed, blacklisted and desperate. Since they were filming after the event, Ivens and his partner Henri Storck were forced to reconstruct episodes of the strike in the nature of the case. The sit-in technique in the face of eviction had been used by Pierre Duclot, a blacklisted miner. In *The Camera and I*, Joris Ivens describes how he reconstructed this in the scene we have just screened:

> We wanted to show this event in our film and the only way to get it was to re-enact it in his very house with his wife and neighbours. We rented two gendarme uniforms from an opera company in Brussels and our first problem was to find two miners to play the roles of the police, the enemy. Not being an actor no real miner was willing to portrait the character of a gendarme, accomplice of the mine owner. But once this objection was overcome we made an honest, straight re-enactment of the sit down action preventing eviction.[2]

Compare this with Ivens's remarks about shooting RAIN:

> On the big central square of Amsterdam I saw three little girls under a cape and the skipping movements of the legs had the rhythm of raindrops. There had been a time when I thought such good things could be shot tomorrow as well as today; but you soon learn that this is never true. I filmed those girls without a second's hesitation. They would probably never again walk at that hour on the square, when they did it would not be raining, and if it was raining they would not have a cape, or skip in just that way, or it would be too dark or something.[3]

At first sight there seems to be a real, and clearly defined, gulf between these two situations. In the one, the event before the lens would not be happening without the direct instigation and intervention of the filmmaker; whereas in the other, the skipping children would be skipping whether Ivens was present with his camera or not. This clear distinction, however, masks the realities of normal filmmaking practice. Ivens did not report whether or not he had any conversation with the children but if he had – if, for instance, he asked their permission to film – would that vitiate the documentary quality of the shot? Would the documentary 'essence', if you will, be destroyed if he asked them to repeat some skipping steps? Or if he asked them to continue to play for his camera after they stopped playing for themselves? Conversely, in BORINAGE, is the record vitiated by the fact that the two gendarmes are fake when all the other participants, the location, and the action are real?

When we consider reconstruction as a documentary technique, we are actually simply dealing with situations which we can place towards one end of a filmmaking continuum. We can think of this continuum as starting with non-intervention of any kind – the filming of, say, natural disasters – at one extreme, and finishing with total intervention – that is, the completely fictional representation of people, locations, and events – at the other. At one end, TRAIN ARRIVING AT STATION, at the other STAR WARS. We can move on this continuum from unfilmed interactions between filmmaker and subject (the asking of permission to film, for example)

- through specific unfilmed requests made without prior research to repeat or delay action
- to specific requests to re-enact actions witnessed during the research process
- to specific requests to re-enact actions witnessed by the subject or others in the past (what we may call history)
- to specific requests to re-enact actions witnessed elsewhere during the research process performed by other people of the same type as the subjects (what we may call the typical)
- to specific requests to enact actions which are possible but unwitnessed
- to specific requests to 'act' (that is, to perform before the camera at the direct behest of the filmmaker without the legitimization of any witness in ways unrelated to the subject's actual behaviour and personality).

NON-INTERVENTION
PERMISSIONS
     DELAYS & REPETITIONS
        RE-ENACTMENT OF WITNESSED ACTION
           RE-ENACTMENT OF HISTORY
              RE-ENACTMENT OF THE TYPICAL
                  ENACTMENT OF THE POSSIBLE
                      ACTING
TOTAL INTERVENTION

This last is unambiguously fiction, but all the others can and have been considered legitimate documentary practice. Beyond this last, however, dividing the continuum so that on one side we are dealing with fact and on the other with fiction is as vexed a business as it has ever been.

Today, I want to examine the most complex section of the continuum to ask if anything of documentary 'essence' or, to use Grierson's phrase, 'documentary value' can have been legitimately claimed for the re-enactment of the typical and enactment of the possible?

Humphrey Jenning's war-time British documentary feature I WAS A FIRE- MAN, and the shortened version FIRES WERE STARTED which was prepared for general release, come from what might be thought of as the classic pe- riod of re-enactment, the first decades of the sound documentary from the mid-1930s to the late 1950s. A definition of documentary dating from 1948, for example, reveals the extent to which reconstruction became embedded in documentary practice during these years. The documentary was defined as a film using 'all methods of recording on celluloid any aspect of reality in- terpreted either by factual shooting or by sincere and justifiable reconstruc- tion...'[4]

Reconstruction was an 'honest, straight' alternative to factual shooting. At its most extreme, as in the case of FIRES WERE STARTED, reconstruction re- quired careful observation on the part of the filmmakers, which was then transmuted into full treatments complete with snatches of dialogue. Documentarists were driven, as it were, to this procedure by many factors. For example, there was the failure of the documentary to develop modes of representing time and space which were specific to this particular film form, using instead the grammar of representation which had been developed primarily by the fiction film in Hollywood. Moreover, these filmmakers were also heirs to a persistent tradition of re-enactment which embraced NANOOK's building of the igloo or Grierson's construction of the trawler's cabins, and also encompassed the even cruder subterfuges of the earliest days of the cinema when, for example, footage of toy ships shot on a table top were presented as THE BATTLE OF SAN JUAN BAY or the BOXER REBELLION was restaged in a building in upstate New York. We might call this 'insin- cere but (commercially) justified reconstruction' – 'dishonest, crooked re- enactment'. Synchronous sound made re-enactment or reconstruction of necessity a routine during this period. The equipment would allow for nothing else. As Ricky Leacock noted of Flaherty's LOUISIANA STORY, shot four year after FIRES WERE STARTED (1946-1948):

> I saw that when we were using small cameras [to shoot silent footage], we had tre- mendous flexibility, we could do anything we wanted, and get a wonderful sense of cinema. The moment we had to shoot dialogue, lip-synch – everything had to be locked down, the whole nature of the film changed. The whole thing seemed to stop. We had heavy disk recorders, and the camera that, instead of weighing six pounds, weighed two-hundred pounds, a sort of monster. As a result of this, the whole nature of what we were doing changed. We could no longer watch things as they developed, we had to impose ourselves to such an extent upon everything that happened before us, that everything sort of died.[5]

Although silent footage could be shot on smaller cameras, feature film sound equipment cemented, as it were, feature film techniques in place for the documentary. Documentary synch sound scenes required scripts, rehearsals, multiple takes – just as their fictional equivalents did.

I WAS A FIREMAN is a feature length documentary on the work of the Auxiliary Fire Service (AFS) during the first London blitz, which began on 23 August 1940 and lasted throughout that autumn and winter. The film is entirely reconstructed because, as with the strike in the Borinage, the blitz was almost over in the form of high explosive and incendiary carpet bombing from manned aircraft, at least for London, by the time Jennings began to film in April and May of 1942. The film shows how the Auxiliary Fire Service was organised during the earlier period. It had been totally changed in August 1941 into a National Fire Service which integrated all the various different forces and commands but Jennings does not reflect that, not even in the treatments he is writing in the winter of 1941/42 – despite these various iterations all being headed, 'The NFS (National Fire Service) Film'.[6]

Jennings certainly uses 'real firemen and women'; that is, those who were involved in either the London Fire Brigade (LFB), the pre-war professional fire service, or the newly recruited AFS and who had fought the fires of the London blitz. The auxiliaries were the subject of some fairly intense rivalry with the LFB men, not least because they were paid less than the fireman's wage rates – another reality not mentioned by Jennings. There were also women firefighters, a further source of tension and another factor simply ignored by Jennings. However, none of the 'actual firemen' in the film is actually playing themselves. They all have fictitious names, for example. Barrett, supposedly an advertising copywriter, is actually the author William Sansom – who was, though, (let me repeat) actually, an auxiliary fireman during the blitz. Johnny was actually a one-time taxidriver called Fred Griffiths, whose life was so touched by his experiences in the film that after the war he made a successful career for himself playing loveable cockneys in British film and television. And so on.

One sequence was shot in a school commandeered by the film as the location of Substation Y.[7] I have found some references to studio sets being used but I believe that is not true. Sub-fire stations were located in schools and other buildings but this location is not an actual one any more than the site of the big fire which is the film's climax was actually started by the Germans. Edward (Teddy) Carrick is credited with the sets for the film.

Nor did Jennings ever observe firemen singing 'One Man Went To Mow' in a recreation room, although, they did have sing-songs, as he had seen in other substations, 6W in Chelsea for example, where he had been doing research on 11 November 1941.[8] An ambulance driver had written to him in

February 1941 suggesting a film about her life which reported that: 'after a meal in the canteen we would frequently hold a sing-song.'[9] Actually, Jennings had heard 'One Man Went To Mow', a well known old English folk song, spontaneously sung in an air-raid shelter in Liverpool. So here we have a group of men, who spent the London blitz as auxiliary firemen, but who are given false names and who never served together, sitting about a recreation room created by some filmmakers in a school got up to be a sub-fire station singing a song which they were never heard to sing before. And they had to sing it all day. In a BBC documentary on Jennings made by Robert Vas in 1970,[10] Fred Griffiths remembered the day they shot 'One Man Went To Mow' in these terms: 'I've started at half past eight in the morning and we go on singing all the way through. A break – half an hour, forty minutes for lunch. Start again. At 5 o'clock – cut! He [Jennings] comes over to me, he says: "I think your voice is going". I'd been singing for nine hours and he said: "your voice is going."'

If you like, all this constitutes the case for the prosecution. The creative treatment of actuality on display here is so overwhelmingly creative that it would be easy to dismiss any lingering actuality as being of no significance whatever. But that is exactly what I do not want to do – and for the following reason. The war time documentary features such as FIRES WERE STARTED were very often matched by full-scale fictional feature films on the same topics. Carol Reed's THE WAY AHEAD has its counterpart in the documentary COASTAL COMMAND. The Ealing film SAN DEMETRIO LONDON parallels WESTERN APPROACHES, a documentary; ONE OF OUR DESTROYERS IS MISSING echoes Noel Coward's IN WHICH WE SERVE; but most closely of all, FIRES WERE STARTED marches in fantastic lock step with a Tommy Trinder vehicle, his second 'straight' film for Michael Balcon at Ealing – THE BELLS GO DOWN. So close are these two films that the same title was at one point suggested for both of them. In the Jennings papers at the BFI there is a 'Bare first treatment of National Fire Service story' titled 'The Bells Went Down'. This document is dated 'Denham Studios, 4 January 1942'. The Ealing production, THE BELLS GO DOWN, directed by Basil Dearden and starring James Mason as well as the comedian Trinder, began in April. The 'National Fire Service story' became I WAS A FIREMAN (eventually recut for release as FIRES WERE STARTED) and was shot at the same time.

By comparing FIRES WERE STARTED and THE BELLS GO DOWN we can begin to make a case for documentary difference; we can lay out some elements of documentary value even in a situation where the re-enactments go beyond the observed and witnessed to encompass, as in the sequence we have seen, the typical and the possible. This comparison can be reinforced because the original version of the documentary, I WAS A FIREMAN, was some seventeen minutes longer than the released version, FIRES WERE STARTED. The basis for the recut was exactly that the documentary elements were felt to drag on the narrative. Simply to note them, then, is to list what the filmmakers themselves thought made up the documentary essence of the work.

The structure of the documentary and the fiction film is virtually identical. Both are set on the docks. A motley crew of firemen is introduced. Daily life in the station and a training session is shown. A major fire is tackled, and in each film, central characters die bringing it under control. Each film ends with a church service. There are overlaps with the fiction film containing documentary footage of training and, conversely, the documentary utilizing numerous fictional techniques and elements including the false 'death' and burial service of a fireman. There are also a number of fictional plotting devices in FIRES WERE STARTED; for example, a number of references to the fact of a moonlit night, signifying the increased danger of a German raid, are 'planted' early in the film. The essential sunken barge is similarly planted in a completely fictional film style because it will figure crucially in the climax.

But these similarities and overlaps mask considerable differences in the level of narrative complexity generally, the fiction film being very much more complex. I want to suggest that a general lack of narrative complexity is one element of documentary 'essence'.

The plot of the fiction film starts before the war and runs up through the 1940/41 autumn and winter blitz. It offers a number of sub-plots – a couple postpone their marriage because of the outbreak of war, then marry, then produce the child who is christened in the last sequence of the film. Another character is stealing barrels of Guinness from a ship on the dock. Tommy Trinder appears to steal James Mason's girl. There are also various fires raging, ranging from a comic blaze involving heavily-stereotyped Italian cafe owners to the climatic conflagration.

Compared to this, FIRES WERE STARTED offers only one plot line and one fire; and we learn very little of the firemen's backgrounds. Jennings' actors exist only in the civil sphere; their personal lives are unexamined. There are, thus, elements in THE BELLS GO DOWN which have no place in FIRES WERE STARTED – they are not, therefore, pertinent to the documentary essence. They include personal relationships of all kinds, including romantic entanglements (still an area largely untouched by the observational documentary mainstream, even in its most popular docu-soap form). So, in defiance of a documentary's normal tone as – to use Nichols's phrase – a discourse of sobriety, the fiction film goes in for comic relief. In yet another subplot, Tommy Trinder acquires a very unsuccessful greyhound and is given space for his 'cheeky chappie' routines.

So, a second major element in the 'documentary-ness' of FIRES WERE STARTED, after simplicity of plot, is the limitation of personal relationships to the public sphere as compared with the feature. Let me emphasize that it is not that Jennings fails to present such relationships at all. Indeed, much of the film's strength as propaganda arises from the realism and humanity of these interactions. Only the bad language has been omitted, for example, in the exchange which realistically highlights the unheroic and humdrum nature of the firemen's daily routine – a glimpse of alienation which allows the spectator more fully to believe the uplifting message of the rest of the film. This is a real characteristic of English propaganda dating back at least to Shakespeare. In Henry V, he has the king in disguise visit the common soldiers on the night before Agincourt. Harry argues that it is a great thing to be in the Royal service with the King but one of the cockneys replies that he wishes the king were 'in the Thames up to his neck and I by him'. I think this level of realistic negativism is what makes such propaganda really effective; it promises a realism which, of course, it does not then deliver. Instead, you get heorics but I suggest one notices that less.

The most important and third documentary element is located in the film's treatment of the very business of firefighting. This means that despite the feature film's title, which refers to the alarm bell in the fire station and the men sliding down poles to get to the engines, there is far more specialized language in the documentary. Hoses are 'branches'; the area the fire station is responsible for is its 'ground', and so on. There are more references to detailed procedures such as emergency water supplies or trivial facts such as hatchet handles being painted different colours according to the owner's rank in the service. We have already seen how Trinder deals with the vital telephone links in the control room. In contrast, there is a painstaking attempt to show the various levels of control in FIRES WERE STARTED, often with a certain resultant confusion. (Without question, Jenning's attempts to explain the by-now abandoned structure of command are the least successful parts of the film. It is quite difficult for the viewer to know which level of control is being pictured.) But it is this patina of detail which nevertheless, gives FIRES WERE STARTED its documentary value. It reinforces the authenticity of the fireman and the location – those factors which might be considered as the fourth and fifth elements of the documentary essence.

The clearly absurd action in the feature film has no place in the documentary. Let me say a word about the accents – especially the women's accents in both films. In FIRES WERE STARTED there are middle-class accents, especially among the women in the district headquarters. This represented a reality because well-brought-up women who would not have entered the pre-war work force did, indeed, work in all sorts of jobs – including being actual fire-fighters, as I have said. In the feature, however, the supposedly cockney girl has an aristocratic accent you can cut with a knife. It was an absurd convention which persisted well into the late fifties. Proletarian English accents were deemed to be utterly inconsistent with any sort of sexual glamour.

Let me come back to the main theme. We must not assume that the climactic fires in both films do not have a great deal in common. They do, despite the fact that Jennings famously burnt warehouses on St. Katherine's Docks for a number of weeks to make his film whereas Dearden worked in the studio. My point here is that the differences between actors and firemen, studio sets and real locations alone are not enough to distinguish the documentary element. It is the context of authenticity, if you will, provided by Jennings at the level of language and in the picture of a complex organization which finally makes the difference – what I am describing as the third element.

Let me just add that it was exactly this content of documentary detail and the interactions of the men that Jennings and his editor Stuart McCallister trimmed by seventeen minutes from the original version of I WAS A FIRE-MAN. They did so in order to enhance the narrative drive of the film or, to put it another way, ever more clearly reveal the simplicity of the plot line. I would argue that the comparison of these two versions further reinforces an analysis of documentary essence which concentrates on detail, public-sphere interaction of subjects, and plot simplicity, as much as on the authenticity of the documentary actor, his or her actions, and the locations. This allows us to refine somewhat the usual basis for this discussion, that is, that the documentary uses real people and real locations doing what they usually do – none of which really apply, at least in a straightforward way, to FIRES WERE STARTED. The real people have assumed names. The locations are actual places, but they are not what they seem, having been converted into the typical by the filmmakers; and the people are not doing what they usually do, but what they did or, even, what others like them did.

In terms of the continuum I suggested earlier, Jennings is clearly making specific requests to his subjects to re-enact actions witnessed, either by himself or by his various correspondents, during the research process. He is also prepared to make specific requests to re-enact actions witnessed by the subject or others in the past, an absolute necessity given that he is portraying a situation which no longer exists – the London blitz and the fragmented Fire Services response to it. This leads him to the typical – specific requests to re-enact actions witnessed elsewhere during the research process, performed by other people of the same type as the subjects, the 'One Man Went to Mow' sequence being but the most famous example of this in this film; and, beyond that, to the enactment of actions which are possible but unwitnessed – as, for example, Jacko's death. Nevertheless, I would argue that Jennings does not cross the line into fiction because of the various elements I have highlighted. This remains, Ivens put it, an 'honest, straightforward re-enactment', sincere and justifiable reconstruction, clearly and obviously distinct from its fictional alternative or counterpart.

Let me conclude by saying that the next stage of this argument, which I cannot deal with here, is whether or not FIRES WERE STARTED is a dramatic documentary rather than a documentary proper. My sense of the dramatic documentary is that it uses actors and sets to re-enact situations otherwise unfilmable, and its claim on documentary legitimacy comes from the authenticity of its script. Ideally, this means an actual transcript as from a court of law or, at a minimum, very full memoirs and minutes. Without this, it is not dramatic documentary but drama even if it is dealing with 'real' people and 'real' events. Do not forget that Macbeth was a real king of Scotland but that does not make Shakespeare's play a dramatic documentary. Conversely, I do not believe that FIRES WERE STARTED and all the other documentaries of its type fall within this definition. Moreover to make them do so, it seems to me, is actually to privilege the observational documentary's inflated claim on the real – that is, you are in effect saying that the observational film's relationship with its material has a greater claim on reality than does the classic documentary with its re-enactments. I do not think the observational documentary's pretensions can be sustained. But that is another story.

Joris Ivens and the Legacy of Committed Documentary

Thomas Waugh

As a teacher of film history, I believe in always starting with the moving image. I shall try to replicate this cinematic departure point with the following brief descriptions of the film and excerpts I will refer to in what follows:

MISÈRE AU BORINAGE (Joris Ivens & Henri Storck, Belgium, 1934). Striking Borin miners dramatize for the camera an earlier solidarity procession, complete with a portrait of Marx at the head. Supporters line the route fists upraised. But the fictional march turns into a real one, and police are shown cycling to the scene to restore 'order'.

INDONESIA CALLING (Joris Ivens, Australia, 1946). This film, one of several of Ivens's masterworks to be virtually inaccessible (myself not having seen it in almost twenty years), also resorts to dramatization, thanks to the politics and economics of its semi-clandestine context. This resilient story of Australian labour militants backing up the effort of Indonesian nationalists to defend their newly independent homeland, is full of oratory, city and harbour scapes, and above all, dramatized anecdotes of sit-downs and demonstrations. It culminates in the rousing march over the Sydney harbour bridge that rhetorically unites all of the national contingents in this tale of international solidarity.

LE JOLI MOIS DE MAI (C'EST LA RÉVOLUTION PAPA) (Ateliers de recherches cinématographiques, France, 1968). The Left Bank is surging with a flood of protesting students, intellectuals, and workers, flaunting banners and slogans, and confronting the police. Hand-held cameras capture the demonstrations, battles, and pursuits from the centre of the action, with images often jostled or blurred.

DOCTORS, LIARS AND WOMEN: AIDS ACTIVISTS SAY NO TO COSMO (Jean Carlomusto and collective, USA, 1988) A hand-held video camera records a demonstration of angry ACT UP women before the New York head office of *Cosmopolitan* magazine, which has just run an article falsely reassuring their women readers about HIV transmission risks. They then invade TV talk shows and confront both the article's author and a media hierarchy that silences 'non-expert' (i.e., women's) voices.

A PLACE CALLED CHIAPAS (Nettie Wild, Canada, 1998). The camera crew follows a group of unarmed Mayan refugees who have returned in a group to their original village, now occupied by paramilitary thugs. Only the camera presence prevents this public confrontation from escalating into a massacre, and the peasants are allowed (temporary?) access to their homes.

A NARMADA DIARY (Anand Patwardhan and Simantini Dhuru, India, 1995). Demonstrators whose ancestral villages are threatened by the Narmada Dam superproject, financed by the World Bank, demand a meeting with the World Bank president, who is attending a fashion show in Bombay's luxurious Taj Mahal hotel and thus refuses to meet them. The villagers and camera both invade the fashion show.

Judging from this film and these five film excerpts, from six different countries and dating from the thirties, forties, sixties, and the last decade, one would think that there is nothing new in the realm of the committed documentary. And indeed there hardly is. At least, that is what I shall try to argue based on the astonishing symmetry and assonance, both textual and contextual, of these sequences produced over almost seven decades. These clips may well reflect the radical disjunctures in the political and cultural history of the century, and the evolving agendas and constituencies of the Left, but they also testify (selectively excerpted, I admit) to the remarkable continuity in the textual and political strategies of artists intervening in that history, artists making documentaries to change the world.

If, for me, this sounds like a familiar tune, it is because I made a similar argument fifteen years ago when I produced an anthology on the militant or committed documentary film, called *Show Us Life: Toward a History and Aesthetics of the Committed Documentary.*[1] But before proceeding, certain misunderstandings that arose in the original discussion period in Nijmegen impel me to clarify my use of the term 'committed' (originally inspired by the French *engagé*), as well as the basic assumptions underlying this committed paper about committed documentary in honor of the centenary of a committed filmmaker. By 'committed' I am referring to activist cultural interventions on the Left, situated along the continuum that that ideological label evokes. 'Committed' documentary has its own continuous and autonomous history of more than eighty years in the cinema, as well as its own recognizable repertory – iconographical, aesthetic, ethical, tactical, and technical. I dispute the possible insinuation that propaganda is propaganda, right or left, and have demonstrated in the past[2] the left documentary's distinctiveness in relation to activist documentary on the Right (the latter notion is paradoxical, it could well be argued). This is all the more true since the history of right documentary has, until recently perhaps, been mercifully sporadic and, with a few exceptions, inconsequential. I would be happy to demonstrate how the last decade's AIDS activist video current in the English-speaking world, exemplified above, is distinctive, and substantively so, from the pro-life, anti-abortion work mentioned in the discussion, were this not a digression from the task at hand.

Show Us Life took stock of the vagaries of the committed tradition over several generations, from founding parents Dziga Vertov and Joris Ivens to Santiago Alvarez and Anand Patwardhan. In my 1984 preface, I undertook to affirm and analyze documentary's continued priority as radical political and cultural discourse, and to inventory, historically as well as taxonomically, the forms it had taken since the heady days of the 1920s, when Ivens had not yet got his feet wet. My stance was somewhat defensive in the early eighties, for those were of course years of great geopolitical stress. The Reagan empire engaged in its genocidal war on the Sandinista revolution, and its lunatic race in star wars weaponry. In academia itself, the orthodoxies of post-structuralist agnosticism and pseudo-Brechtian formalism added to the stress more than any kind of 'Reaganacademics', for the current attack on the humanities and the arts in North America was hardly felt yet – or at least not in Canada. (As for the 1989 *New Criterion* attack on *Show Us Life* in terms of Soviet-style double talk, false-consciousness, and the communist 'infiltration' of academia – honouring me by unmasking the strange bedfellows Erik Barnouw and Annette Michelson as my co-conspirators – this would only arrive much later, laughably the same year as the fall of the Soviet empire of which we were pawns and dupes.[3])

I masked my defensiveness in 1984 by a cheery celebration of the Central American solidarity films that were then current, and avoided dealing with the inescapable fact that we were in a bit of a slump. Outside Central America, the Latin American front was eerily quiet, and the Cubans seemed to have abandoned a stirring documentary heritage. Elsewhere in the North, the New Left experiment in documentary activism of the late sixties seemed far in the distant past. In fact, the legacy of May 1968 militancy had been utterly renounced in France, the country that had once been its crucible. (I discovered this when I asked for permission to reprint one of the essential balance sheets of French militant cinema for my anthology, only to find that what I would sarcastically term in my introduction the 'Gallic intellectual ritual of repudiations of all former positions every leap year' had taken its toll on French *cinéma engagé* as well. Guy Hennebelle, once its high priest, could not believe he had once written those things and opined that Marxism was inoperational even on the therapeutic level![4]) Thus in the dark years of the early eighties, political documentary once more seemed to converge on the cultural spectrum with the avant-garde, just as Ivens had declared in 1931 at the time of the release of PHILIPS RADIO, as he was preparing to leave for his second Soviet trip.[5] I was thus able to draw consolation from a vantage point of history that showed this and other cyclical patterns, from that hoary Marxist 'certitude', as Ivens put it at the time of BORINAGE,

> that a strike is never lost, that even a provisional defeat is only a stage of the struggle and that the struggle continues...[6]

Now, fifteen years later, this radical heritage seems slightly less under siege due to the academic publishing boom on documentary (a new book is imminent on Emile de Antonio, for example) the international flurry of documentary festivals; the stepped-up infusion of European television money into transnational documentary; and the still-proliferating video rental market – offering access to our documentary past that earlier practitioners (and myself, the young Ivens researcher of the seventies) would have died for. Yet, there are clouds on the horizon: a new world media economy based on super mergers, deregulation, privatization, and the closing down of public space everywhere, as John Hess and Patricia Zimmerman have chillingly described it,[7] together with the global demoralization of the Left predicated on the alleged death of Marxism and the alleged end of history, and often expressed in a postmodern cyborg aestheticism.

My recent experience on the programming committee for an international human rights documentary festival in Montreal[8] has given me an optimistic viewpoint on the matter, despite working with a committee of activist filmmakers whose sense of radical film history goes back no further than Barbara Kopple, most totally oblivious to the precedents of Vertov and Ivens, let alone Newsreel and 'Challenge for Change'.[9] The reports of demoralization are premature. I found the sense that, despite everything, there has been an extension of the legacy, however unwitting, by hundreds of eager young documentarists out there, eager to denounce injustice and change the world by the force of their art. The guard has changed and the new shift are all busily reinventing the wheel as zealously as their grandparents had done under the Popular Front, and as their parents had done again in the late sixties. Haven't these green-haired multiple-pierced young activists heard the news about the end of history? As for the necessity that they reinvent the wheel, no doubt this is a blessing in disguise, for, as Ivens discovered as soon as he started making political films, it is the process rather than the recipe that is the key to a significant political cinema.

This, of course, is a cyclical view of documentary film history that is non-teleological, non-canonical, and perhaps even non-materialist. It is *non-teleological* in the sense that Bill Nichols's evolutionary dynamic (which should not be taken too reductively as a Darwinian model of documentary evolution, but which I affectionately caricature, all the same, as the expository mode connected to the observational connected to the interactive connected to the reflexive connected to the performative) is reflected in this trajectory not so much as shifting structural cores or discursive consensuses, than as optional stylistic or technical veneers on a stable subject-centred ideal and rhetorical constant.

It is *non-canonical* in the sense that – the dead white male names I have evoked notwithstanding – we are talking of a trajectory with few auteurs and fewer masterpieces, and even fewer works available on video. As I stated in 1984, this is a trajectory of anonymous journey work that meets few criteria of conventional aesthetics:

> Instead of meeting the criteria of durability, abstraction, ambiguity, individualism, uniqueness, formal complexity, deconstructed or redistributed signifiers, novelty and so on, all in a packageable format, political documentaries provide us with disposability, ephemerality, topicality, directness, immediacy, instrumentality, didacticism, collective or anonymous authorship, unconventional formats, non-availability, and ultimately non-evaluability.

In other words, the aesthetics of political use-value, as I put it, makes writing the history of the art form difficult, and doubly so in a climate where graduate students are understandably feeling pressured to write theses on name brand documentary auteurs Frederic Wiseman, Errol Morris, Trinh T. Minh-ha, and Chris Marker rather than the ephemeral anonymous variety that have constituted the common fund of our activist legacy.

It will be already obvious that I have chosen to refer to these foregoing five clips alongside INDONESIA CALLING because they all belong to the generic 'demonstration' trope. They are flirting, on the one hand, with the deadliest, most formulaic cliché of the committed cinema. The demo is the trap for all bad filmmakers and literal-minded sectarians, and the fodder for parodic deconstruction and mythic intensification by filmmakers of every political stripe, from Joyce Wieland to Woody Allen, not to mention lapsed leftists from Sidney Lumet and Bernardo Bertolucci to Jean-Luc Godard himself. Yet, on the other hand, these clips show that the demonstration trope is also one of this tradition's most evocative, still fresh as the day it was born, lending itself, no matter how formulaic, to an astonishing variety of cultural and ideological gradations, and still capable of riveting us to the screen. Indeed, INDONESIA CALLING, a no-budget reconstruction of events from the immediate past, is so fresh fifty-odd years after its production because it seems like one long demonstration trope from beginning to end.

Indeed, the demonstration is not only a cinematic trope but a political resource of great transformative power. For all six of these works constitute not only documents of collective actions of public defiance, but also performative engagements with those collective actions, active interventions by filmmakers and consequently by spectators into the political worlds of the films. As Ivens had said of his famed demonstration scene in BORINAGE (or rather as his brilliant and unacknowledged ghostwriter Jay Leyda had him say):

> We joined the procession with our camera... and the people forgot that it was for a film. Spontaneously the whole community gathered and our staging turned into a real demonstration... Thus the whole concept of the film reached a new level and we felt ashamed to remember that we had originally come here to film facts. Facts became engraved in feelings...[10]

Or, as Jean Carlomusto said on the soundtrack of DOCTORS a half-century later,

> I was torn in a way, because, being in the organizing process, I wanted to be part of the demonstration. But when you have a camera in your hand, you have to think about documenting; so part of you has to be cool. And frankly, at that point, I lost my cool... So you see a lot of my feet in the rough footage because my hands were up in the air and I was chanting along with everyone else...

In the camera's loss of documentary 'cool', the demonstration stops being a shorthand record of dissent, and becomes, as in all of these six films, a subject-centred cinematic performance of political action – respectively, of a community coming together to support a strike in Wasmes, of labour and Indonesian activists symbolically staging an anti-colonial coalition in Sydney, of students and workers confronting the state on the Left Bank, of feminist and AIDS activists storming the New York media, of Mexican peasants re-occupying their homes and fields, and of rural environmental refugees invading a Bombay 5-star hotel to stop a dam. Ivens said 'Our staging turned into a real demonstration'. But since demonstrations are already by definition staged, he should have said '*Our staged staging turned into a real staging*'. 'Staging' thus loses the pejorative connotation it once had, in the mouths of *New Criterion* red-baiters and cinéma vérité apostles alike, as the interference with the experiential truth value of a documentary. Instead, 'staging' acquires the innuendo of street theatre, of political performance,

Still from BORINAGE: a staged demonstration.

Still from INDONESIA CALLING: a real demonstration.

and by extension, since theatre is transformed into the real, of performativity in the public political sphere.

A demonstration has also to do, by definition, with public space, with territory, since the demonstration occupies the streets where the state stages its authority. The demonstration shows its force and commits ritual speech acts that perform territorial possession and liberation, however temporarily, before the 'cops' come to chase them away or beat them up (as they do in all six films I have mentioned, whether off screen as in INDONESIA CALLING, A PLACE CALLED CHIAPAS, and A NARMADA DIARY, or on screen as in MISÈRE AU BORINAGE, LE JOLI MOIS DE MAI, and DOCTORS, LIARS AND WOMEN: AIDS ACTIVISTS SAY NO TO COSMO). As I said, the filmic act both performs and represents the demonstration. As performer, the filmic process alters the relations of power. Often, it erects a protective shelter against violence around the demonstration space, or, conversely, it invites the retributive restoration of order. Or else, the filmmakers are the *metteurs-en-scène* for the staged demonstration in the first place (in this sense, are the women of ACT UP simply imitating Ivens from fifty-five years earlier, with the exception that their territorial claim is not only to geography but also to the discursive space of magazines and talk shows, that is, representation itself?). As representer, the filmic process infinitely extends the discursive space of the original demonstration: the original speech act not only proliferates through this magnification but is also changed qualitatively. In A PLACE CALLED CHIAPAS, Nettie Wild's voice-over calls the Zapatista revolution she is filming the first postmodern revolution because of its shrewd use of the Internet. Perhaps. But the challenges of cinematic discursive space that Ivens already faced in the 1930s are still recognizable in Wild's negotiations of cyberspace: for example, the temptations of techno-fetishism and techno-privilege, the commodification of abjection, the sellouts and trade-offs around personal charisma and collective stakes, short-term and long-term objectives. Are today's anguished compromises around getting foundation funding or accessing mainstream circuits ultimately any worse than Ivens's old 1930s obsession with exactly the same goals, no matter how much the technology and mediascape have been transformed?

The lure of cyberspace notwithstanding, the demonstration is first and foremost about local space and its indexical recording. Wild's Maya villagers reclaiming their homes know this all too well, looking worriedly back at the crew as if to remind them that the cinematic *here* is preceded, for all its postmodernity, by the staking out, penetration, reclaiming, and defence of the historic *here*. Of course film and video in their materiality capture that historic *here* so well – and that is the magic of indexical audio-visual forms, especially when the operator loses her cool and shows the texture of the

Manhattan pavement, Paris paving stones, or Mexican earth, or enacts the blurry kinetics of standing the line, of nervously standing *behind* the front line, or of strategic flight.

Significantly, in all of my examples, the reclamation of local space is directed against the nation state, against its agents of occupation. The genre of committed documentary where the nation is synonymous with revolution, community, or justice, as in Ivens's SPANISH EARTH or Cuban films, or in the Sandinista films I was including in 1984, or the other films of postcolonial national liberation, has undergone a permanent eclipse (although the cyclical view of history does not allow us to use the word *permanent*). The discourse of local space is addressed not nationally but globally, to transnational discursive space. 'Think globally, act locally' may well be another cliché of the Left, but it is one that these works test and verify. The filmic subjects of the South know this even better than those of the North. The stormers of the Bombay hotel – and indeed the subjects of that entire very lively subgenre, the anti-dam, anti-development film that thrives from China to the Cree territory of Northern Quebec[11] – know full well the importance of the World Bank and the other planetary webs of corporate neo-liberalism, and their role in propping up the national oligarchies' desperate superprojects at the expense of local livelihoods.

I am reminded of the journals of one of Patwardhan's compatriots and contemporaries, Manjira Datta, who, like him, is fiercely committed to the local as site of projection as well as of politics. Datta's film SEEDS OF PLENTY, SEEDS OF SORROW (1992), dissects the Green Revolution and indicts the complicity with Intellectual Property Rights that has lined pockets on the national and corporate level and poisoned lives, communities, and soil on the local level. The film, internationally financed by the BBC and transnational development money, had a screening on a dark and stormy night in the South Indian state of Kerala:

> ... People here have heard about the Rio Earth Summit but did not know anything about GATT, IPR, etc. The screening is packed, 200 men, men only. It is held inside a shed under some palm trees, the film soundtrack competes with the drumming sound of the rain on the tin roof. Despite all this the para-dubbing by Mohan is loud and clear. However, towards the end he obviously gets tired and loses the thread completely, and misses out on some of the critical portion about global economic demands, etc. The generator starts acting up and the film speed fluctuates but there is hushed silence and total concentration from the audience.

The first question is why the disaster wrought by the Green Revolution isn't shown more visually, graphically. My reply is that, in the areas that I have visited and filmed in, the ill effects of the Green Revolution are just now being discovered by farmers. The film has been made as a warning, it has been made to generate more active discussions.

Somebody clarifies for me what has happened in Kerala land reform...

Someone asks why the local political struggles weren't shown... why only development and environment were highlighted: local politics is very important. I replied that when I had made the film, local protests hadn't started so in that sense the film was a bit dated. Yes, I agree that local struggles are very important but under the sweeping reforms of the New World Order it has become imperative to understand the strategies and tactics of global politics which are bound to influence local level politics in the future. Politics have to be addressed today at two levels. Protests and movements have to be at the global level as well as at the local level. I feel it is about time people in India started talking more and more widely about the connections between development strategies and environmental effects.[12]

The resemblances to the discussions Ivens had with his audiences in the Soviet Union in the early thirties are, of course, striking:[13] local issues from elsewhere, are filtered through lenses specific to the local reception context, for example housing and the buying power of wages, and on this basis global dialogue and alliances are formed.

In Ivens's day, the global meant the humanity that will be saved by the dictatorship of the proletariat, as the last title of BORINAGE put it. In fact, the political discourse of Ivens's work right up to 1968 was shaped by an international context dominated by the institutional left, specifically by the peripeteias of the international communist movement to which he loyally but discreetly subscribed. This may be explicit only in BORINAGE and the Cold War films among Ivens's entire oeuvre (and then, often subliminal or disingenuous), but it is a structuring absence everywhere else. If BORINAGE's intransigence was dictated by the Comintern's sectarian paranoia of the early thirties, and if INDONESIA CALLING's manic triumphalism was shaped in disavowal by the postwar rout of the communist movement in the West and the Cold War, already underway, my four post-Ivens examples testify to entirely different contexts. If the May 1968 images are energized by the oedipal revolt against the organized and monolithic Old Left, the images of the last decade are characterized by its utter absence. The disappearance of the relation to the Party as a cinematic issue may thus be the single factor that distinguishes Ivens's work most from that of his grandchildren.

The Party is over, but, as I have said, there remain surprising constants in the way its grandchildren are articulating the relationships of local space to the global. One important way these are expressed is through the quantum proliferation of networks and constituencies for the documentary commit-

ted to radical change as we head for the next century. This is another observation I made in 1984 and *The New Criterion* took great delight in mocking
the 'ragbag army of malcontents' I listed at that time as the constellation of
constituencies to whom the radical documentary was addressed:

> Both those working within the framework of the traditional left and workers' move-
> ments, and those within the progressive mass movement of the seventies and eight-
> ies: the women's movement; minority, anti-racist and national movements; the
> environmental/anti-nuke/peace movement; lesbian and gay liberation groups; and
> other resistance movements enlisting prisoners, consumers, welfare recipients, im-
> migrants, the handicapped, the elderly, the unemployed, and others on down the
> endless list of those disenfranchised under patriarchal capitalism.

Of course, the traditional proletariat are still critically at the core of the committed documentary vocation, though their classical embodiments within
the cinegenic primary resource industries or manufacturing, as in BORI-
NAGE, are increasingly swallowed by information industries, demoralized
and marginalized as Michael Moore discovered in ROGER AND ME, or else
displaced to the deregulated and de-unionized 'free trade' zones of the
South. Otherwise, the army is still lively and very malcontent indeed, and I
would only make some further additions to the list, thanks to the HIV pan-
demic, the proliferating politics of subjectivity and identity in the North, the
intensification of the environmental movement, and exacerbated immise-
ration in both North and South. Among many urgent new rags in the bag:
the infected and the medically destitute; the sexually marginalized; the
drugged and psychiatrized; the poisoned, indigenous and displaced; students and young people without jobs or hopes of jobs; intellectuals and cultural workers, increasingly marginalized and censored; and in the South,
rather than the postcolonial *clients* of so-called development as seen in
Ivens's DEMAIN À NANGUILA (1960), its *victims* as seen in the work of Datta
and Patwardhan.

Some of these new constituencies have consolidated emerging or re-animated documentary genres such as the autobiographical film and the media deconstruction; new technologies have also re-animated the ideal of
subject-produced non-professional radical culture that has been around
since the agitprop trains of the Soviet Revolution. And if these new genres,
constituencies, and technologies have led to the multiplication of potential
distribution outlets and formats, none of this has fundamentally altered the
structural relations of producer to constituency, the disappearance of cen-
tralized Party networks notwithstanding. This is the wheel that the green-
haired youths have been constantly reinventing: not the relations of cultural

commodification, but the specifically subject-centered political relations of analysis and mobilization, of linking local space to global solidarity.

I worried earlier that my sense of film history in this article might turn out to be a non-materialist one, as any pan-historic juxtaposition of images threatens to be. But, in fact, it is the materiality of subject-centered film distribution, of the relationship of image-producer to image-receiver, of receiver as producer, that also binds my six instances together, beyond the iconography of the demonstration that I have highlighted. My three excerpted works of the last decade have deployed a wide range of distribution tactics, from the classical Ivensian models of parallel theatrical release and the local shed-and-generator community screening method, to public television. But most promising may be the video blanket approach shared by the Indian independents and ACT UP alike. This approach consists of blanketing constituency networks, both pre-existing and customized according to the issue at hand, with cheap or free copies of the work, on cassette – or increasingly on the Net. Intellectual Property Rights are the latest weapon of international corporate capital, and it hardly behooves committed filmmakers to play their game. These tapes are made for pirating!

Perhaps this is a fitting note for a conclusion. Upon the centenary of a committed film-maker whose relevance continues to amaze and inspire, I call on the Ivens estate to profit immediately from the example of ACT UP and the Indians, and to reconsider the cautious inertia that has held back the circulation of Ivens's work since his death. I call on the guardians of the hoard to immediately release cheap if not free copies of twenty of Ivens's most immediate political works to the community networks who are his proper constituency and heirs. The young practitioners of committed documentary who are reinventing the wheel deserve full access to the works of this founder of their art form. At one hundred, the youthful Ivens belongs not to the archivists and lawyers but to the greenhairs and the whole ragbag army of malcontents.

A Special Relationship: Joris Ivens and the Netherlands

Bert Hogenkamp

In 1995 the one hundredth birthday of film was celebrated. In the Netherlands this joyful event was the occasion of the issue of two special stamps. One showed a scene from TURKS FRUIT (1973), the film that drew one of the biggest audiences in Dutch film history. For director Paul Verhoeven, filming Jan Wolkers' novel meant the breakthrough which was to take him to Hollywood, where he has achieved a lot of success the past ten years. The second stamp portrayed a young Joris Ivens behind the camera. The designer used a black and white photograph from the thirties. The connotation that Ivens was the Dutch national filmmaker was made clear by the choice of the supporting colours red and blue (the Dutch flag is red, white and blue). A few months later the politician Frits Bolkestein, leader of the moderate conservative Liberal Party, said in an interview that Ivens was 'a *pur sang* communist, a propagandist of an inhuman system'. Bolkestein added: 'For me he equals Leni Riefenstahl, the Nazi filmmaker.'[1] The politician said that he did not feel like licking Ivens's behind and would therefore try to prevent the issue of the stamp. It had already been for sale at the post office for months and, consequently, had been licked by many tongues. This incident makes clear that in his native country, Ivens has remained a controversial figure even after his death.

From the end of the twenties, Joris Ivens himself showed great interest in the legend of the Flying Dutchman, the man who had broken Christian standards and had to pay for it with eternal exile on the high seas.[2] But where the Flying Dutchman could not bring spokesmen or defenders into action to plead his case, Ivens managed to mobilize supporters again and again.[3] In a Machiavellian way it could be said that this was his most successful directing work. But there was more. A day at the Deutsche Film- und Fernseh-Akademie Berlin in February 1974 acquired the motto 'Von Joris Ivens lernen' (Learning from Joris Ivens) which had nothing to do with the filmmaker's vanity in the first place, or the need to create a personality cult. For Ivens, holding up his own artistic experiences as an example was a matter of course, just as the course of his life had been an example. His two autobiographies (*The Camera and I*, Berlin-GDR, 1969, and *Joris Ivens ou la mémoire* d'un regard, Paris, 1982) bear clear witness to this. In the prologue to the brochure *Joris Ivens 50 jaar Wereldcineast*, published in 1978 on the occasion of the exhibition of the same name for his eightieth birthday, he wrote that the visitor 'discovers NEW EARTH, his own BREAKERS in his own life, personally and socially and builds bridges, THE BRIDGE. But also his own war, Laos. And even sometimes needs his own BORINAGE, when decisive choices have to be made'. In this way Ivens's reputation was continually at stake. The result was a fascinating struggle in which the arguments put forward were of a political, aesthetic, and even humanitarian nature. Among the participants there were, besides Ivens himself, of course, politicians, civil servants, journalists (film critics in particular), but also film archivists and scientists.

Between 1928 and 1930 Joris Ivens developed into the great promise of the independent Netherlands film art.[4] He was born in Nijmegen in 1898, the son of C.A.P. Ivens who owned a chain of photo shops bearing the name of CAPI. Predestined to succeed his father, he had studied in Rotterdam and Berlin and had served his apprenticeship in Dresden and Jena. Working in the Amsterdam CAPI branch, he surrendered himself to the artistic life of the capital. In 1928, he presented his first film THE BRIDGE, a study of the movement of the railway bridge across the Koningshaven in Rotterdam, to the Film League audience. This league which vowed to promote the art of film, had been established by Ivens the year before. The performance was a great success and THE BRIDGE was distributed by Ufa. This film was followed by the short films BREAKERS, RAIN, a filmic poem about Amsterdam before, during and after a rain shower, and a long documentary for the construction workers' union, from which Ivens distilled two separate films: PILE DRIVING and ZUIDERZEE. These films were widely reported in the press, both in his own country and abroad. He was praised by the likes of Germaine Dulac and Vsevolod Pudovkin.[5] At the beginning of 1930, he travelled to the Soviet Union and became a communist. He did not report this to the press (only in the communist newspaper *De Tribune* was he sometimes given the title of 'comrade') which he extensively spoke to after his return. In 1931 followed his first sound film, PHILIPS RADIO, an assignment for the electronics firm of the same name. Ivens also laid the foundation for the first serious film academy in The Netherlands, the Filmtechnische leergang (FTL). Among the participants, offered by two Ivens collaborators Willem Bon and Frans Dupont, were several future filmmakers.[6]

In 1931, his first book appeared: *Het cineastisch werk van Joris Ivens* (*The filmic work of Joris Ivens*). It contained some thirty drawings, photographs of him working and filming, preceded by an appraisal of Ivens's films by film critic L.J. Jordaan. It contained a striking thesis that 'in Ivens one does not only honour the person but most certainly also the principle'.[7] In it, he refers to the principle of independent film art as announced by the Film League. At that time, this reference could also be found in other film publications, in which Ivens belonged to the Film League although as a first among equals.[8] The fact that he made SONG OF HEROES (also known as KOMSOMOL) in the Soviet Union in 1932 – his critics later launched heavy objections to this film – was rather an affirmation than a breach of faith. Even completely stripped of its political message, the Soviet film was declared the 'absolute film' by Film League ideologist Menno ter Braak.[9] With such reasoning it was, therefore, a great honour but also a logical step that Ivens was to make a film in the country that had produced Eisenstein and Pudovkin. Even in magazines that could rouse little sympathy for the bolshevik regime, the news about Ivens's stay in Magnitogorsk, where SONG OF HEROES was filmed, were generally positive.

In the seventies, Ivens proclaimed BORINAGE as the film that had completely changed his career. It was a film that forced him to say goodbye to his aesthetic opinions and forced him leave his homeland. Together with Henri Storck, Ivens had filmed BORINAGE in the autumn of 1933 in the Belgian mining district of the same name, where Vincent van Gogh had been active as a lay preacher some fifty years before.[10] March 1934 saw the first screening of the film, first in Belgium, and then shortly afterwards in the Netherlands. The reactions in the Dutch press were mixed. Some newspapers condemned the communist version of the events in the Borinage, which was all the more reason for the communist newspaper *De Tribune* to praise him. Incidentally the film, in contrast to what Ivens wrote in *The Camera and I*, was never banned in the Netherlands for the simple reason that it was never put before the Central Board of fim censors.[11] However, the *Nieuwe Rotterdamsche Courant* discovered a more essential omission: 'Joris Ivens's principle to reduce the activity of the camera to register factual reality as objectively and neutrally as possible, is in strong contrast to the principles of the art of filming that have always been defended here.'[12] It is true indeed that Ivens definitely departed from Film League aesthetics with BORINAGE. These aesthetics came under fire precisely in that period from the Dutch feature film industry. Producers did not set store by filmmakers with a Film League background, who, by the way, did not have any experience with directing actors and had considered narration a sin. This fate was experienced by among others, Mannus Franken, co-director of BREAKERS and RAIN, who, out of desperation, left for the Dutch East Indies. Jan Koelinga, another Film League disciple, even had himself filmed while standing in a dole queue together with hundreds of other unemployed workers!

The need to break with his father to enable him to join the Soviet 'workers' paradise' played a big part in Ivens's decision to leave the Netherlands.

The period from April 1934 until the beginning of 1936, which he spent in the Soviet Union, belongs to the least documented part of his life. The communist newspaper *De Tribune*, which was the only one to report on him with any regularity, probably surpassed in the number of words what Ivens himself wrote about this episode of his life in his autobiographies: not one word (*The Camera and I*) and two pages (*La mémoire d'un regard*) respectively. Considering that his name surfaces in the protocols of the 'party purge' executed in the summer of 1936 among German writers living in exile, the question remains whether Ivens would have escaped the Stalinist terror unscathed had he not left for the United States in January 1936.[13] At the end of the same year, he returned to Europe to make a film in Spain with American financial support. For six months, a civil war had been going on between the legally elected republican government and the rebels under the leadership of general Franco, who could rely on military and financial support from national-socialist Germany and fascist Italy. That Ivens, who had found a good partner in the author Ernest Hemingway, was on the side of the republicans who were supported by the Soviet Union was obvious. After a successful first screening in the United States (in the White House for president Roosevelt and his entourage) and a series of successful performances in Hollywood, THE SPANISH EARTH reached the Netherlands in November of 1937 through the good offices of cameraman John Fernhout. Here, film censorship did not bother itself so much with the film's political opinions as with the references to Germany's involvement in the conflict. If they were to be left in then the country's neutrality would be at stake, opined civil servants and even the Minister for Foreign Affairs, who came to see the film especially for this purpose. He took his wife along with him because 'going to the pictures' was, of course, a family affair. Every reference to German involvement in the conflict (like Hemingway's famous comment upon the wreckage of a shot down German Junker, 'I can't read German either') was carefully removed.[14] Nevertheless, THE SPANISH EARTH received a positive reception in the press. Although Dick Vriesman inevitably referred to Ivens's Film League past in his book, he also presented a new aspect, the creative use of sound in THE SPANISH EARTH.[15]

However, apart from THE SPANISH EARTH the oeuvre that Ivens realized between 1937 and 1944 in the United States was for the greater part to remain unknown in the Netherlands as a result of the German occupation. THE 400 MILLION (1939), his film about the struggle of the Japanese in China which initiated his great love of that country, was not released until 1945. The other films were never to be shown in Dutch cinemas. The Dutch authorities in exile showed great interest in Ivens the person, all the same, during the war. They had little choice in the matter however, because apart from Ivens's cameraman John Fernhout no good Dutch filmmakers were available. They were stranded in the Netherlands, during the German occupation, or in The Dutch East Indies, which had been conquered by Japan in 1942. Loyal to the party line, Ivens sided with the allied *war effort* only after the German invasion of the Soviet Union. In 1944, he made his film NEW EARTH (a new version of ZUIDERZEE with music by Hans Eissler and a voice over – commentary by Ivens himself) available to the Netherlands Information Services. The third act of NEW EARTH, in which Ivens heavily criticized the capitalist system that first reclaimed land from the sea and then threw the grain growing on this new land into the sea, was removed. Under the title of NEW EARTH the film was released as proof that the Netherlands was a country that fought the sea and not its neighbours.

In September of the same year, Ivens was approached by representatives of the Dutch East Indies government for the job of Film Commissioner of the Dutch East Indies. His task would be to film the liberation of Indonesia and subsequently, to initiate a documentary film production system with Indonesian filmmakers. Ivens, surprised that he had actually been chosen, hesitated, but the assurances of authorities that he, and nobody else, would be able to translate the democratic aims of the government, won him over. As 'a dangerous communist', however, the filmmaker was monitored by the FBI and was subsequently refused the right (the *re-entry permit*) to return to America. His status of suspicious person also meant that he was refused entry to the war zones of the Pacific. Yet, Ivens still decided to leave for Australia, where the members of the Film & Photo Unit of the Dutch East Indies government received him with anything but open arms. After the proclamation of the establishment of the Republic of Indonesia in August 1945, the gulf between Ivens and the Dutch authorities became even wider. On 21 November 1945, he announced his resignation as film commisioner at a press conference, referring to the Atlantic Manifesto and the Indonesian right to self determination. Ivens then managed to rouse support among the Australian Waterfront Workers' Union for a film about the harbour strikes against Dutch military transports. It became a cinematographic pamphlet made with a ridiculously low budget called INDONESIA CALLING. His resignation and the film had a large impact on relations between Ivens and his homeland.

In February 1947, Ivens returned from Australia. In his *La mémoire d'un regard* he created the impression that he had been received as a 'pariah', a 'traitor' and that even the communists thought of him as 'no more than an adventurer'.[16] Yet, during the short stay in the Netherlands, he was offered several assignments (even by the government), while in the following years, the communist press in the Netherlands used only superlatives when describing the films he made behind the Iron Curtain. None of these films, however, was to receive normal screening time in the cinemas, which excused the film press from writing about them.[17] The fact that Ivens was active in Eastern Europe during this time aroused great commotion. From 1948 onward, the Dutch embassies made it difficult for him to have his passport renewed. He was mostly granted a three months' extension or a *laisser passer*. Ivens sometimes admitted that this was why he was forced to make (mediocre) films in Eastern Europe.[18] However, in *Gevaarlijk leven* (*Dangerous Life*), the recent Ivens biography, Hans Schoots reveals that it is true that there was some mention 'of a rare harassment by the authorities, which deeply insulted Ivens... [but that] in that same period he [was able to] travel from East to West and back without hindrance'.[19] Although other Dutch communists were equally troubled by similar 'harassment', involvement Ivens's and his alleged anti-Dutch attitude in the case of Indonesia certainly did not help matters. The ultimate provocation was ofcourse the film INDONESIA CALLING, which was like a red ray to a bull. As far as it was within their power, representatives of the Netherlands abroad tried to put a stop to showings of the film. Sometimes they were successful (Locarno, 1948), sometimes they were not. Thus, in 1963 (!) the influence of Mr. Joseph Luns, Minister for Foreign Affairs, the later NATO Secretary-General, was not sufficient to stop a screening of the film in Münster.

In 1958, Ivens won the great Cannes festival prize with LA SEINE A RENCONTRÉ PARIS. A year later, he visited the Netherlands in connection with the screening of this film at the Arnhem Film Festival. Critics appreciated the film, but also Ivens's colleagues paid tribute to the film. For many of them he was still the creator of THE BRIDGE and RAIN, films that, even during the Cold War, were regularly shown in the Amsterdam cinema, 'De Uitkijk', or in the Netherlands Film Museum. The idea of filming a subject in everyday life with stylistic camera work and editing was a method that Bert Haanstra and Herman van der Horst, the celebrities of the Dutch Documentary School of the fifties, had successfully used in their films which were also appreciated abroad. In the Netherlands, LA SEINE A RENCONTRÉ PARIS was, therefore, not interpreted as a French film. On the contrary, it was considered proof of the aesthetic principles of the Dutch Film League being right, thus a Dutch film through and through. It was therefore no coincidence that enthusiasm for the film and its creator was biggest with the Dutch Association of Professional Filmmakers. This organisation evolved out of the artists' resistance during the German occupation, and it felt strongly about the ideas of the Film League, and welcomed Ivens with open arms and appointed him an honorary member. One of the friendships Ivens made at that time was with Bert Haanstra.

Nostalgia or invitation? Joris Ivens in Paris, 1950.

In February 1964, Ivens was again in the Netherlands to celebrate his sixty-fifth birthday, which he had celebrated in Leipzig in November 1963, once again. On this occasion, the Netherlands Film Museum (NFM) under the direction of Jan de Vaal had prepared a retrospective of Ivens's work. After the estrangement in 1968 between Ivens and the GDR, which seemed to have a monopoly on the celebration of Ivens's birthday invariably taking place in the penultimate week of November during the Leipziger Dokumentarfilmwoche, it would become a tradition to celebrate the jubilee years in the Netherlands: 1968 – NFM and Filmacademy: retrospective and a legendary party in De Brakke Grond, 1978 – NFM: retrospective and the exhibition *Joris Ivens 50 years world film-maker* mentioned before; 1988 – the town of Nijmegen: retrospective and exhibition, publication of a book and tribute at the Town Hall.

The role of the NFM was a remarkable one: by regularly organizing performances of Ivens's films it constantly reminded the outside world of his existence. That was important for, with a single exception, none of the films Ivens had made in the sixties and seventies was given normal circulation.

Some (e.g., LE PEUPLE ET SES FUSILS) were shown in the so-called alternative circuit by the political film distributor Cineclub, others were broadcast on television (e.g., HOW YUKONG MOVED THE MOUNTAINS). The NFM showed those films at least every five years, even though the museum did not always have all copies with Dutch subtitles.

Ivens's films from the sixties and seventies paradoxically impressed his colleagues less and less. In the sixties, young cinematographers had finally put the principles of the Film League to rest. Several of them (e.g., Johan van der Keuken) continued to maintain good relations with Ivens, but the admiration was focused on the person rather than on his aesthetic opinions (which, by the way, had undergone some changes in the course of the sixties). Ivens was the prototype of the anti-establishment figure who rebelled against the 'ruling class', i.e., the Dutch Authorities; a Provo, though it is true that that movement did not want to have anything to do with Ivens the communist, and rather compared itself to the Beggars fighting against the Spanish rulers in the Eighty Years' War.[20]

In contrast to the Cold War period, the press cultivated an interest in Ivens and his films from 1964.[21] In general, the filmmaker could rely on great sympathy from among film critics and journalists. Only one newspaper consistently turned against him, Amsterdam's *Het Parool*, which was founded in the resistance and was led by conservative social-democrats for whom anti-communism was self-evident. There was often good reason to write about Ivens: he celebrated a jubilee, had just returned from journeys to Vietnam, China or some other faraway country, a new film was being screened, a new autobiography was published, or he was being honoured with an important medal. Special attention was given to the relation between the filmmaker and his homeland. In 1963-64, people were indignant about the fact that the government had refused Ivens a film assignment about the Delta works. When in 1969 the Minister for Culture, Marga Klompé, invited Ivens to make a short film in accordance with his own views, it provoked much comment in the press, all the more because the filmmaker had decided to approach the offer with caution. After several years, Ivens finally handed in a synopsis for a feature film about 'The Flying Dutchman'. Another incident occurred in 1978, when during the presentation of the Dick Scherpenzeel Award Minister de Koning ventured some critical remarks on HOW YUKONG MOVED THE MOUNTAINS. Ivens thought this inappropriate, and remarked that on the presentation of the European Cup you do not tell the coach of the winning football team that he could have coached the team differently and could have fielded other players! Although during the eighties, Ivens and Loridan implicitly recognized the truth of what the De Koning had said, the press condemned the Minister.

Joris Ivens and his close friends Jan de Vaal (founder and director of the Netherlands Filmmuseum untill his retirement) and Tineke de Vaal, 1985.

The incident was seen as the umpteenth time that the government had
'something' against the filmmaker.

In September 1985, the minister for Culture, Elco Brinkman, flew to Paris
to present the 'Golden Calf', the culture prize of the Dutch Film Festival to
Ivens personally. On that occasion, Brinkman, referring to the Indonesia affair, confirmed that 'history agrees with you more than with your opponents at that time'. They were the words that Ivens had been waiting for, for
over forty years, and he readily accepted the extended hand. His joy increased when the Production Fund and Dutch television announced that
they were willing to contribute a large amount to the film Ivens and Loridan
were in the process of making in China. This time, it was not *Het Parool* that
showed its disapproval, but *Intermediair*, a weekly paper for university
graduates. In a lengthy article, Michel Korzec and Hans Moll opposed the
'canonization' of the winner of the 'Golden Calf'. Using two films, SONG OF
HEROES and 600 MILLION WITH YOU, a report on an anti-Western demonstration Ivens had filmed in 1958 in China, as examples, they demonstrated that
Ivens had lent a helping hand to two mass murderers (Stalin and Mao). According to Korzec and Moll, Leni Riefenstahl's contribution to Nazism was
a 'myth', whereas Ivens's was a 'fact'.[22] They did not leave Ivens at peace

concerning the Indonesian affair either. In the historical magazine *Skript* of December of the same year, Jan Willem Regenhardt published an article in which he claimed that Ivens had actually been dismissed before he gave his press conference in November 1945. What was the truth? Ivens supposedly accidentally left a briefcase with documents in a bar (!), containing the script for this anti-Dutch film, the future INDONESIA CALLING. The Dutch authorities were informed of this and were thinking of a way to 'get rid of' the filmmaker in a decent way, when Ivens himself handed in his resignation. The civil servants involved were bitter because Ivens had passed the buck to them. In 1988, Regenhardt repeated this version about the 'reversal trick' in the weekly *Hervormd Nederland*.[23]

Where Korzec and Moll had only too carelessly and easily quoted from Ivens's own autobiographies, Regenhardt had gone about his research differently. He had gone to the State Archives, delved into the records, and produced several important documents about the problems concerning the *re-entry permit*. However, Regenhardt based his weak accusations of the 'reversal trick' on the oral statements of one man, and that someone had been a sworn enemy of Ivens since 1945. Yet Regenhardt's article initiated a change in research procedures. He made it clear that only thorough research of the source material in the records could shed light on certain episodes of Ivens's life. Historian Eric van 't Groenewout, who was convinced that Regenhardt was wrong, saw this as all the more reason to see what relevant material was available in various ministries. He found the relevant documents relating to Ivens and the 'case' by which he clearly demonstrated the inaccuracy of Regenhardt's statement in his doctoral thesis.[24] Another historian, Hans Schoots who shortly after Ivens's death decided that it was time to write a biography of the film-maker without him constantly looking over his shoulder, went even further. Assisted by the fall of communism, he was allowed a peek at Soviet documents about Ivens's first trip to Russia, had the FBI file about the film-maker sent over, and, something Regenhardt had failed to do, listen to the accounts of witnesses from both sides. In 1995, his *Gevaarlijk Leven. Een biografie van Joris Ivens* of more than 500 pages appeared. This book will not be the final word on Ivens, however.

Far into the eighties, the memories of the filmmaker had largely determined the image that was sketched in the books about him. And although Ivens had an excellent memory, it was not infallible, as is true for any other human being. In the sixties and seventies, various authors had used the separate collection of Ivens documents that Jan and Tineke de Vaal had collected with great enthusiasm at the Film Museum. It was often material collected by the filmmaker's (ex-)wives. Ivens himself had also consulted this collection intensively, for among other things the exhibition about his work and life and in the writing of his second autobiography. During the eighties, when the NFM felt the pressure of spending cuts, it became difficult to extend the collection any further and to receive visitors in an appropriate manner. In order to make the collection available again, minister Brinkman decided to furnish 100,000 Dutch guilders in 1985. It would take twelve years, however, before the archives, now in the custody of the European Foundation Joris Ivens in Nijmegen, could be consulted by bonafide researchers without preconditions (as is appropriate for an institution financed by public funds). Besides the fact that the political culture during the nineties was not in his favour, the unavailability of the Ivens documents was the main reason why there was hardly any publications about the filmmaker, except for the Hans Schoots' biography.[25]

The importance of a filmmaker is not only decided on the basis of his written legacy, but also on the basis of the films he has left behind. Some films had already been given to the NFM during the fifties together with the collection of the cinema 'De Uitkijk', other films had been collected by Jan de Vaal in the course of years as the result of exchanges with foreign archives. By the beginning of the nineties, the NFM board thought it was high time to re-evaluate the collection of Ivens films in the possession of the Museum. There was still the possibility, it was argued, to put the nitrate copies in optimum condition with the help of new laboratory techniques (wetgate-printing). The NFM called in its associated archives and collected hundreds of copies that were compared in the technical centre in Overveen. Practically all the films until 1954 (when the switch from nitrate to acetate material was made) were transferred to new material. The project rendered surprising discoveries as well, for example, a version of THE SPANISH EARTH with spoken commentary by Orson Welles, which was always thought to have been lost. The same film had been shown for years although, without the shots of the German writer Gustav Regler. These had been removed from the film during the fifties in the GDR, when Regler had become persona non grata. The material cut from the film had been carefully kept in a film tin bearing the heading 'Ivens in Poland'.[26]

Hans Schoots' biography, the beautiful new copies of the early films and the opening up of the document collection seemed to be all factors in the reconsideration of the importance of Ivens and his oeuvre in his hundredth year of birth in 1998. However the contrary also appeared to be true as the anti-Ivens lobby manifested itself more vociferously than ever. These forces even suggested the renaming of the Ivensplaats (Ivens Square) in Nijmegen.[27] Although they referred to Schoots's book, their argumentation seemed to come directly from Korzec and Moll that Ivens had sided with the 'hangmen' Stalin and Mao. Condemnations rather than explanations were what seemed to matter.

More fundamental, however, was the doubt that some critics cast upon the value of the filmmaker's oeuvre. The argument ran as follows: at the beginning of his career Ivens made a few masterpieces (THE BRIDGE, RAIN, ZUIDERZEE), but after he had sold his soul to the devil (communism), he never created anything worthwhile again.[28] According to supporters of this view, little can be 'learned from Ivens'. In this context, the declining interest in Ivens among the younger generation of Dutch filmmakers was referred to.[29]

Yet this explanation hardly seems relevant in a discussion about the 'special' relationship between Ivens and his homeland. It seems more like an expression of the growing distrust about claims that the documentary shows reality (and nothing but reality). Ivens, for that matter, is not the only star in the history of the documentary who fell victim to a similar form of *debunking*: his Scottish colleague John Grierson – who cannot be accused of communist sympathies at all – experienced exactly the same thing ten years ago.[30] In short, other arguments were now playing a role in the struggle for Ivens's reputation, but that struggle is still as fascinating as in the preceding decades.

Music and Soundtrack in Joris Ivens's Films

Claude Brunel

The music and soundtrack in the films of Joris Ivens, like the other elements of his oeuvre, are the reflection of one century of cinema. This has been the case since his first silent films in the twenties until he began using synchronous sound in 1968, beginning with LE 17ÈME PARALLÈLE. They are also reflections of Ivens's political, geographical and artistic environments. Their style, unlike that of the images, which always remained recognizable, evolved, adapted and are determined by the sensibility of the various eras and places visited by the director of KOMSOMOL, SPANISH EARTH, POWER AND THE LAND, and LA SEINE A RENCONTRÉ PARIS. We can distinguish three periods: the silent film period, the 35mm sound film period and the synchronous sound film period.

The Silent Films Period

The silent film period begins with ÉTUDES DES MOUVEMENTS (1928), THE BRIDGE (1928), continues with RAIN (1929), BREAKERS (1929), PILE DRIVING (1929), WE ARE BUILDING (1929), CREOSOTE (1931), ZUIDERZEE (1930-33), and ends with the first version of BORINAGE (1933). Except for BREAKERS (BRANDING), which is half-fiction and half-documentary, for which an accompaniment was played in the theatre, all the original versions of these films are silent. The main characteristic of these silent films, especially THE BRIDGE, is the musical construction of the visual track. As the avant-garde French filmmaker, Germaine Dulac wrote in January 1930, after the first projection of THE BRIDGE in Paris: 'I saw a moving symphony with harmonies, chords organised in different rhythms, I felt a musical idea of which the sensitive resonance was overtaking the object, I found the visual music of the future...' This meant that the organization of the cinematographic visual sentence is constructed in a similar way as the music. To develop the sentence in a permanent relationship between the instant (in music, the note or the chord, the instrumental or vocal timbre, in cinema, the shot with all its elements: faces, gestures, architectures, landscapes, light and darkness, black and white, colours, frame, etc.); the value (value of the note or chord in music, value of the shot in cinema), and the development of these elements in the time; that is to say, to practice the musical editing as Eisenstein defined it and practised it.

This kind of musical writing, this awareness of the sensitive power of the musical editing will remain a permanent impression which characterizes the style of all of Ivens's films.

The 35mm Sound Films Period

This period begins in 1931 with PHILIPS RADIO, with music composed by Lou Lichtveld. In this film, Joris Ivens who was in total support of socialist ideals, succeeded in shifting the initial purpose of the commissioned publicity film for Philips, with a powerful mixing of image and sound. He juxtapositioned the tired faces, the repetitive gestures of the workers with the magnificence of Philips's commercial products.

As early as KOMSOMOL or SONGS OF HEROES (1933), Joris Ivens was already using the soundtrack as an extension of the visuals. The soundtrack was composed to support the political, social, or pedagogic discourse of a filmmaker who, like most of the intellectuals and artists of his generation, believed, or wanted to believe, in the emergence of a just society, based on equality, which was the aim of the Soviet socialists.

With NEW EARTH (1934), which is a revised version of ZUIDERZEE and was made after the great international economic crisis of 1929, Joris Ivens, who wrote and narrated the commentary, opened the door to militant commentary and affirmed his committed choice for documentary cinema - a cinema in which the filmmaker affirms his human, social, and political convictions with images and words.

He often provided commentary written by well-known authors or journalists who shared his convictions, such as Ernest Hemingway for SPANISH EARTH (1936); Dudley Nichols for THE 400 MILLION (1938); Catherine Duncan for INDONESIA CALLING (1946), THE FIRST YEARS (1947); Vladimir Pozner for THE SONG OF THE RIVERS (1954); and Alberto Moravia for ITALY IS NOT A POOR COUNTRY (1960). Joris Ivens denounced capitalism in the Soviet version of BORINAGE; the monopoly of American capitalism in ITALY IS NOT A POOR COUNTRY (L'ITALIA NON È UN PAESE POVERO); colonialism in INDONESIA CALLING; and fully exposes men fighting for their liberty in SPANISH EARTH, THE 400 MILLION, LE 17ÈME PARALLÈLE; he shows his belief in a better world in THE FIRST YEARS, THE SONG OF THE RIVERS, FREUNDSCHAFT SIEGT, PEACE TOUR; or sings, with images and sounds, with Jaques Prévert, Chris Marker, or André Verdet, in LA SEINE A RENCONTRÉ PARIS; or the sounds of the seaport town in ... A VALPARAISO, 1962; or the wind that lashes the land and its people in POUR LE MISTRAL, 1965.

As omnipresent as the commentary is in these political films, Joris Ivens never forgot how music and concrete sounds helped to affect the spectator. He also never forgot the power of the human voice, like the voice of Paul Robeson singing 'Old Man River' in THE SONG OF RIVERS; nor forgot instrumental music's power, with the music of Hanns Eisler in SONGS OF HEROES, THE 400 MILLION, NEW EARTH; or the music of Shostakovitch's in THE SONG OF RIVERS, or that of Cuban composer Gramatgès for CARNET DE VIAJE or PUEBLO ARMADO; and he never forgot the impact of popular songs which he uses in SPANISH EARTH or KOMSOMOL; nor the importance of the concrete noise which he organizes, associates, and conducts in a precise synchronized relationship with the images, as he does with the ominous noise of planes releasing their bombs over Madrid in SPANISH EARTH or on Shanghai in THE 400 MILLIONS.

When he returned to the West in 1957, Joris Ivens began to exchange the political commentary for social and poetic commentary, but he remained a spokesman for the dispossessed and the oppressed, or simply 'the people': those along the banks of the Seine (LA SEINE A RENCONTRÉ PARIS) or in the villages of the Provence (POUR LE MISTRAL), or in the hills of Valparaiso (...A VALPARAISO) or the people of Nanguila learning of their independence (DEMAIN À NANGUILA, 1960).

The Synchronous Sound Period

The Vietnam war pushed Joris Ivens into a militant stand. LE 17ÈME PARALLÈLE is one of the most moving, and yet optimistic denunciations of war and shows the resistance of the Vietnamese people against the American agressor, and daily life in a Vietnamese village over a period of three months with Marceleine Loridan. It is here that he began to work with the 16mm camera and synchronous sound. There is no music, instead we hear a very complex soundtrack produced by Marceline Loridan, with all the noises of war; a very realistic but also very visual soundtrack. The recorded sounds fill the foreground and background to reflect a terrible war, where death comes down from the sky all day and all night. But there is evidence of also a resistance in which the will to live and the courage of poor country people triumphs over the world's most powerful nation.

In HOW YUKONG MOVED THE MOUTAINS (1976), Joris Ivens and Marceline Loridan use all the possiblities of direct sound and the handheld camera. The film aimed to answer occidental questions about China's cultural revolution. Each of the twelve films was prepared in France by Marceline Loridan with a systematic questionnaire. All the questions were designed to allow the Chinese people to speak for themselves, among them people of Shanghai in THE PHARMACY, the Shanghai generator factory workers in THE GENERATOR FACTORY, students and teacher in THE FOOTBALL INCIDENT, a Peking mother in A WOMAN, A FAMILY, and the artists of the Peking Opera in REHEARSAL AT THE PEKING OPERA, etc.

A sober and precise commentary gives information about the geographic, economic, social, context and history of this complex people of China. The music, diegetic or not diegetic, provides episodic lyric breathes.

In UNE HISTOIRE DE VENT, the last film of this period, Joris Ivens himself thinks aloud about the meaning of human life, the importance of the wind – breath of the world – in the eternal China 'decors', in the China of sand deserts and living myths, while Michel Portal's clarinet plays, as an intermittent and light musical commentary, fragments of a repeated melody which echoes and spreads as a frail, secret, inward song.

In this long cinematographic career of the Flying Dutchman, marked by the history of mankind and the evolution of the image and sound techniques, we have chosen to analyze three films, exemplary for his different approaches and treatments of the soundtrack: SONGS OF HEROES, LA SEINE A RENCONTRÉ PARIS and ...A VALPARAISO.

SONGS OF HEROES (or KOMSOMOL)

Produced in 1932 by the Mezjrabom studios of Moscow, SONGS OF HEROES is the fruit of ten years of artistic and political developments, which characterized the European avant-garde of the twenties and thirties. The avant-garde, according to Walter Benjamin, was the answer that artists try to offer to the appearance of the masses on the stage of history, and an attempt to adapt to the enormous changes in daily life which industrial society has brought to the experience of the individual.[1]

Joris Ivens was the son of a bourgeois Catholic trade family in the Netherlands, who during his studies and internships in photographic equipment factories (Leica, Zeiss, Ica), developed his revolutionary ideas on an the artistic as well as on a political level, which fed into the havoc of the Germany of the twenties; out of which also emerged the likes of the Bauhaus movement, Mondrian, Brecht, Piscator, Fritz Lang, Wiene, Ruttmann, and those that inspired the anarchist and communist demonstrations, social conflicts, and police oppression.

Back in the Netherlands, Ivens filmed ÉTUDES DES MOUVEMENTS, during a trip to Paris, where he also befriended Sergei Eisenstein. THE BRIDGE and RAIN followed, films that establish Joris Ivens as one of the leading figures of the European avant-garde according to among others, French filmmaker Germaine Dulac and Soviet filmmaker Vsevolod Pudovkin, who presented his film THE MOTHER at a Film League meeting in Amsterdam. Meeting Pudovkin was important for Joris Ivens. Pudovkin eventually proposed that the Association of Soviet Filmmakers invite Ivens to present his films in the Soviet Union. In Moscow, Ivens met Dziga Vertov, Dovzjenko, Donskoi, and he stays in Eisenstein's apartment, who was filming in Mexico, and crossed several Soviet republics during three months.

The warm and enthusiastic reception by intellectuals, artists and workers when Ivens returned, encouraged him to continue in the direction he had chosen with THE BRIDGE, RAIN, WE ARE BUILDING, ZUIDERZEE, the path of a filmmaker who 'captures life with the lens of a camera, like the eye captures the spectacle of life' – following Dziga Vertov's definition. Vertov knew the power of images, framing, and montage and was one of the filmmakers to sign the manifesto along with Eisenstein, Pudovkin, and Alexandrov concerning the necessary audio-visual couterpoint in sound cinema.

When Ivens returned to Moscow in February 1932 to make a film 'that provides an answer to the questions of many people in the West concerning socialism and the Soviet Union', he has to solve two problems at once: the choice of a meaningful subject, and that of his relationship as a non-Soviet filmmaker, with the Mezjrabom studios, which were already dictated by the bureaucratic and 'correct thinking' of the Party. Helped by Pudovkin, Ivens choses to concentrate on the youth movement – 'the best symbol of socialism in progress'[2] – and more precisely, on the building of the blast furnaces of Magnitogorsk by the Komsomol youth: 'youth and steel, that is exactly what I was looking for'.[3] The complete building of the blast furnaces, and the city around them, was initiated, executed and controlled by the Komsomols, the communist youth organization, in the framework of the first Five Year Plan.

Ivens formed his crew, which was supported and controlled by the Komsomol organization. One of their members, Andrejev, became Ivens's assistant scriptwriter. He asked his friend Hanns Eisler to do the soundtrack. The shooting took three months, and was mostly done in

Magnitogorsk, under difficult circumstances. Magnitogorsk, 'the new socialist city', was nothing more than some barracks and Khirgiz tents in the
middle of the Ural steppes; a desolate landscape on the border between Europe and Asia, where its riches, iron-ore, lay buried. The workers, technicians, architects, were all volunteers; members of the Komsomol – the oldest
being less than twenty-five – 'all driven by an inner energy of will and pride
to contribute to the construction of socialism, and to fight the forces of nature.'[4]

Not long into shooting, Ivens realized that the music had to take into account the 'infernal' reality, of the sounds on the building sites – a necessary
part of the superhuman and epic dimension of the work done by the
Komsomol youth. He, therefore, asked Hanns Eisler to join him in
Magnitogorsk.

The collaboration between Ivens and Eisler began with the shooting of
the first images in Magnitogorsk. Every element of the soundtrack was su-
pervised and organised by Hanns Eisler who wrote several years later:

> I saw right away that I could not write the music from behind my desk, so I started
> working as a 'musical reporter'. I first needed detailed information on the realization,
> then I recorded the indigenous music of the national minorities, the sounds in the fac-
> tories. The work was not easy for me – for I was not in the habit of climbing up like a
> mechanic on top of a blast furnace to find the best place for the best sound of this
> enormous uproar – so I am always very proud to have recorded more than seven-
> hundred and fifteen metres of noises and the music of national minorities in a very
> unusual atmosphere for me. The second stage of my work was done in Moscow,
> where I composed the film music, which I recorded at the Mezjrabom studios. First,
> with comrade Tretjakov, I composed the 'Ballad of Magnitogorsk' of the Komsomol.
> The text was very simple:

> Ural, Ural,
> City of the Magnet Mountain,
> There is much steel.
> The Party says:
> Give us... steel!
> The Komsomols answer:
> Within the ordered time,
> We will give you steel![5]

The result of this collaboration between the composer - who called himself a
musical reporter – and the filmmaker – who, from the first day of filming in
Magnitogorsk was thinking about the soundtrack – is unique in Ivens's oeuvre. SONG OF HEROES is, in fact, the only film of Ivens's which was conceived,
from the start, as an audio-visual counterpoint. The problem of commen-

Still from SONG OF HEROES.

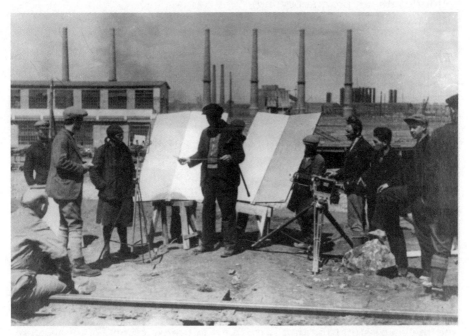

Hanns Eisler (sitting, far left) and Joris Ivens (standing, left) working on the sound
recordings of SONG OF HEROES.

tary does not impose itself, yet Ivens can still use intertitles, as he did in silent films. These intertitles can give very punctual information on geography, economics and politics.

The film can be regarded as a real audio-visual partition: while the images reveal men at work - their faces, their smiles, their gestures, their efforts, their comings and goings, their conversations, their moments of rest and shared joy, during the various stages of the building of the blast furnaces. At the same time, it explains the consequences of this construction work – the mining and processing of the iron-ore into steel, the functioning of the blast furnace and the products it makes possible – the soundtrack, composed of sounds from different work sites, sounds of hammers, drills, steamengines, train wagons, chains, as well as of instrumental and vocal music, written or recorded by Eisler, follows its own rhythm and architecture. This soundtrack, alternating concrete music with symphonic music, also plays with the synchronicity of the images, or, rather, like in a polyphonic piece of music, with the superimposition of two melodic lines (here, image and sound), which periodically harmonize (sound with image).

Let us give some examples:
- harmony between the images and sounds of the blast furnace (in the fourteenth minute and beyond)
- harmony between the gestures of the worker and the drill (twenty-fourth minute)
- harmony between the images of the women passing over the bricks to those who lay them, and the light sounds that accompany their gestures and labour
- harmony during the spoken passages at work or on the telephone.

These harmonies are sometimes the result of a desire for realism, realized in the studio. For example, the sound of the metal bricks, sliding through a shaft, or the sound of the footsteps of the workers running and shouting that the blast furnace is on fire. Apart from these harmonies, the sounds are composed as a partition for an orchestra, with accents, rhythms, pauses, timbres; with its 'forte' and 'pianissimo, its 'crescendo' and 'decrescendo'.

The instrumental and vocal music, recorded on location (the young Khirgizian playing his flute, facing the steppe; the popular song) or the music composed by Eisler in Moscow, comes into play in a more traditional way, to stress the lyrical and symbolic dimension of the images, to underline the political message, to celebrate the great march of communist youth and the success that the first Five Year Plan must bring. The music composed by Hanns Eisler comes into play at four different stages:

1   During the title sequence and introductory scene of the film; very symbolic, for it shows repressed demonstrations, the progressive victory of the workers, the triumphant march of the Soviets that evolves into the march of the Komsomols. This music sets the tone of the film: determination, enthusiasm. With its hammering rhythm it is easy to note, and it will serve as a basis for the other orchestral sequences in the film, of which the rhythms and melodies are variations of this introductory march, with the exception of the final sequence, which is completely taken by the 'Ballad of Magnitogorsk'.

2   During the recruitment of the young Khirgizian; to express the importance of the work with the Komsomols, as well as the determination of this young man.

3   During the work reunion and the evaluation by the Komsomols, in which they express their satisfaction regarding the work done and their collective determination.

4   During the final sequence, in which the 'Ballad of Magnitogorsk', a strong, vigorous and simple song, expresses the triumphant joy of the Komsomols, and, metaphorically, the machines at the service of Man and, of course, the Party.

We thus witness true fireworks, offered by the images and the orchestral and vocal music, with the rhythm of a montage sequence of metal, steam, gestures, movements, shadows and lights, until the last image, that of a giant and proud blast furnace rising against the sky, liberating its own music, the power of industrial breath.

It is a unique case in Ivens's oeuvre, because it occurs at the turning point from silent film to sound film. Ivens still uses intertitles instead of commentary. The film SONG OF HEROES allows the music, its sounds and tones, to play its contrapuntal role, and the spectator to experience a true audio-visual work, in accord with the way that Eisenstein defined it in 1929.

LA SEINE A RENCONTRÉ PARIS

In Spring 1957, Joris Ivens arrived in Paris, the city he would leave regularly, to fight misery, war, injustice, and in search for the true communism. His confidence in the Soviet system, he was willing to step back; having just spent ten years in Eastern Europe, filming, more or less free, less and less convinced by the 'construction of socialism' he witnessed. But now he rediscovered Paris, and his French friends: Georges Sadoul, Jacques Prévert, Serge Reggiani, Simone Signoret, Yves Montand, Betsy Blair...

Ivens always loved Paris, the Seine and its boulevards. Georges Sadoul presented him with the idea of a film about an encounter between the river and the city, which would evolve into a film about Parisians and what they do along the Seine, and what the Seine offers them. Joris Ivens dove into the Paris of the fifties, wandered along the banks of the Seine, observed the water, the sky, the clouds, the bridges, the quays and the ports, the boats that come and go, the monuments, and the people. He began to film, wrote a visual poem, the river as its theme, lively, majestic, now wild, then tranquil, the Parisians, mariners, small business-men and -women on the banks, lonely dreamers, fishermen, Sunday painters, young couples, children, excited and cheerful. He recorded all of these images of popular Paris in the fifties; the city of photographer Robert Doisneau, celebrated by Jacques Prévert with love. He remembered images by Renoir, Vigo, Carné, the music of Kosma – everything that makes up French poetic realism.

Ivens again produced a film without obligations, a film first and foremost made by the director about water, rain, heavy skies. He became the director of bridges, docks and machines, mixing in faces, gestures of people at work, the looks and laughs of women and children. And with this he returned to the perfect musical montage of his silent films.

The images of LA SEINE A RENCONTRÉ PARIS were organized by the idea of a passage through Paris, from east to west, aboard a small boat. They were also organized according to the contrasts of day and night, the world of labour versus the world of rest and play, the industrial quarters to the east versus the peaceful and idyllic Cité and the rich and superficial quarters to the west. And when the images were finished, Ivens began to dream about the soundtrack. Who better than Jacques Prévert – the scriptwriter of Marcel Carné's films: DRÔLE DE DRAME, QUAI DES BRUMES, LE JOUR SE LÈVE, LES ENFANTS DU PARADIS, but, even more well-known and popular French contemporary poet – to write words that would, like the images, express at the same time the beauty and the cruelty, the tenderness and love, life, joy and suffering along the Seine, of Paris and its people?

Joris Ivens showed the film to Jacques Prévert. Jacques Prévert wrote a poem and said to Ivens: 'Do what you want to.' The poem functioned as a counterpoint to the images: the words express what the images show but only before or after or even later – out of synch, in other words. This enhanced and explained the social message of the film, guarding its own musicality; that of the words, inspired by the images. Ivens also recalled the magic that was created on the screen, but also offscreen, by the duo Prévert-Kosma; the harmony between the words of Prévert and the music of the composer of *Enfants qui s'aiment*, and of *Feuilles mortes*; the link that binds the poetry of popular Paris with the accordion in a rhythm of false nostalgias, played on the piano, assumed by the clarinet or the violins.

Ivens commissioned the composer, Philippe Gérard, to write a music in the vein of Kosma - which would periodically accompany and extend the images and words of the film. Clever and nostalgic, tender, light, playful and even funny; a music that could make rain, water, boats, cars, and silence audible.

The nostalgic leitmotif, presented at the beginning of the film, dominates; a slow waltz, based on a melody one remembers (fa# se re si do# re mi fa# mi si do# re do# si la# sol# la# si...); obsessional, declined then by the accordion, then by the piano, then by the flute or the strings, sliding through Prévert's verses, between the noises of construction, dominating the rumours emanating from the boats, and sometimes disappearing, but always reappearing on the faces of the men; this love song.

An other kind of music played an important role: it is the one we hear for the first time after the passing of the metro near Quai de la Rapée, played on a piccolo flute – jumping, nasal – as we enter La Cité, and the text states: 'It's a song from the headsprings, it's a voice of youth...', the one that is based on the childrens song *Il était un petit navire*, when the images of lovers, of fishermen, of Sunday painters pass by; when children are playing, tramps are shaving, and lawyers are running – music whose tempo slows down to accompany the Notre Dame and its towers, the Louvre, and the Eiffel Tower.

Let us not forget the music of the harpsichord that, as a break, so unexpectedly and playfully, accompanies the model photography session, the picnics, the tourist photographers, the sleeping men – legs in the air – the beautiful strolling ladies walking their dogs; this music that flows out from the diegetic music from a young man with a guitar, humming that nostalgic leitmotif. Let us not forget the seductive and rhythmic jazz which is introduced by lightning, on the Pont Alexandre III, and then continues through the rain and storm. This jazz extends the images of the rain and the people that seek shelter from it, and then ends as the sun reappears, when the main accordion theme returns.

Thus conceived, filmed and edited, LA SEINE A RENCONTRÉ PARIS had all the elements to seduce the French, as well as international audiences, to make them fall in love with Paris. That was what happened at the Cannes Festival in 1957, when Joris Ivens received the Palme d'Or for best documentary.

...A VALPARAISO

In 1962, Joris Ivens was invited, upon the instigation of Salvodor Allende –
whom Ivens had met in Cuba, and who was leader of the Chilean opposition at that time – to teach Documentary Film at the department 'Ciné Experimental' at the University of Santiago de Chile. Ivens accepted the
appointment and decided to teach these youngsters, without training, 'on
location'. He filmed ...A VALPARAISO with them:

> It was the richest port of all... A snip of the scissors in Panama put it back in its place...
> It is still a port... Not the richest, but it lives. It lives well... at the foot of the hills, is the
> life of a commercial town. Up in the hills there exists another town. Not a town: a fed-
> eration of villages, one on each hill. Forty-two hills, forty-two villages... Two worlds
> connected by ramps, stairs, lifts.[6]

The images, all impregnated by the sun, light, and shadows of Valparaiso,
the dignity of the inhabitants of the hills, are organized by the climbing up
and down the stairs and the funiculars between 'two worlds'. They take us
to the border of the sea, the harbour, its boats and businesses, its seagulls, to
the beach with its dolphins; they show us the past and present of the trading
town; they make us climb, descend, look from far and from close up, from
different angles, panoramas, and movement, the stairs, the houses, the
squares and little gardens, the games, and performances up in the hills.

These images reflect the tenderness Ivens felt toward the inhabitants of
the hills: young and old, women and children, their difficult lives, but also
their joys, their loves and their luck. And suddenly, these images began to
recall, in colour, how much ancient and recent history of Valparaiso had
been linked to violence and blood.

Back in France, Ivens edited the images and commissioned someone to
write an original commentary but ultimately that did not meet Ivens's expectations. Discouraged, a few days from the final mix, he accepted the invitation of friend Chris Marker to help him out, while he entrusted Gustavo
Becerra to write the music. In 1962, Chris Marker was already a film critic, a
writer with a reputation, but, above all, a well-known filmmaker and an author of commentaries for documentary films. Marker wrote a commentary
for ...A VALPARAISO which is, at times very precise, informative, but also poetic – without lyricism – and always added a touch of humour. Here, as in
his own films, he made the text extend the meaning, the place and the
rhythm of what the images reveal, with so much intelligence and vision that
nothing was redundant. It was as if he was not the author of the images.
Marker wrote his commentaries as a filmmaker *and* writer, knowing where

Stills from ...A VALPARAISO: 'Forty-two hills, forty-two villages'.

the power of each starts or ends. The images offer the power to show and move (in every respect); while the words have the power to explain and create links between the present and the past, to control the emotions with humour and an apparent lightness.

Using the notes, editing plans and images of Ivens, Marker wrote a commentary that creates a distance which, far from lessening the power of the images, their beauty, their tenderness, or their violence, actually brings in a dimension of reflection, of the objectivity of the first spectator. Still, the film hinges on the coincidence between images and words. For example:

–   At the beginning of the film the images of the unloading of bananas in the harbour coincides with the text 'The port is down there. It was the richest port of all...'
–   The images of a hearse, solemnly passing through the steep sunny streets coincide with the sentence 'It's Valparaiso. Val Para-iso, the Valley of Paradise. For the sailors who gave it its name it was the Paradise of a stretch of sunlight after the nightmares of their voyage. Or else it is the last stretch *before* Paradise.' (A text accompanied with the song *Dies irae, dies illae*.)
–   The images of the rich women who let out their penguin coincides with 'All the women in Valparaiso come out with their sunglasses on to walk with all the penguins in Valparaiso.'
–   The long take that shows the activity in the harbour and the work of the dock workers coincides with the text 'It's truth is the sea.'
–   The images of the playful descent and the difficult climbs, of which the first image shows a one-legged man coincide with the text: 'A one-legged man climbs the stairs. 121 steps. He knows how many, he counts them. You need a stout heart and a good memory too. The ramp takes you down ten times faster than the steps. You come down ten times faster than you go up. You laugh as you come down. You gasp for breath as you go up. It's funny, it's exhausting, it's ghastly, joyous, inhuman, solemn, ridiculous, strange.'

The third structural element of the film is the music of Gustavo Becerra which is based on the song *Et nous irons a Valparaiso*, sung by Germaine Montéro. This music, with its seducing rhythm, bursts out, lightly as the images of the fireworks illuminate the harbour of Valparaiso at the beginning of the film and wafts about between the orchestra, the images, the words, during the rest of the film. It returns with force at the end of the film; first tenderly murmured, polished by the flute and the harp (with images of children playing with their kites), then, a new bursting out, introduced by a roll on timpanis, as the song is sung by Germaine Montéro, in all its splendour, until we see 'The End'. The song is the main musical theme of the film and is orchestrated differently and more subtly than the images and the text.

In ...A VALPARAISO, there is no counterpoint between the images and the soundtrack, but an audio-visual structure in which every element, every group of images, words, and sounds exists in close relationship to all the others; in which every element cannot be separated from the rest, and which advances our comprehension to allow us to make understand the poetic, the social, the political, and the philosophical dimensions of the film.

Three films: three ways to associate images with sounds; three ways to present the spoken word; three ways of chosing and using the music, but always the same style and the same music of images: Ivens's style.

A Key to the Metaphysics of the Wind[1]

On UNE HISTOIRE DE VENT

Sylvain De Bleeckere

> It has no shape and no name
> Its genesis is before Heaven and Earth
> And till today it is not finished.
>
> (From *The Four Writings of the Yellow Emperor*, about 190 BC)

On the occasion of his last film Joris Ivens used the word metaphysics regularly.

> In my very long life, I discovered that metaphysics and dreaming are a form of reality, that metaphysics is a bridge between the past and the future.

> There will always be other horizons. Horizons are fine, there is always one after the other, and again another one, so the Chinese say. If you get into that theme, wind becomes metaphysical.

Ivens's words cause surprise. Had the man who had been a confirmed communist for years, become a metaphysical filmmaker toward the end of his life? The answer to this question is UNE HISTOIRE DE VENT. That answer comes from Joris Ivens and Marceline Loridan. UNE HISTOIRE DE VENT is not their first film, it is their last, however, about China.

Thinking Proceeding from Nature

With UNE HISTOIRE DE VENT, old cinematographer Joris Ivens certainly did not adhere to the classical metaphysical distinction between nature and supernature. On the contrary, in their film, Ivens and Loridan focused their attention in an original way on ancient Chinese thinking, which is deeply rooted in Chinese civilization. Chinese civilization is steeped in a metaphysical attitude which involves an intense surprise regarding the presence and meaning of the wind. The most important pillar of Chinese thought and culture and the oldest document philosophical thinking known to mankind is the Chinese book of oracles the I Ching or *The Book of Change*, written about 3,000 BC, which verifies this cultural concern about the wind. The I Ching details the notions of reality as a correlation between yin and yang. This notion permeates all schools of Chinese philosophy.

Originally, the words yin and yang were geographical indications. Yin indicates the dark side of a valley, the north side of a hill, the cloudy sky, and so, everything dark and wet. Yang indicates the opposite: the bright side of a valley, the south side of a hill, the clear sky, therefore, everything clear, bright and warm. Here it becomes clear how the profound association with nature and the unpredictability of the climate nurtured Chinese thinking. Compared to western metaphysics, the heart of Chinese metaphysical thinking consists of refusing to think in absolute categories. Yin and yang are relational notions that complement one another without establishing a rigid hierarchy.

In UNE HISTOIRE DE VENT, Ivens understands that Chinese thinking emanates from a unique metaphysical experience of the wind. Here 'metaphysical' does not mean the doctrine of the supernatural order of existence, but rather the very special nature of the penetrating experience that comes into being when the wind-force of reality touches man and sets him in motion. With the compass of his film camera, the machine that follows the movement of reality, Joris Ivens followed this metaphysical intuition. It made him the Flying Dutchman of the twentieth century, who through numerous ideological escapades penetrated the reality of the wind, and in China found the ancient confirmation of the suspicion that he himself cultivated with the film camera in China. It is definitely no coincidence that a major scene in UNE HISTOIRE DE VENT presents the Chinese guard who unlocks the chest in which the magic wind-mask is kept. The wind is the key that Ivens himself had been seeking almost his entire life. Together with his wife and artistic partner, Marceline Loridan, he let the world know that he had finally found this key in UNE HISTOIRE DE VENT.

Structural Layers

Ivens's self-portrait using the notion of invisible wind has a multi-layered structure. The lowest layer forms the framework of the film and consists of an old man waiting for the wind. For this waiting scene he travelled to

China, where in the West Chinese Taklamakan Desert, he and his camera sought out the wind. That waiting for the wind occurs in three film-symphonic movements. In the *first* movement, the image of the waiting itself under a burning sun is the dominant image. In the *second* movement, the old man is still waiting patiently through day and night. Finally, exhausted, he collapses into unconsciousness. The *third* movement and the final movement reveals the revived old man, awaiting the arrival of the wind in a tent. He is helped by an old Chinese woman who comes to write a magic sign in the sand. Finally, the wind appears.

In a second structural layer, the film looks like a modern montage of images and sound. In between the three movements, Ivens and Loridan edit in two large montages consisting of a mosaic of scenes, dream images and purely poetic, but dramatic audio-visual impressions. Within each part, the rhythm of images and sounds spring from a direction of the wind of their own. Sometimes, the fast, even stormy rhythm in which images and sound follow one another hastily and chaotically, transforms into the sedate rhythm of the soft autumn wind or the dancing rhythm of the playful, frivolous spring wind. It is not only to that rhythm that these two large montages undulate in the wind. They are also thematically dominated by the wind. They are interwoven into the narrative motive through the search for traces of the wind. The central image of the figure patiently waiting for the wind does not only occur in the desert. This figure has an active side as well. He is also seeking, through waiting, a figure whose presence has been hinted at in other parts of the film. He finds these traces in the Chinese myths about Hou Yi and Chang'e and the mythical wind-mask of the Chinese sculptor Guangzhong; as well as in Chinese history during the dynasty of the emperor Qin Shihuangdi, in the Chinese Kung Fu tradition with the taijiquan, in the tradition of the monumental Buddha statues and in the metaphysical flying kites, but also in the peculiar landscape of the Yunnan Province and the sacred mountain of Huang Shan.

Feng Bo

The invisible expressive power of wind has left deep impressions upon the ancient landscape of Chinese thinking and culture. Joris Ivens and Marceline Loridan find their oldest traces in Chinese myths and legends. A major Chinese mythical figure named Feng Bo is the Count of the Wind. The myth offers insight into how man's life on earth strongly depends on the rhythmic changes that occur in the heavenly landscape. If the sun shines too

Still from UNE HISTOIRE DE VENT: waiting for the wind.

much – yang – then everything withers away; if dark clouds, pregnant with rain, dominate, then darkness rules – yin – and everything is in danger of being washed away.

Already early on in the film, by the beginning of the first montage, Ivens and Loridan reveal the presence of the wind in the way that the old Chinese man moves. In a Kung Fu school, Ivens visits an old Chinese taijiquan master. This defensive martial art is based on the very rhythmical, but asymmetrical, movement of the body. Ivens discusses the secret of breathing with him. The Chinese master controls his breathing so well that his movements look like those of a bird riding the wind. He moves like the paper kites with which the Chinese children make the wind their playmate. Ivens actually edited in images of kites.

In the sequence with the Tai Chi master, Ivens mentions his asthma and his fear of exhaling. Ivens presents himself as someone who, as a result of his asthma, has a very special, existential experience with the wind. The wind brings oxygen and supports breathing. Ivens has come to China to learn something about the art of breathing. The Chinese master teaches the 'Flying' and 'Filming' Dutchman that the secret of breathing can be found in the autumn wind. Then the old master demonstrates the meaning of his words in a dance. The taijiquan is the calm experience of Kung Fu and aims at sensing both balance and energy in a spiritual way. The wind, therefore, is also an anthropological notion in which mental health and physical control over breathing are closely linked. Images of a mountainous Chinese landscape reveal how mountains have bodies that dance with the wind in the same way as the Tai Chi master does. The wind appears as a sculptor of the Chinese body, both in the cultural as well as corporeal sense.

The Dragon

In China, Ivens discovered that the metaphysics of the wind was grafted onto the great miracle of life which crystallizes in the image of the dragon. In the Chinese dragon, wind and life are one. In China, the dragon is the oldest mythical beast. He represents the fertility of the earth and, in the past, the positive power of the emperor. The dragon is yang, male, and powerful. The dragon dances that are still performed in China have their origin in fertility rites. As early as 1958, Ivens filmed an exuberant dragon dance for the coming of spring in BEFORE SPRING. Ivens interest in Chinese mythology goes back a long way as is evident in the sequence in his first Chinese film THE 400 MILLION from 1939, in which he photographs the four sculptures representing the four directions of the wind in a Buddhist sacred place.

It goes without saying that the Chinese dragon is the mythical representation of the wind. His fantastic, twisting tail and his mostly open and blazing mouth represent the power of the wind that offers protection from the burning sun, brings rain to the land, and thus signifies life. The dragon is the wind that allows the earth to breathe. That is why in China they say that the wind is 'the breath of the earth', and that the dragon inhales in the summer and exhales in the winter.

But the wind also has a yin side. In the film's key sequence involving the wind-mask, the dragon and the phoenix together form a yang-yin whole. The maker of the mask explains the image by recalling an ancient Chinese legend of a dragon living in the south and about a phoenix residing in the north. They are the two characters of the wind: one comes from the sea in the shape of a dragon and after having arrived on land, changes into the mythical bird that rises from its ashes again and again.

The yang side of the capricious wind also holds the Chinese secret of the origin of UNE HISTOIRE DE VENT. The film owes its existence to a unique meeting of the two cultures, the West and the East, as well as to the existential and artistic bond between the two poles of man and woman: Joris Ivens and Marceline Loridan.

Still from BEFORE SPRING.

The Buddha of Ta-tsu

Buddhism also finds its place among the cultural traces of the wind that Joris Ivens and Marceline Loridan follow. The film's first sequence ends with a direct reference to Buddhism in China. First, Joris Ivens visits the monumental Buddha that comforts the devout with a thousand hands and gazes with a thousand eyes in the caves of Ta-tsu. The sequence with the Buddha of Ta-tsu is very strong. The scene opens with an image of Joris Ivens directing. He is sitting beside a camera lunging forward. With a look of great concentration, he directs the camera lens toward the large statue. Then the Buddha itself comes into view. Ivens alternates long shots with close-ups. There is a meaningful bird's eye view in which the Buddha almost fills the screen with the ant-like Joris Ivens at the bottom left. This composition offers the viewer an idea of the size of this Buddha. At the same time great respect speaks from the complete scene for the religious sense the statue has borne witness of for years. In another short scene, the old man is sitting on a chair before the statue. He rests his head on his two hands which are holding a walking stick. His shadow is outlined on the floor of the cave. For a moment, he assumes the pose of the thinker, as the French sculptor Rodin once represented him. In the sequence a movement is initiated in a portrait of the old cinematographer Ivens himself. He is shown filming and gazing at the statue, he sits down, thinks, becomes introspective and then lifts his head to gaze at the statue again. Joris Ivens makes connections between his own life in general, but also the film camera in particular, and the age-old nation of spiritual seeing, the contemplative vision of all great religions. The meditational attitude of the Buddha is evidence of this. Joris Ivens clearly does not approach this statue as a cultural tourist. The ancient statue literally creates spiritual space for wide-angle vision, a stirring vision that offers a rhythm between vision and contemplation. The camera lens is the extension of the human being, an inspired eye that is capable of seeing not only the outside, but also the inside of things. As a director who had travelled around China and had witnessed twentieth century history with his camera, he realizes here in front of the great Buddha that the materialism of seeing is a yang without a yin. The Buddha expresses the remarkable many-sidedness of seeing. The Buddha gazes with a thousand eyes simultaneously.

The aspect of the hand also catches the eye in the Ta-tsu sequence. Buddha comforts with a thousand hands. This comfort shows the grief and pain that belong to every human's life, whereas the hands show involvement and help. Buddhism developed from a deeply felt suffering and sorrow, the storms in the inner land of man. In meditation and asceticism, Buddha found comfort. In a sense, it is therefore an atypical Buddha. Buddha's hands are almost always in a meditative, resting pose. But here they are helping hands.

It is by no means a coincidence that Ivens and Loridan chose this Buddha from the many Buddhas of Ta-tsu, and chose this one over the equally monumental one of the sleeping Buddha. The latter represents the Buddha reaching nirvana which is an old-Indian word literally meaning 'extinguished, blown out', a compound word made up of the negative 'nir' and the verb 'va' which means 'blow'. This implies that the Buddhist nirvana implies a negation of the wind and of life. This kind of renunciation of sentient life is not an option for the engagé Joris Ivens. Hence, his preference for the Buddha with the one thousand hands.

In the Ta-tsu sequence, Joris Ivens also asks the metaphysical question about the meaning of suffering. For him, this question is a double-edged one for it is both an existential and a historic one. As a ninety-year-old asthma sufferer, Ivens knew that death was near. He faces the question of the meaning of life head on. In UNE HISTOIRE DE VENT he takes that question, formulated it, and searched for an answer in the metaphysics of the wind. But in the metaphysical question of life's meaning he also feels the reverberations of history. Looking at it from this perspective, it is not too absurd to state that in the history of film, Joris Ivens was the pioneer who continually had an eye for the suffering man. He was inspired by the first Soviet films, especially those by Vselevod Pudovkin, whom he became acquainted with personally, but also those of Charlie Chaplin. They inspired him to use his film camera to expose the suffering of humiliated and maltreated human beings in an engagé way. He never let his hands rest; they were always clutching his camera. In that sense he was no Buddhist looking for comfort by avoiding and fleeing. No, he preferred an engagé, involved, and compassionate existence. Several of his films remain permanent stirring documents of the suffering twentieth-century man.

With the Buddha of Ta-tsu, Joris Ivens realized that he had been looking for the foundation of sympathetic compassion in Marxism. He came to an understanding of its limitations. Atheistic materialism refused to recognize the other side of suffering, the other wind, the religious and metaphysical side. Communists do not have any exclusive answer to the question of suffering. They even pretend to be able to remove suffering and lead believers to a permanent paradise, although that was already a key element of other non-communist ideologies rooted in eighteenth century Enlightenment. In UNE HISTOIRE DE VENT, Joris Ivens makes a complete break from those modern ideologies without renouncing his sympathetic hand.

The image of the hand forms an important visual rhyme in UNE HISTOIRE DE VENT. In the first sequence, Joris Ivens lends a helping hand to the fallen old master of taijiquan. In the second sequence, he shakes hands with a Chinese child.

The Magic of the Imagination

In the second sequence, more precisely in the film studio scene, Joris Ivens writes another anthropological chapter of the metaphysics of the wind. In this important sequence, he mounts the film camera in the heart of that metaphysical aspect. The film studio appears to be the space where the magic wind of the imagination is blowing. Like the wind, the imagination knows no bounds and cannot be restrained by political oppressions. The doors of the film studio are opened by means of a magical incantation, uttered by the person with the made-up face, a figure with whom Joris Ivens identifies himself in the final frames of the scene. The figure opens the doors to the studio and a bright light descends, together with a strong, youthful wind. That playful spring wind is shown in the numerous children getting off the bus and entering the studio laughing and playing. They bring the breath of life into the studio. Ivens and Loridan show how, in fact, life is at home in the studio: the playing children, the loving couple getting married, the couple from the Beijing opera saying goodbye, aspects of everyday life, as well as sports, the arts, and work are represented. These are the kinds of small seemingly inconsequential details of ordinary life which the communist seems to deny, Ivens seems to say. But he fails. The elusive, made-up figure undermines the speaker, so that the various scenes can gather their own dynamics. In the end Ivens and Loridan focus on a group of girls where it becomes clear that they form a choir. The playful anarchy with which they entered the studio, like a spring wind, has completely disappeared. Standing in line, they sing a militant party song. In this scene, Joris Ivens exposes the tragedy of an ideological dictatorship. This dictatorship would like to curb the imagination that belongs to life itself. In order to do so, it uses and abuses the children, those in whom the magic of the imagination is still intact. By identifying with the made-up figure, Ivens expresses how they have not been able to curb his imaginative power. In the final analysis, the reason seems to lie in the metaphysical wind-force of the art of film itself and is present in the figure in the film studio. That wind-force represents mankind's free, collective imagination, which again and again escapes everything that wants to lock it up. Some party or group may own the film studios, but ultimately, the film belongs to life itself. Further along in the film, the director confronts the censor of the imagination in a similarly very direct way. He battles with the prejudiced bureaucrat who manages the terracotta army of the Emperor Qin Shihuangdi. In no uncertain terms, Ivens lets the stubborn Wang know that 'I fight for my art, for freedom of expression'. Over Wang's protests, he responds with the whirling wind of creativity. In-between the sequence of the desperate negotiations with Wang and the one with the soldiers brought to life, Ivens and Loridan insert some images of the stormy wind. These images throw light on the inextinguishable fury with which the director encourages his fellow workers in a game that finally develops into a beautiful aesthetic dance. It is remarkable that in this section, Ivens, acting as the imaginative director, is seated in a wheelchair. His body may have become weak, but his imagination is still as young as a child's, friend of the playful wind.

Still from UNE HISTOIRE DE VENT: King Ape.

Still from UNE HISTOIRE DE VENT: soldiers brought to life.

Sun Wugang

The strange, made-up figure makes regular appearances in the two large sequences. He appears for the first time during a visit to the Kung Fu school, and for the last time during the preparation for the dance of the terracotta army. His appearance is peculiar because, in fact, he is invisible to others, like the wind. He personifies the elusive wind. His make-up and clothes identify him with a well-known character from the Opera of Beijing. His name is Sun Wugang or King Ape and he is a popular hero from the classical sixteenth century Chinese novel *Journey to the West*. In this adventure novel, the author incorporates China's Buddhist history in which Chinese Buddhist monks make a pilgrimage to the west – that is, North East India – to study the original sources. But the author also incorporates ancient Chinese legends into his story. One example is King Ape who lives in heaven and wishes to remain there. The other heavenly Kings, however, think he is too wild and too arrogant. They put him in prison, but release him again on the condition that he will return to earth to accompany a monk on his journey to the West in search of the holy books.

The figure of the rebel King Ape plays an important role in what UNE HISTOIRE DE VENT expresses. He accompanies, as it were, the old man on his journey to the East in search of the sources of the metaphysics of the wind. As the playful spirit of the capricious wind, he is the good spirit of the breath of life, the guardian angel of the main character Ivens. He represents the rebel and playful spirit that brings movement where rigidity rules, creates space for life where death is imminent.

A Testament of the Twentieth Century

At a certain moment, just before the episode of Mr. Wang's vicissitudes, Ivens listens to the wind as it speaks in the first person in various languages. The voice of the wind says, 'My secret will never be told. All honour to the keepers of the secrets.' By the end of the multi-voiced monologue of the wind, it becomes clear in which direction the vane of the metaphysics of the wind points as indicated by the Hebrew epilogue: 'I am the breath that hovered over the waters on the first day of creation.' With this clear reference to the opening verse of Genesis, Ivens and Loridan identify the wind with the metaphysical secret of the elusive, divine spirit of life on earth. There is the great secret of never-ending movement, of the breath of the earth. The spirit is the breath of life of creation. That breath of life is the most fundamental *arché*, not only of the Chinese landscape, Chinese culture, but also of the whole of creation. The wind, warranting life, is the archè whose power surpasses every logos. No man, no regime, no 'ideo-logos' can claim that metaphysical archaeology. Joris Ivens and Marceline Loridan clearly understood this with UNE HISTOIRE DE VENT. Their remarkable film has left its special mark on twentieth-century history. Owing to its uniquely biographical character, the film also looks like an important and unique testament of our late twentieth century. Its adventures are reflected in the life and work of Joris Ivens, born in Nijmegen, but driven to travel all over the world as if on the wind. The twentieth century becomes visible to us as 'une histoire de vent'. It is a history that forms a runway for the flight to the next century and to a newly evolving cultural period. At this moment, the airplane is still on the ground, like in the film's epilogue, but it is preparing for take off for the twenty-first century to be carried by the metaphysical wind-force.

Articles by Joris Ivens

Notes on the Avant-garde Documentary Film (1931)[1]

I

The documentary film is the expression of reality in her causal and inevitable state. Firstly, I must establish that the documentary film is the only means that remains for the avant-garde filmmaker to stand up to the film industry – not the film industry as such, but insofar as the documentary film expresses reality like it is, whereas the film industry usually expresses itself through bad films that compete for the favour of the audience by adjusting to the bad taste of that audience – yes even drawing inspiration from it – without trying to generate a reaction or stimulating any activity.

The avant-garde film is a film that aims at raising the interest and the reaction of the spectator. For me, avant-garde films are films that take the initiative of progress and keep it under the banner of the cinematographic sincerity.

The independent film, indeed, has the ability of self-criticism that leads to progress, whereas the industrial film has no other standard than success, meaning, the judgment of a badly-educated audience.

II

The sound film is the starting point for all future possibilities of radio and television. All the more reason to stand up to the tasteless inspiration which forms a continuing threat to the film industry.

III

The documentary film allows the avant-garde filmmaker to work in a positive way. Being a representative of the masses, a mouthpiece of the people that are represented through him, it allows him to put as many personal things in his work as possible.

Because the documentary film mainly thrives on commissions – and for industries there is no better way of advertising – the documentary filmmaker only has to deal with one man: a businessman, an outsider in the field of filmmaking. Therefore, it is in the interest of that director to make a good film using truth and the documentary's character as the sole criterion.

Should he work for the film industry, however, he has to deal with a board, artists, and censorship. He is no longer independent, he is bound; he is more or less a slave. To break free from this slavery, he has to be absolutely sure of the production and also be able to convince his spectator, whether it concerns someone from the industry or not.

IV

The documentary film in the current state of affairs, is the best way to find the road to true film. There shall be no danger of it decending into theatre, literature, music hall, in a word everything that is not film.

This is a very old thesis, but it seems useful to point to it once again and to repeat myself, because the sound film of today encounters the same dangers as film did at its birth – dangers it gradually was able to break away from.

Filmmaking is a trade. The independent filmmaker is a professional. He possesses the necessary technique, which does not have to be detrimental to the spirit or the intellect. That is why the film industry also has its good side. A good American cameraman makes a larger contribution to a film than a poet. He resembles a medieval craftsman, who, on a large scale, gives shape to the design of the intellect by his perfect knowledge of the material he works with. A good cameraman makes a better film than a poet because he has a better understanding of material and technique, and because this advantage leads to new opportunities. I am biased to say that the idea of a poet can only be right by accident, because he lacks the indispensable cinematographic line of thought.

V

A documentary filmmaker cannot lie, cannot harm the truth. No treason can be committed in this regard: a documentary film requires the development of the personality of the filmmaker, because only the personality of an artist separates him from commonplace actuality, from simple photography. A good filmmaker stands in the middle of the matter, in the middle of reality. At every occasion, he only chooses to interpret part of that reality. The success of his film depends on the trust of the masses in his personality, and, as a result of that trust, on the personality of an individual who has chosen for – in his view – an important part and not more than an important part of reality – putting the rest aside.

With other films, this realistic as well as important criterion to estimate the personality of the filmmaker at its true value does not exist.

VI

The documentary film should not only be a motive for emotion, a literary ode to the beauty of matter, but it also has to stimulate lingering activities to evoke reactions.

An overdose of individualism and an overly-artistic attitude makes Europe reject the social effect of the documentary film. Therefore, I think I can only attain the development of my ideas, and of my cinematographic ideals, in Russia, where every day the masses become more familiar with these activities and come to a better understanding of the social realism of the documentary film.

The Artistic Power of the Documentary Film (1932)

My speech at this congress¹ is a sort of exception, because, in a way, I start on the border of our subject matter. The border on which we otherwise stop in our discussions: how are your scientific and technical inventions and studies applied?

Here, we are bringing in a new factor: artistic power. The design of our technical and scientific achievements happens because of the creative powers of the artist. Unfortunately, from the beginning, this design was almost exclusively controlled by the issue of productivity and generation of capital. Unfortunately, the design was distorted by this issue and its actual development slowed down. The commercial film industry is the guilty party. It made incorrect use of your technical and scientific work and created a sort of 'art inflation'. The film avant-garde - the film brigades - fights this art inflation.

Some ten years ago, this avant-garde started her work, first in Germany and then later in France and other countries. Here and there independent artists from outside the film industry went in their own directions. They looked for, and found, the path to the pure cinematographic design of a theme. They worked on the artistic, aesthetic, and social side of film. There was little opportunity in the industry at that time for this kind of work, and even now, except in Soviet Russia.

The industry imagined that the works of the avant-gardists were produced only for small audiences. The avant-garde does not do battle with the film industry because it is an industry; it fights it because, on the whole, she regards the production of the industry as being of low quality. What is the task we independent filmmakers assign ourselves? Cinematography has to answer for her own existence in the most perfect manner possible. Cinematography is the art of the moving image. So a film's final design has two tasks: to concern itself with the moving image as a series of static moments; and to concern itself with movement itself, or in other words, the organization of thousands of images.

The tasks of the static image are of a photographic, optical, and mechanical nature. Some topical film problems such as aspect ratio, colour photography are separate issues.

Let us now talk about the subtle side of cinematography or its movement – the basic element of a synthetic image of film art. I do not mean movement in the mechanical sense, but, let us say, movement in the artistic sense –

rhythm. The laws of rhythm, which also control music, painting, literature, and dancing, are also the major determinant in cinematography, however, the application is very different. In any art, including film art, artistic power is brought in when these laws are applied. We try to apply the laws of rhythm to films without being influenced by literature, painting, theatre, etc. We seek our own cinematographic rhythm, with its own laws concerning time and place. Over the past few years we have acquired an excellent ally, sound – sound film – which has shown us new directions to rhythm.

Film rhythm is a notion that is hard to define, harder than precise objects, like a lightbulb, although that is also difficult. Rhythm in films is determined by the logical trains of thought that preceeds the design, the sequence of notions and emotions, and the closeness of the whole. And I believe that the contemporary genre of acted films slows down, transforms, and sometimes even destroys the pacing of a film. And unfortunately, this rhythm in acted films is usually dictated by elements outside the film, usually afilmic, literary elements. Film director and audience should not see the white projection screen in the same way that they see the white pages of the books in which they find their sources. The healthy development of film is slowed down in the acted film. Meanwhile the acted film has gained a crass popularity. I am not even talking about bad influences, but about commercial calculation that speculates on the false sentimentality of the public.

I believe that, in this period of film development, it is better not to tie the filmmaker beforehand to false, anti-filmic regulations, but to give him carte blanche where he can discover the appropriate filmic rhythm by utilizing his filmic talent.

This field is unfortunately called *documentary film*. The documentary film has to be regarded as a category of films that is closer to cinema newsreels, reports, and cultural films than to acted films. It is not a series of external ideas, but the objects themselves which indicate their sequence in place and time. The filmic form originates in the relation of the recorded images to on another – only those images that are true and direct are eligible to be called documents. In the documentary film, the filmmaker is forced to be honest and open towards his objects. Only then will he find the right cinematographic design. And with this power, the documentary film should technically lead the way into the future for acted films and so it is here that real film drama will be discovered.

Contemporary acted films generally have, in their dishonesty, a numbing, negative influence on people. Their false romance distracts people from the real serious issues of our time. The documentary film and the new form of acted films need to have a stimulating effect on the spectator, they need to offer him positive energy. That is the large task that the film industry and the avant-garde should be working on together.

On the Method of the Documentary Film – in Particular the Film KOMSOMOL (1932)[1]

During the Litotdel[2] session of 21 February 1932, the plan submitted for the film KOMSOMOL was accepted on the condition that some aspects be altered. I was asked to submit a production plan and an article on the method I would use to make my first film in the USSR on the proletarian front. An evaluation of this working method would have to take into account my own development and transformation into an active fighter in the class struggle, as well as the development and character of my film work in capitalist countries.

During and in my first works, I was a representative of the leftist avant-garde movement. Contrary to other representatives of this movement, my technical education and much practical work experience prevented me from being torn away from the masses and daily economic circumstances. Unlike other countries, Holland was a country without war and revolution, which, for me, meant it would not favour my class-conscious work on the proletarian front.

My first film, THE BRIDGE, is characterized by a strict formal method and was much acclaimed by the progressive press as a protest against sentimental and commercial feature films. Like the other films of this period (RAIN, BREAKERS, PILE DRIVING) this was not a class conscious film. My film work then, had no clear relation to my ideological development then. These films concentrated on the form and the control of the pure technical filmmaking processes and were, as avant-garde works, a protest against the middle-class cinematography of Hollywood, Paris, and Berlin.

In 1929 came the films WE ARE BUILDING and ZUIDERZEE WORKS, which is a technical documentary film. By strictly following the building process of the biggest sea dam and the biggest sluices in the world, I distanced myself from pure formalism and started (of course I was encouraged by the producer of this film) to elaborate social elements in the film.

This method took me, in 1929, away from contentless formalism – the revolutionary work of the so-called 'leftist' film avant-garde. However, along with this social awakening came the realization that the working conditions were becoming more difficult for me. The capitalist sponsors more tightly controlled things and did not approve of these different methods and social tendencies in my work; they could see that I was moving towards the revolutionary film front. The artistic and technical level of my work, and the fact that I was regarded as the leading documentarist of the West European avant-garde, guaranteed work for me, but I could not use my ideas about new documentary methods in film. My last film, a company film for the Philips radio factories, had to be made under strict restrictions. I did, of course, develop my skills and sound techniques, and only now and then, among the many formal things, I could point to the atmosphere of this rationalized capitalist multinational company. Although the film was highly acclaimed in the foreign art press, the Philips people were not satisfied.

Along with this film work for capitalist companies, I also made films of demonstrations, agitation films for the communist press, protest films against bad housing policies, agitation montage-films from bourgeois newsreels, and led the work of the agit-prop group in Amsterdam.

This rich experience – on the one hand, the films for capitalist companies, and on the other, the class conscious agitation films – gave me an important advantage for my work in the Soviet Union. Here, I was given the opportunity to make a film with communist content according to the methods which I had developed under the above circumstances. That is why I think it was necessary for me to sketch this part of the development of my work.

To develop the content of my new work, I had to use new means to make advances with my new method, which resulted in a harmonic unity of form and content in our Soviet film.

If one needs to classify my film, then call it a documentary film, or, better yet, a publicitary film. I hesitate to call it a documentary film, for many understand this to mean events and facts recorded without intervention from the director (who only gets to intervene in the editing process). You will notice that I do organize, and reconstruct events and facts. Among non-fiction films, there are many sub-genres which are difficult to distinguish such as the documentary film, publicity film, film poster, agit-prop film, art film, newsreel, educational film, instructional film, sketches.

What mistakes do I and others make in our documentary films? First of all, the creative method seemed rigid, and was not dynamic enough to represent the progress of socialism in the Soviet Union. It led to formalism and schematism, and falsely concentrated on outward appearances of facts and processes, or it became a mere recording of events. A director was to have no involvement in the documents – meaning a superficial and generalized film, lacking a concrete form, in other words, lacking the why and the wherefore. You will seldom see the man involved in the production, and when he does appear, you are prevented from bonding with him because he remains an impersonal part of the whole. You see how a man works, but you cannot feel empathy. What are his ideas about his job? What does he do after work? How does he live? Is he a Party member? What does his brigade do? Has he got a name and an age, like the rest of us here in the screening room?

The method I want to use will attempt to actively involve the spectator with the documents. This can be affected by concretely positioning one or more people in the middle film. In this way, the spectator will get to view the greatness, the value and the relation between the recorded events and the facts. I also want to show the Komsomols in the village, on the Magnitostroj,[3] in Berlin. One will learn their names, how he lives, what his friends do while he is studying, how he participates in the military work-ing-group, who his rivals are in the socialist competition. Will he receive a premium when he becomes a Komsomol member? These simple, concrete facts will, of course, be put into the general context. When we show the Komsomol while he is studying in the military working-group, we will re-veal this through images that give an impression of the general work of the Red Army.

This method requires that one does not limit oneself to the recording of accidental events, occuring at the moment of recording, but that one also in-cludes short episodes and reconstructed events that occurred in the plants or the construction of these factories. These events, of course, must have taken place at these same locations and concerning the same type of activi-ties. The relationship of the worker to his work, to the socialist working methods, to the Party, to the socialist build-up and to the cultural develop-ment must be made clear.

It seems to me that people have been too afraid to make such organized recordings on location (although they had no fear when it came to the edit-ing, where they severely and sometimes even falsely organized events). I am convinced that reconstruction – organization of past events at the same location using the same workers doing the same activities – is essential for the further development of the documentary film and, when correctly orga-nized, that it will not lessen its documentary value.

As for how the recordings are organized; this is the main aspect of my working method by which it can be distinguished from other directors.

A documentary film, as I produce it, has no elaborate script. Although it does have a plan, which reveals the political views and structure of the film, and which sketches the directives which determine the different recording locations and the actual recordings. From this plan a production plan emerges, in which locations, metres of film to be shot, the composition of the group, etc., are determined. It is only on location where the right material is chosen that matches the plan's directives, and from this, the recording schedule will be created (a kind of shooting script) which indicates in great detail what will be recorded.

This creation of the recording schedule on location is a very important stage of work. It is here that the organization of the directives is placed into the context of the found live material. Strict directives and a politically correct attitude towards the film will guarantee that the material will not dominate the political perspective. Consulting with the Komsomol, and informing them of our work will help interest them in it, and this is of the utmost importance.

The recording method is different from the method used for feature films. I will show this later in relation to the libretto. Along with the recordings, I will also utilize newsreel material as documentary evidence (for example, in the part which shows the crisis in the capitalist countries).

Sound will be employed in the film KOMSOMOL to enhance the effect of the images. In a short section of film, sound makes it possible to show the dialectic value of the shots more effectively than in a silent film. I will clarify this with a few examples. There will be calculations, statistics, and titles in the film, e.g., as with the Lenin speech on the occasion of the Third Congress of the Youth Federation (October 1920). He states:

> The generation whose members are now in their fifties, cannot count on experiencing a communist society. That generation have passed on by then. But the generation that is now fifteen years old will witness as well as built this society themselves. And they must know that their task in life is in to create this society.

Periklitschka

On the basis of the plan for the Komsomol film, I can now best explain my work methods. I submitted a plan, where I indicated that I also wanted to treat the main areas that focussed on the socialist front during the last years of the Five Year Plan such as the coal and steel industries, machine construction, as well as village life (see illustration).

The Periklitschka is from the start meant to give the spectator the right feeling, so he can readily acknowledge the influence of the work by the Komsomol in the film. He will learn why the work was done. He will understand the struggle and the difficulties of socialist development in the last year of the Five Year Plan, the leading role of the Party, the Komsomol as aids to the Party and the coherent, systematic work applied to the socialist work schedules. The spectator will sense the construction of the film. In the Periklitschka questions will be asked which will be answered by the film. Other plans mentioned explain their difficulties and shows the struggle to solve the problems. The spectator's interest will be aroused about future scenes.

For example: the Komsomol explaining the steel front is in Magnitogorsk. He explains the difficulties, the technological progress and tells us about the construction progress on the new blast furnace. Later, when Magnitogorsk comes into view, we see how workers qualify themselves, how a brigade that works is formed, a socialist competition, and the construction of the blast furnace. The final format of the Periklitschka mostly depends on the material which I will record. It will be a general introduction. Image, speech, music, noise and multiplication – everything will be used to create this introduction. By doing this, I will be assured that the different sections of the film will not be isolated from the whole.

In the section about steel production, it will be stated that the production demand in 1932 was 9,000,000 tons; the plan presented by the steel workers, was 10,000,000 tons. It will also be stated that this steel is needed for the machine industry and for the Soviet Union's independence from other countries, and that the coal demand is connected to the capacity of the smelting works.

Such a Periklitschka makes it possible for me to elaborate my work scheduled for the rest of the film.

Komsomol on Magnitostroj

In our shooting schedule, we see that it is the same Magnitogorsk Komsomol who appears on different occasions in the film. He presents some episodes regarding life and work among the Komsomol. He is not an actor, but a Komsomol from Magnitogorsk. We will give his name and age; the spectator will get to know him. We will film several episodes with him and his brigade, in order to show his development from an unqualified village worker to a qualified employee with a conscientious, socialist attitude toward work – the New Man. Through the Komsomol it is possible to show the concrete living conditions, their studies and cultural activities -- at home, in the socialist city, in the barraks, the clubs, the Red Corner, the military activities – nothing will be vague and generalized. This is the concrete positioning of which I spoke earlier.

These simple facts in the film will be connected to the general context. When we show the Komsomol's house, on Magnitostroj, it will be directly connected to the socialist city. This will be done in the same way with other facts. Not just in Magnitogorsk, but also in the village, in the coal mining

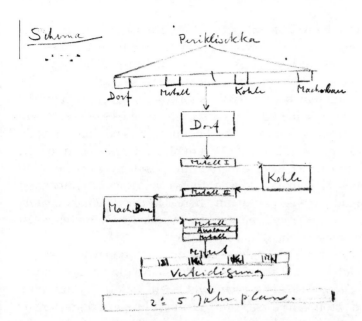

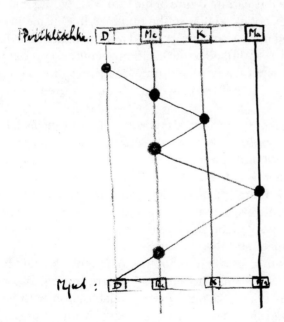

The Periklitschka

area, in other nations; he will be one of the many Komsomols to act in the film. The young German comrade who lives in Berlin, on such and such a street, and who has been unemployed since 1929, etc. This will be shown together with the chronicle about the crisis and the class struggle.

You will understand that, because of the short shooting period, it will be necessary to reconstruct some episodes, because some of the events will have obviously occurred before we arrived on location. The Komsomol on Magnitostroj, for example, will already be a qualified employee in reality. To show his development, we have to include an episode in which he is still working in the mines. He will have to wear the work clothes of a miner and join the mining brigade so we can film him there. The documentary character of the shooting must, of course, be strictly controlled, because that must be the influential element of the film for the spectator.

The possibilities for reconstructing of episodes with non-actors will, of course, not be overestimated. If you allow him to act in a too complex capacity it will give it a dilettantish atmosphere and it will look unnatural. With our method trained actors can be used but you must film short characteristic events – without complex psychological tensions and scenes of the mixed actions of two or three actors – that bear the action of the episode.

In the context of the whole film it should be realized that the Magnitogorsk Komsomol will not be the leading figure of the film. This would make for a bad feature film in concept as well as in the final result. Our method would be falsely represented if the Komsomol played a scene which was invented; only the episodes directly linked to the location events and his daily work must be filmed. That is why any plan with a description for scenes would be false for this film, and therefore dangerous for our documentation methods.

The conscientious socialist attitude towards work and the enthusiasm of the Komsomols gives us the opportunity to pursue our production method. This attitude makes the Komsomols understand the value of such a film. A conscientious, active attitude towards the film's realization is only possible in the Soviet Union, because the Komsomol's job and our film work have the same goals. This conscientious, active attitude toward the film assures that during shooting, an active collaboration and a natural relationship is established between the camera and the workers.

From the above it follows that, before the shooting starts, the plan will be Thoroughly discussed with the Komsomol committee and the Brigade, so that everything is clear. This plan develops in close collaboration with the Komsomol and is immediately linked to the daily life of the Komsomol. The film will, therefore, have a vivid documentary character.

To summarize: my work here is also determined by my agitprop work and political education as a Party member, and by my film work in other countries and the rich experience in the production of documentary films.

The method I use in the Komsomol film is based on the notions of dialectical materialism and has developed from my experience with earlier methods, from self-criticism, and the criticism by others, and from my personal contact with the Komsomols.

This work will be of major political importance, in the USSR as it will be abroad; it will be the first publicity film on the Komsomol with historic value – the work of socialist development of the proletariat under the leadership of the Communist Party in a period of global importance.

Hollywood (1936)

1936 – Hollywood, summer

In the hill garden on the lowest terrace down from the bright white house of my host, next to the well-shorn lawn lies the symbol of the Hollywood life-style to the outside world, the Swimming Pool. (This is not a kidney-shaped or fancy pool – just an ordinary square one with underwater lights for night dips.) I am in Movie Mecca now, coming from the East after a lecture tour.

My host and director, pops up out of the water after an elegant dive. 'Hey Joris, we got the sponsoring committee going for the showing of your film.'

The invitation cards:
'You are kindly invited to a showing of Joris Ivens's documentary films in the Film Art Theatre.
Sponsors: Lewis Milestone, Dorothy Parker, King Vidor, Frank Tuttle.'

The Show:
Many Hollywood directors, producers, actors, writers, and all had a good look, many of them for the first time, at documentary films.

My first peek at Hollywood too.

In the lobby after the show:
'Not so different from travelogues.'
'Pretty arty.'
'Give me a camera and I'll do a dozen of those.'
'Is this for school use only?'
'Let's stop making pictures here.'
'This is the real stuff!'
'I wonder how much re-enactment there was for that eviction scene in the coal film.'
'No theatre will run them – it's pure propaganda!'

This last one must have connected with a sly, well-known and disliked gentleman who wrote down all the names of those attending the show. The next day, the front office boys from a big studio called in three of its writers and reprimanded them for having attended that leftist radical show.

The show had other repercussions as well. Many a writer and director wanted to see these films at their studios and talk about how they were made and the relation between documentary and fiction films. They, in turn, taught me a lot about their creative work and struggle for good film in The Millions' film production called 'The Industry'.

My flat swimming-pool perspective of my first days here in film town had been wrong.

Notes on Hollywood (1936)

To us in Holland, and most of Europe, Hollywood appears as a strange empire, with its embassy palaces and consulates in every country, city, and hamlet of the world. Whoever enters one of these palaces (and he must pay) is on neutral ground: one's sorrows, insecurity, protest-demonstrations, struggles, and war are left outside. Inside is darkness. An endless series of false illusions flicker across the screen, and the cunning director, with the help of a Clark Gable, Jeanette MacDonald, or Shirley Temple, tries to prove to the whole world – the American coal miner as well as the Dutch peasant – that human nature never changes.

It is clear in whose interest such a perversion of fact and reality is perpetuated. Who owns the screen? The talkie? The loudspeaker? Think of the thundering bellow of culture across the world each evening – and then also think of the following story.

In British-ruled India, there lived a strong isolated tribe of mountaineers who did not like continually having to pay taxes to the London bankers. They took their rifles and marched against the authorities. A bright English officer proposed to his general to send an airplane with the world's most powerful loudspeaker over the camp of the mountaineers who were so audacious as to defend their liberty. A well-paid Hindu priest assuming the voice of God of the Mountains announced through the silvery amplifying tubes that he wanted the tribesmen to bring all their rifles, weapons, and gunpowder to the river bank. The people complied, and were conquered. Today, some of their young warriors are studying radio engineering and aviation in order to be able to deliver their own message.

I

Hollywood seemed to use us in far-off Holland as well, and we are much farther away than the film centres of London, Moscow, Paris, Berlin. With these centres, our own independent film groups and audience organizations maintained regular contact. Celebrated European directors spoke at our public meetings on their conception of film art and their methods of work such as René Clair, Pudovkin, Renoir, Eisenstein, Pabst, among others. But Hollywood remained distant. Our only contact with it through the years was its many mediocre and awful movies. You can imagine what a distorted idea of American life the Dutch, French, and English received. A country full of gangsters and G-men; every office girl with a chance to marry her boss; the old fairy tale that every boy has the opportunity to become a millionaire; Negroes who were merely clowns with nothing to do but dance and sing all day long. All of this, time and time again.

Things took a turn for the better much too slowly. Every year four or five good films (of course far to few) came out of this dream factory where films – 500 per annum, 65 percent of the world's production – were made on a conveyor belt. Names like King Vidor, Milestone, Mamoulian, Von Sternberg – later John Ford, Capra, Cukor, Hawks, La Cava, and Le Roy – and those of a few good actors and actresses, appeared. Films began to be made which could no longer be derisively labeled 'box office', 'religion and sex', 'war and sex'. One had to differentiate. We now saw some good films. Hence, there were obviously some good people out there, creative forces, artists who wanted to create something beyond cheap entertainment.

II

During my first few weeks in Hollywood, as a craftsman I naturally concentrated on the marvelous working places. Hollywood is indeed a magnificent place in which to produce movies – a mild, even climate, for many a bit too monotonous – a lot of sun, little wind, scenic variety, and, in addition, the best technical equipment in existence. People from all over the world come to observe the studios in operation and to study their perfected methods of production. (Shumiatsky, for instance, came to Hollywood while in the preparatory stages of building a gigantic film centre in the South of the Soviet Union). Visit these studios for a few hours and compare them with London or Paris, the dependability, the speed and calm of the directors, cameramen, stage and electrical workers and carpenters. Here, one finds a working method of the utmost efficiency, systematic mass production, a concentration of the whole population of a city for one end – to produce films.

Technically, everything is possible. The lenses pan across the scene faster than the eye of the interested visitor. The microphone hears more acutely than the ear of the snooping publicity agent. In twenty minutes, one passes through twenty different streets, through a few thousand years of human history. Indeed, a marvelous place in which to produce pictures.

Then, week after week, one suddenly remembers that this apparatus, technically so marvelous, only produces four or five good pictures a year. It is not as efficient as we thought! One realizes the discrepancy between the technical possibilities and the result. Why?

In the scenario department, the inbreeding of ideas proceeds on an unprecedented scale. Every year, an endless row of variations on boy meets girl or the Cinderella story. Experiments in direction and shooting by director or cameraman are impossible, or emerge mutilated from the cutting

room. An actor has to fight for his life to escape being typecast; once a dancing girl, gangster, or butler, always a dancing girl, gangster, or butler. In
Hollywood, one is not permitted to evolve. One is not permitted to make
use of the rich American life outside. And it lies right next door – all around.
Do not forget: Hollywood borders on Los Angeles, a city of two million,
with the greatest aviation industry in the United States, the greatest fruit orchards of America, the second greatest centre for rubber and oil. But between Hollywood and Los Angeles lies a boulevard, which separates the
motion pictures from reality.

In the scenario department, the last word in contact with life is a short
story from the *Saturday Evening Post*, or a book. Sometimes even a good
book. But the pages are juggled, and often wiped clean of their texts, leaving
a blank white sheet to be used as a movie screen!

III

There are certain things in Hollywood, however, which are not hampered
by restrictions. One is the censors. You get the feeling that these all-power-
ful and ignorant midwives have been involved in each film from its incep-
tion and that is why they hover over each meeting of boy and girl armed
with the vetoes of religious and moral decency.

The curiosity of the public is similarly unlimited and unhampered, stimulated by the fan magazines, whose Myrmidons scurry like rats in and
around private lives. Diaries, bedrooms, gardens, are all open to them. They
dutifully help to make the atmosphere of Hollywood fatal for true talent.
Many writers succumb in the struggle and become businessmen, more so
than in any other film centre I have observed and worked in. Most of them
come to Hollywood with a modest package of ideas, but the package is soon
emptied. Life in Hollywood makes a writer soft. 'Of course, I only came for
three months, to make a pile. Soon I'll quit and do what I want – write a book
– a play – or study – or make my own films.' But if you ask these writers (or
actors) how long they have been in Hollywood, they answer, 'Three years –
four years'.

Among them there are those who really had something to say. But after
three or four years they dried up – like the sea in Holland – slowly, pain-
lessly, in a marvelous climate, in a house with a view and a good car. Only a
few of them can indulge in the luxury of permitting themselves individual-
ity. The producers have their problems with this sort! The better type of production requires strong, original talent. The producers engage writers who
are known to possess it and then have to nullify the very qualities they need
so badly, because in most instances, the writer turns up with a scenario far
too powerful, too original, too honest. ('Controversial topics are barred.')

The producer has other problems. He has to get writers into some sort of collective relationship, because it usually takes more than one to turn out a script on a picture. I experienced one typical case. The collective did not gather around the theme or the idea of the film, but around the prospective title - four words. (The producer assured me, 'Every letter is worth gold.') I shall not divulge it, it was something like *Love on the Moon*. Four writers, the producer and the title – a brilliant gathering! A very strange process with four writers brooding like roosters over an empty eggshell, making a full egg of it, and the public having to swallow it!

The writers are divided into various categories. After the *Love on the Moon* collective has done its work, the gagmen and the heavy dialogue men are called in. ('And I have three idea men – fine fellows. No, they always do the same kind of work.') Once I was almost run over by the first aid doctor. 'Help! One of the idea men has suddenly developed into a laugh man!'

Such a 'collective' is a vulgarization, a profanation of collective work as I have experienced it in Moscow.

IV

Instead of resorting to such travesties of the creative process, Hollywood should turn to the rich, full life right at its door, life in which a Balzac or a Zola would revel! I saw a fruit pickers' strike – three thousand Mexican workers – which offered material for at least two *Viva Villa*'s. In la Habra, I was present at the birth of a fighting song, the circumstances of which, if incorporated into a film, would have had ten times the strength, and directness and optimism and would probably have been more of a popular hit than the usual Hollywood epic. Yet how many Hollywood film employees were aware of this heroic primitive struggle in the fruit orchards, where trees seem to be better cared for than men?

In San Francisco, it should not be necessary to fake an earthquake to create an interesting theme. San Francisco provides other themes for pictures besides earthquakes. On any ordinary day there is more tension in this harbour than in any Hollywood superfilm. One is conscious of five continents meeting in the harbour and international complications can offer great cinematic material.

The writers must add depth to their work, they must tell more than they do at present. The screenwriters were right to organize. It was and is necessary. They must defend not only their salaries but their professional honour and integrity.

Fuller and richer scenarios would not have to wait for good directors and actors; they would be there because they *want* to make better films. There are great artists and experts available; I realized it again when I saw Capra shooting LOST HORIZON. It is artistic love, the love of a craftsman for his profession that guides him. He directs a mass of one thousand people or the wrinkled brow of one of his actors with equal intensity. He notices with equal acuteness the mistakes of five extras in a mass of a thousand, or an incorrect fold in Ronald Colman's Chinese gown. And he corrects everything himself. He does not trust his eye, and controls the screen picture in the finder of the camera. One would almost think he had the screen with the completed film on it right beside him while he is shooting. I asked him whether he cut the film himself. 'Of course. I consider that part of the director's job.' Capra is one of the few directors in Hollywood who are free from front office interference. In his studio there reigns the quiet, intense atmosphere of devotion essential to the making of good images, which I also found with René Clair in Paris and Pudovkin in Moscow. The same is true of others here whom I watched at work such as Vidor, Milestone, Mamoulian. The calm confidence of men who are the complete masters of their art, their craft. One becomes furious at the thought that such talent does not have the freedom necessary for the further development of film art.

One might think that Hollywood would be a marvelous greenhouse for actors. On the contrary. I have already commented on how each actor is typecast. Only with the help of courageous directors or perhaps an intelligent producer, can they escape this fate. All too rarely do they get to work earnestly at their profession. They always have time and energy for a physical workout, tennis, polo, etc., but only rarely to study their roles, the character they are playing, before work on the film is begun. I had expected a great deal; I had thought that at least something of the methods of the Russian film actors had reached Hollywood, or that the modern American theatre would have exerted some influence. Such was not the case. At times, I saw an astounding lack of discipline among most of the leading actors and stars. They lacked the power or desire to submerge themselves in their work. Concentration is impossible.

At home, their calendar is full of engagements. I tried to remain calm when a star with a yearly income of at least two hundred thousand dollars complained earnestly to me: 'Thursday night and Saturday night, no date, no invitation!' (Invitations are the barometer of popularity.) One must not wait! Call yourself! That is the first straw one clutches at. (Modern courtroom atmosphere.) Publicity manager. These are her problems. Her final goal is a footprint in the concrete at the entrance to Grauman's Chinese theatre. Madam has worries indeed!

The young cameraman working for years without advancement has greater worries. No promotion possible. In certain companies, a small group of older cameramen is in control and effectively block the way. No younger man, however talented, is allowed a chance. Tired musicians tell me of long working hours and bad pay. Matters are even worse among the army of extras. The Central Casting Bureau reports that of the 15,275 people offered jobs during the first six months of 1936, 13,463 earned less than $200. This is the Hollywood about which the fan magazines never write.

V

When I said that Hollywood was shut-in and isolated, I did not mean that it was not completely dominated and controlled from the outside, and that it was not being used as a powerful medium to reconcile the masses to the insecurity of their daily lives by giving them cheap entertainment as an escape from reality. To my mind, Hollywood is the world's greatest centre of agitation and propaganda. One has only to remember how in 1917 the war spirit was worked up with miles of celluloid and a few telegrams and meetings. Would not such a thing be possible again today?

The mental attitudes of those who work in this centre of propaganda are not simple. Meeting different people in Hollywood taught me to understand better what Donald Ogden Stewart said at a public reading of *Bury the Dead* about the profession of screen writing. There are many fine, charming people in Hollywood. At home, they play with their children, read a great deal, take an interest in art. But at the office, they write and produce bad films which their own children, and the rest of the world as well, will see. They distort, consciously or unconsciously, the fundamentally healthy illusions of human beings, and project them on the screen as a new kind of reality. Their work constitutes a moral disarming of the masses.

If one asks the producers or film magnates: 'Why entertainment on such a low level, why so few good movies?' they always hide behind the box office, which they insist represents the wishes of the masses. The masses become a sort of big brother. 'My big brother likes it that way.' But 'big brother' is becoming wiser, more conscious of his own life. He spends his earnings to see these pictures. And he finds them too empty. The industry's answer is not better pictures, but the double feature. Still, my 'big brother' is not satisfied. The pictures give him nothing for tomorrow, or to mitigate his nine-to-five. And the industry's answer? Screeno, and Bank Nights! Still not enough? Then give away a car! What will they give away next year, producers, and directors?

It is a pity that a few of the leaders of the film industry could not accompany me on my tour where I showed the films of independent film groups in Holland and Belgium. They would have marvelled at how widespread and lively is the desire for better films in all circles, among students, intellectuals, and workers. The honest film critic could render great service by voicing this too little expressed desire.

All those who wish to raise the American screen to a higher level should heed the example of the young new theatre movement in America. No other country except the USSR can show such a steady growth of modern theatre as America. (In Germany, by contrast, the theatre has withered away under the Nazi dictatorship.) Playwrights, directors, and actors in New York sense a great task. The American screen must follow their example; the days of merely cursing or deploring Hollywood are over.

Hollywood can produce such films as THE INFORMER, MODERN TIMES, MR. DEEDS GOES TO TOWN, FURY, PASTEUR. Good artists in Hollywood need the help of the public so that the box office risk of such pictures can be reduced. The producer must sense a new terrain with new possibilities. Educational, youth, peace, and labour organizations could support such productions, could stimulate the demand for progressive films and form a bulwark against anti-labour, fascist, and war tendencies in pictures.

It must be made possible for Hollywood writers, directors, and actors, and with them the public, to face the real problems of life. The film must take part in the cultural development of the people, as must the theatre, literature, music, painting, and radio.

Why shouldn't directors, screenwriters, and actors found an experimental studio for a systematic examination of the fundamental laws of the art of the film? This is essential. This studio would shoulder the cost of the experiments which the producers of feature films do not want to assume. Special studio films intimately associated with the reality of the world would enrich their aesthetic sensitivities and give new vitality to their work.

Independent film groups are already engaging in courageous pioneering work with already excellent professional results: Nykino's LABOR MARCH OF TIME, American Labour Films' MILLIONS OF US. This must continue. For the public good, films are indispensable in their struggle for life. Films with the power, the artistic level, and the social function of books like *Don Quixote*, and *Uncle Tom's Cabin* are long overdue in America. A young film movement must open the way.

Speech after the Screening of THE SPANISH EARTH (1937)

Summer 1937, Hollywood, the home of Fredric March

Now you have seen what it looks like.

There are some things we could not get in. The way the ground rocks and sways under your belly and against your forehead when the big bomb falls. That does not appear. Nor the noise kids make when they are hit, although there is a sort of foretaste of that when the child sees the planes coming and yells 'AVIACION!'

Then, too, when they are hit some kids are very quiet until you move them. We do not have any pictures of the full streetcar after a direct hit in the Gran Via. There were 32 people in it. They carried out two badly wounded, and what was left had to be handled with shovels. That was in the town center around noon.

Such a scene is just one of the by-products of the totalitarian war the fascist countries are waging. This war was originally meant to terrorize the civil populations in order to break their morale. It was a war against the *people* of a country instead of a war between warring armies. It has now developed so that it includes taking deliberate planned murderous vengeance on the opposing civil population whenever the fascist armies are defeated in the field. Hemingway and I watched this kind of murder being engaged in for a long time. For much too long a time.

You have seen something of it and you have also seen the faces of the men who are opposing it. We have lived with them behind the lines and in the trenches. We have gone with them on the attack and we have seen them wounded and we have seen them die.

In the last few weeks we have lost many friends whom we loved very much. This is the camaraderie men only experience in battle. They were such good friends that it is hard to talk about them now. These men all knew what they were fighting for.

You all know what they were fighting for. It is an old story and we do not have to go over it again. It is our fight as much as it is theirs. If fascism is to be stopped from spreading across the world, it must be fought and defeated in Spain. These men you see are fighting our fight for us now.

Since last month, the republican army has been on the offensive. Yesterday, today, and tomorrow and the rest of this summer and this autumn, men that you have seen in this picture will be killed and wounded. Tomorrow morning, while we are in bed, they will be fighting on the road to Navalcarnero. Hemingway and I are going back to be with them. The issues are so clear that we have no choice. But we cannot go back without bringing what we came here for – the only excuse we have for being away from Spain.

In war, for every man killed in battle there are, normally, six to eight wounded. I do not know whether you have ever been wounded. It differs from an operation in that there is no anaesthetic and you never know whether your stomach is full or empty when it happens. The chances are that it is empty. When it happens, unless the bullet or the shell fragment hits a nerve, and even then it may numb it, it is not very painful. It is more like being knocked down by a club and clubbed in the belly or the legs or the neck or the shoulders or the feet or almost everywhere. If you are clubbed in the head you end up not knowing anything about what happened. But in about half an hour, when the shock has worn off, the pain starts and when the pain really gets going and the ambulance is slow in getting there, you will truly wish you were dead. The wish to die, to make the really unbearable pain stop, will make one man ask another to do him a great favour and shoot him in the back of the head.

It takes twelve ambulances per brigade to properly handle the wounded of that brigade in action. In a bad attack out of 2500 men, from 300 to 800 men will be wounded or killed. Half a dozen shock brigades now have twelve ambulances. Some have seven. Some have five. Some have none. The hell the wounded men go through in a brigade with no ambulance I will not try to describe for you.

They are lifted off stretchers into trucks, and they try not to scream when they are pushed in as gently as men can be piled on top of each other with their broken bodies, haemorrhages, bones grating, dressings loosened so they begin to bleed again and the short unrepressible scream changes to a groan and then to a moan and then to nothing but a man's life quietly dripping away from lack of care. That happens.

The trucks are bad enough, but the wounded in trucks are lucky compared to those who have to make the trip in carts or those who simply wait to die on the side of a hill, under fire, because there is no transport for them.

You can support their struggle in Spain, under existing neutrality regulations, through the channels which the North American Committee has worked out by supplying ambulances.

If you give nothing, the war will go on just the same, New York will go on just the same. Men will be wounded and die there every day, and men and women will work hard and make money here every day. But if you do give money, men who otherwise would die may live and the suffering men will remember your names gratefully.

This is a war in which there are no rewards or medals. Wounds are the only decorations and the only reward is that of a good conscience. I think that those who do what they can do this year will sleep a little bit better at night than those who do nothing. I know that money is hard to make, but dying is not easy either. If you would like to keep hundreds of fighting men from dying between now and Christmas, you can do it with a dime, a dollar, 10, 100, 500...

Documentary: Subjectivity and Montage (1939)[1]

The documentary film in general, I think, is a most distinguished form. The first films were generally produced using factual information, and this is still the root of the documentary. On the one hand, you have fiction or acted films, on the other, you have the newsreel, and between those two you have the area covered by the documentary film.

You know that we cover a broad area. We are involved with a new art form, in a new field of expression and of human creation, and so it is difficult to realistically provide a definition of the documentary film. Now, I said we cover a broad area. There is THE MARCH OF TIME, SPANISH EARTH, THE RIVER, all of which belong to our area, and some people might even include CONFESSIONS OF A NAZI SPY.

As you know, the documentary film was not created in this country, but in Europe, around 1927. It was part of the avant-garde movement, to give film artistic and educational values. The documentary film is part of that great movement that came across the ocean around 1927. In the beginning, it was based very much on aesthetics, and most of us were strongly against Hollywood. We thought, especially before sound films, that they were emphasizing the sentimental angle of cheap stories, as well as the sex angle. We thought they were too distant from reality. There was a very strong and logical reaction from students, artists, and young people in Europe who thought we should fight against that sort of thing and base our work on reality. So that was the beginning of the documentary film.

I believe that the documentary film has had a healthy development, and that Hollywood has learned something from the independent filmmakers. For a while, there was an antagonism between the documentary and the so-called fiction film, but it became less and less so as time went on. In the beginning, however, there was quite an uproar against the fiction film, and even today you will find examples of this kind of protest against the sentimental treatment of what I have called the fiction film.

That we are now regarded as a young art and as an instrument of education has been verified, I think, by the fact that the Museum of Modern Art Film Library organizes different documentary programmes. I think the documentary film has to be very thankful to the Film Library, because it is the first time in history that people can see several documentary films during one programme.

In the beginning – that is, around 1927 or 1928 – we belonged to the avant-garde. We had groups in Germany, France, Holland, and England, and the national character defined the kind of films you got. You can see the German mentality coming through in Ruttmann's films, and you can see René Clair in his films – I mean René Clair of the avant-garde. In the Dutch and Belgian sections of the documentary film movement you find a great deal of realism. You could almost say they were in the tradition of Rembrandt, that feeling of the Dutch and Belgian people for realism, was absorbed into the documentary film.

Soon, we found out that we had to rise above the pure aesthetic approach, because that makes content and form bloodless. I do not know if everybody would agree with that, but I believe it is so. I think a pure aesthetic approach will bring film to an artistic dead end. I consider a film to be much more important if it is connected with a social movement, if it has to do with life.

It was not long before we felt that as artists we had to take part in the social life, in the economic life of our country; that we were dead in the water if we remained on the abstract side of aestheticism. The shift away from this can be illustrated by comparing THE BRIDGE with NEW EARTH, and NEW EARTH with SPANISH EARTH.

We were mostly independent groups back then. We hated what we called big industry. We did not like to work for big money; what we most wanted was to do independent work. We wanted to be able to make our film conscientiously, because we believed that it was the art medium of the educator. It might be interesting for you to know that our sponsors are very special: our Government, our social societies, our trade unions, etc. They are the people who financed our pictures.

Because of this, of course, we were immediately labelled as propagandists, and in a way, I accept that label. In a way, it is true. I say that the same thing is true of a lot of artists. Take Rembrandt again. It seems to me that an artist like Rembrandt just had to take sides, and very definitely did.

I think there is a large field for students in the documentary film. It is a new form of art. Take Breughel, for example. If he were living, I am sure he would be an excellent documentary film man. I think it would be a very good course of study – the relationship between art and propaganda, in both film and painting.

Of course, you find a great problem here, and that is the objectivity and subjectivity of the director. Would you rather see both sides of the Civil War in Spain, or would you rather see it from the loyalist side and fascist side in separate films? Do you prefer to see a man handling both sides of it, trying to give an objective point of view?

I think in such great problems as life and death and democracy and fascism, there is no objectivity for an artist. He gets very weak if he attempts this. You ought to let the artist hate and love, agree and disagree, because that will reflect his work. His work has to be very emotional. I think you might say that the documentary film is an emotional presentation of facts. The audience can try to be objective, but not the documentary film director.

The documentary film should be regarded as a representation of fact; but if you insist on the documentary film as an art form, even as a good educational format, I believe we have a right to be subjective about our themes. As a matter of fact, you will see that our style is changing. The tendency at the moment is to make documentary films in such a manner as to bring them closer to people. They should have elements of persuasive powers. I think the fact that they are made on the spot, with the actual people who live through the given situation, is a great element of the documentary film. It gives a convincing touch that the fiction film does not have. If you see NANOOK, or my next film that I am now making on an Ohio farm,[2] you will feel that you are seeing something that is real.

The film I am making now is for the United States Film Service, about the electrification of a farm in Ohio. We lived on the farm for two months, and we can safely invite you to go out there and see for yourself, if you do not believe our film. If we had leaned to the fictional side of film, if we had hired actors, we would have lost something which is vital to the documentary film.

I want to emphasize a danger for the future of the documentary film: working with non-actors. I think that is extremely important, as well as interesting. The danger lies, of course, in depending too much on non-actors and on too many re-enacted scenes. Documentary filmmakers should face the fact that they are not dealing with seasoned actors. The aim is to be real; the aim is to be convincing.

Now I would like to concentrate on montage, because I think the work in the cutting room is extremely important. I will illustrate this with some of my own work, because I am more closely acquainted with it. I hope you will excuse me, although I would like to say that I am quite critical of my own work.

THE BRIDGE

The first film I want to mention is THE BRIDGE. It is close to my heart, because it was my first film. I made it in 1928. I was a chemical engineer and made microscopic films. In my spare time I worked with a little camera that I bought, always thinking of the films that were coming out of Hollywood, London, and Paris, how unreal they were, and how I would like to make something real.

You know that in music you have to know the meaning of the harmony between notes. In the film we have to know about harmony between movements. Well, I thought about a bridge, about the ships that pass under it, about the constant movement. I would like to study the ABC of movements. Ruttman, in Germany, was trying to discover the harmony of movement with his abstract films. I preferred to take a real object, to discover that harmony of movement. I think in THE BRIDGE that you can see the very simple, visual cutting. There is no sound in this film, but I think you can see the cutting. It is very simple, nothing psychological.

Of course, such a close-up was appealing in 1928 because it was something new then. I tried to find out about timing, about how long an audience would maintain its interest. I tried to discover the interesting and important points in a frame, and work from there to the next shot. Also, I tried to be faithful to the functions of the bridge.

NEW EARTH

Another good example of montage comes from the middle part of NEW EARTH. This film was made for the Dutch Government, about the Zuiderzee. I will not go into the theme, but I do want to note the cutting and editing. Maybe you are more interested in the cutting and editing of THE BRIDGE than the social significance of this film. You will see the development of this visual cutting. In NEW EARTH you get two elements. In the closing of the big dam you will see a struggle between two elements – water and land – and that they were struggling in a kind of boxing match. You are anxious to see the land win, and that is part of the dramatic element in the film. It is of course elementary, this visual expression of the closing of the dam.

THE BRIDGE is static, but NEW EARTH gave me something more to work with. As I have said, I had two elements to deal with. It is still a very visual kind of cutting; there is nothing psychological about it. It is more complicated, composed of a lot of shots, but it has the rhythm of getting this dam closed, against all the powers of the sea. For every shot, there is a kind of critical time. As an experienced cutter, you have to spot how long an audience can sit without becoming bored. The critical time is very important, because that dictates the rhythm of the picture. You will also notice that your attention is in a certain place, and that I build the next shot from there. In other words, I tried to make the second shot grow out of the first, where your attention was originally. Your eye is not jumping all over the screen. I use your attention, in one part, to develop my next scene. Perhaps I could say that one frame is the nucleus of the next frame.

I think the two important things to notice about NEW EARTH are, first, that there is a critical time for every shot; and second, that I tried to work out where the main interest of the spectator's eye would be. If it was in the left corner, then I built up my next shot from the left corner. Or, if I wanted to get you stirred up, perhaps I did just the opposite. If I wanted to excite you about the land and water, I built up my next shot from the other corner. I always tried to have a reason for guiding the spectator's eye.

NEW EARTH was also the first film in which I tried to get music into the film by trying to follow the water's flow with a certain melody. That was my first effort in combining music with a documentary film.

THE SPANISH EARTH

The next film I want to discuss in terms of the editing is THE SPANISH EARTH. Hemingway and I went to Spain, where we stayed for five months with the Loyalist troops during the defense of Madrid. We made a film there. John Ferno, my cameraman, brought it back here, and it was cut and brought into shape by Helen van Dongen, in New York. The music arrangement was made by Virgil Thompson and Marc Blitzstein.

There are two main elements in this film: the irrigation of the land, and the fight for the freedom of that land. You see the trucks, loaded with food, going to Madrid, then you see that we cut back to the irrigation of the earth. You see a man shooting, then you see the irrigation again. You get a kind of daring cutting, I would venture to say. With functions – the irrigation and the battles on the front there is no longer an elementary, visual editing. Psychological elements are coming into the editing.

In one sequence there is a long canal flowing along the screen and then, immediately after that, you see the trucks going to Madrid. In editing, it is important to have three or four links. One very elementary link is that the

Joris Ivens filming ZUIDERZEE.

water comes down, and the main attention of the audience is at the front part of the water. Then, when I cut to the truck, I did so in such a manner that the truck starts exactly where the water left off. Like in NEW EARTH, where your attention is, is where I start the next shot.

Also, it has this deeper meaning of seeing people work to achieve their irrigation goals. You see the water and have a feeling of contentment. You feel how wonderful it is that the Spanish earth is receiving this water. And that is why I show the trucks going to Madrid, to bring happiness to the audience, in the knowledge that the people were going to receive food. You will remember how I linked up the battle for the land, the men who fight for their country, and the people who irrigate the land being fought over. I tried to get a note of optimism in it such as the food trucks going to Madrid, and the successful irrigation of the land.

In other words, a man fights for his land, and at the same time, he irrigates that land – not expecting to lose it. I think that is important. And I do not know what could be more optimistic than irrigating the very land you are fighting for. That is what I tried to achieve through the cutting, which has nothing to do with pure symbolic editing, such as you sometimes see in Russian films. Suppose you see a man in prison and suddenly he becomes happy and you see apple blossoms. That is all very well, but it is purely symbolic cutting. I am trying very hard to convey my point, because it is so important. This kind of cutting is not just symbolic, because it goes much deeper than that. It is part of the theme of the film. It is optimism.

There is another illustration I want to offer, also from SPANISH EARTH. We jump to the middle of the film, during the bombardment of a village. First of all, I want to note the emotional value of sound; second, I want to show you the difference between editing problems in a fiction and in a documentary film.

Naturally, fiction films are based on story and dialogue. If you take away the sound, you get a lot of mute people, looking very stupid, indeed. They just don't talk, and it looks funny, to say the least. In a documentary film, we must concentrate on visual and silent editing. The music makes it more eloquent, that is all.

Even without the sound, I think the sequence of the village bombardment gives a feeling of tension in this village. Naturally, the sound gives it other qualities. We start off with a very natural bombardment sound, but later, when the child comes through the door, we bring it up to a kind of operatic style, to indicate the happiness of the life going on. I think that is much more effective, this feeling of life going on, than the actual bombardment sounds. They are very depressing, to say the least.

Another thing that is interesting is how we do the elementary, visual cutting, with the sound, you might say. Our first idea was to have the real sound, and then an operatic effect, to give a feeling of joy; also, to make it a little smoother for the audience. Bombardment is a pretty terrible thing, so we tried to get away from it as much as possible. That idea that life goes on, we thought was important to keep running throughout the entire scene. That feeling of flowing, I might say, is very important in the documentary film. I think the shots have a very nice visual rhythm – they do not cause you to jump from one thing to another. We tried to make it smooth.

There is a scene during the bombardment when a woman does not know what to do and does not know if her child is badly hurt. You see her wandering through this village, and then you see, very suddenly, some people through an opening in a wall. The logical cut I wanted to insert after that was the woman at her window. You feel her already, before you see her. The jump cut becomes very smooth. You expect that woman, because you have seen a lot of women and mothers before.

One moment, you see a woman looking out a window, so you can easily cut to the wall, and then to the wounded man, because you know this woman is looking for death and destruction. You could say that is the story line, and the logical visual line is when you focus on the window and then look at the other side you see a wall.

You may want to know why the director cut here or there. Well, you have the woman in the bombarded village, destruction, but life has to go on. So you have the children. You have the woman looking out toward the wall, and you pan down to the children. You might ask what the editer could have done. Well, he could have skipped a lot of these images and just given you the barest details. But after all, the most important thing in a war is that life remains, life goes on. We were very happy to have these children there, to give the audience a feeling a reinvigorated life.

The director also wants to show you that the children remain there, but as well he wants to show that the older men are prepared to fight for that life, so you come to the man with the rifle. That gives you the idea that something can and has to be done. As we break off the song, we go to airplanes and see one of them brought down. You would be surprised how enthusiastically people applauded during that scene. Naturally, you get a mixed feeling in an audience. Some are for one side and some for the other.

You remember that I mentioned something about the objectivity of the director. Well, you could have a wall with holes, and show ten dead people. You could cut out the weeping mother and have the bombardment instead, but we wanted to show that life goes on. We wanted that note of optimism.

It would be a terrible thing to show the bombardment and all those dead bodies lying around. Where is your hope? That is why we showed the enemy plane brought down, to stress that hope. Naturally, my idea was to help free Madrid again. I was honest about it. I wanted the audience to see my point. There are many things that could have been done. It could have been made very horrible for the man who hates war. It could have been made very sentimental. It all depends on your approach.

Then, of course, we go into what people call straight propaganda, when we show the German coming down. There was something very interesting when it came to the commentator. I knew there would be people who would not understand those long German words, so I held the scene a little longer, to get them annoyed, and then I had the commentator say, 'I can't read German, either.' In other words, I think you sometimes have to anticipate the feelings of your audience.

One could do anything at all with these images, it depends on what approach one desires. You could edit out a lot of what I put in, but you have to be honest in what you are doing.

THE 400 MILLION

The music for this Chinese film was very carefully conceived by the composer, Hanns Eisler, and it was followed closely by all who worked on the film. In other words, there is a very close relation between the music and the film. We were in China for about eight months, making this film about the resistance of the Chinese people to the Japanese invasion.

I would like to call your attention to the harmony and the close collaboration between music and editing. Helen van Dongen and I worked this film out for the four different sound reels. After hearing the Spanish film, and then this Chinese film, you must imagine that the sound reel is not very simple. It is composed mostly of four or five tracks, all brought together in what we call re-recording. In the case of this Chinese film, we sometimes had five soundtracks, because we have Chinese conversation in it.

We tried to do a little more with the music. Sometimes it is not very complicated, but in the battle we became a little more excited. With the approach of the train, the music becomes heavy and strong. I do not like to make anything grand out of war, because it is a terrible thing; a kind of butcher profession, so Hanns Eisler and I decided not to make the music heroic. Next to the sad things I wanted to evoke the suffering of the people, but also their sense of duty, the power of fighting for your independence. We tried to

Still from ZUIDERZEE / NEW EARTH.

Still from THE 400 MILLION.

show the awful tragedy of the Chinese people. Of course, we could not always do what we wanted to do, but we did strive toward that end with the music.

Now I have come to the end of the things I wanted to say about editing and cutting. I hope I have been able to show you what a large field the documentary film has to cover. I hope, also, that I have clarified some issues regarding the director having both an objective and a subjective approach to his work. Thirdly, I hope that I have adequately presented the fact that we are trying to do more than visual and elementary cutting.

Repeated and Organized Scenes in Documentary Film (1953)

Why did I ask the miners of Wasmes to carry the portrait of Karl Marx twice in BORINAGE? Because it was an important and essential scene to repeat in the film I was making in 1933 together with the Belgian director Henri Storck under the auspices of the film club of Brussels, 'Club de l'Écran'.

The film, a long documentary, had to show the abominable living conditions of the miners in the Borinage, the coal mining region in the South of Belgium, near the French border. The above episode, the last in the film, was shot in Wasmes.

Wasmes is a small mining village among a rolling hills where the miners and the villages lie spread out among the low hills. Difficult to film. The days here are never quite bright. The sunlight always seems filtered through a dusty veil, and when it rains, the streets and houses look hopeless and bare. The grass around the villages is never fresh and green, the sand along the streets where children play is not yellow. The mining companies have never spent any money to make the life of the miners any better. They have built ugly, small houses for which the miners pay an impossibly high rent. Life is hard in the houses which sit so close to the dark mine towers and coalpits.

Everything gets black and brown and dirty, white is a rare colour here. The fresh laundry stays white only for the first moment when women hang it out. The only white is saved for the flowers of the wreaths solemnly carried through the streets at funerals of miners killed in mining accidents. There are many such accidents in the Borinage. The work is dangerous and hard. The mineshafts are old and worn out. No money is spent on the most necessary safety measures for the men down below, because such expenses would decrease the profits of the owners in Brussels. So accidents are frequent and often fatal. The wages are too low to live on while many able men have no work at all. The miners are constantly battling against these factors and often go on strike.

They held a strike in 1932 and Brussels trembled. 250,000 workers went on strike, they marched with their demands written on red banners from the mines to the capital to talk to the government and the bosses. For many years, the Borinage had been known for its militancy and solidarity in the class struggle. Karl Marx had already made this point. One day, during the shooting of the BORINAGE, a miner, taking me to a united front meeting, stopped me just before the Union Hall and said: 'Here, right here, my father was killed, holding our barricade against the gendarmes. I was still a boy then.' Later during the meeting, I heard that the son of this miner had been thrown in prison three months ago. He helped to organize the march on Brussels. When the meeting was over, the men told us we should have been in Wasmes with our camera a month earlier to film the protest they held on the anniversary of the death of Karl Marx. They carried a large, gold-framed portrait of him, painted by a miner himself, around the village. Everybody participated. The gendarmes came, of course, and broke up the protest but they did not dare to touch the portrait.

We asked the organizers of this demonstration immediately, if it could be repeated for the film, along the same streets, with the portrait, with the people of Wasmes. At the shooting, like at all the shooting of this semi-clandestine film, we wanted a minimum of interference from the police, so we decided to start at seven o'clock in the morning, because the gendarmes usually made their daily rounds through the village at eight and they would certainly stop the people from marching and try to confiscate our camera.

The next morning at exactly 7 a.m., the door of one of the miner's homes opened and the portrait of Karl Marx was carried out by two strong miners. While they marched up the steep village street with some comrades behind them, the people came out of their homes and they, the miners of Wasmes, their women and children, without even noticing the camera, spontaneously took part in the demonstration a second time and followed behind the portrait of Marx leading the way. They formed small groups of three, four of five people, having a certain distance between them. They did not march in closed ranks because that would make them too vulnerable to attacking gendarmes. More and more people joined, even from neighbouring villages. The gendarmes came too, of course, despite the earliness of the demonstration, but it went on stubbornly and resolutely and we simply filmed what happened.

The scene which had been especially repeated just for the film, developed into a real scene, a real demonstration, because of the pre-existing tense political situation in the Borinage. Because the film BORINAGE is not known in Poland, the reader must forgive me that I had to give a rather long description of this episode and the general circumstances in which the filming of the 're-enacted' scene took place.

I think that many a director could give similar examples, of repeated scenes which become real scenes on their own. Last winter, a Russian documentary director told me that while repeating an episode of a socialist competition on a Martin Oven among steel workers, they surpassed their production record while re-enacting the original scene.

If such scenes are not artificially rendered, but emerge honestly out of the the filmmaker's reality, life itself will 'capture' such scenes and fill them in with new form and emotion. At the same time, it proves that the choice of the re-enacted scene was right and realistic.

There are many reasons why a scene should be repeated or re-enacted. In the above case of the BORINAGE an important scene was missed, because our film unit was not present in Wasmes when it actually happened. Other reasons for re-enactment are: the original action was stiffly or incorrectly executed, or the cameraman for some technical reason did not capture the action the first time, or the light was unfavourable, or an additional close-up had to be shot, etc., etc. Of course, during those re-enacted scenes the director interjects his directions and suggestions into the action to obtain higher technical and artistic qualities for the film. He tries in certain cases, to obtain more concentrated expressions and movements in the picture than those incidental, arbitrary ones which he often gets during unprepared shooting. One may notice such re-enacted scenes in numerous documentary films; for example, in the recently shown WESOŁA II by Lesiewicz and Raplewaki, which captures mineworkers down in the mineshaft. The documentary film director, Vroctavski and his cameraman Forbert have just finished their film about new developments in the village. It is about a Polish peasant who in the spring visits the Soviet Union and then returns to his hometown of Gruczno. The first evening home, he tells his neighbours and peasant friends all about what he had seen in the Soviet Kolchoses. To film this conversation en scene would have been all wrong. The intrusive cameras and lights and the necessary directorial interference would have gravely harmed the integrity, intimacy, and the propaganda value of Kujama's report to his unconvinced neighbours. Vroctavski had a valuable reason to repeat this episode, which was more essential to his film.

In order to prevent shooting a naturalistic, mechanical reproduction of what had happened, Vroctavski condensed the action to its most characteristic moments, recreated the original atmosphere, and through careful direction and Forbert's discreet camera work obtained a natural atmosphere from his 'actors'. Look at the old peasant woman counting silently, cautiously the great number of granules of the thick ear of Russian corn brought back by Kujama – the peasants show wavering approval of what they hear from their colleagues and begin to believe. Here we touch not only upon the problem of re-enacted scenes but also on the problem of introducing more or less personal, re-enacted scenes. Another question is why do we do this? Before answering this question, it should be clear that many personal scenes should never seem to be pasted on to the reality, they should always correspond with the development of the theme, emerge out of it and, at the same time, reflect it. Now to the question. The documentary film director feels that many personal scenes, are by necessity re-enacted, to give a more realistic and emotional aspect to the theme. They help the public to recognize and understand more clearly the development of the general events. In this way, the documentary film is easier to follow and becomes more convincing.

The personal scenes make the people appearing in the film more real by emphasizing the human element in the action and bringing the men and women who are closely connected with the theme of the film to the fore. Such scenes appeal to the spectator's emotions and through these scenes, thematic developments will more conveniently enter into the range of his own experiences. The actions in the film will no longer seem distant, strange, or exotic – the film will be made familiar for the spectator.

Of course, there are many documentary films where the course of the general events and facts 'carry' the entire film, but we often hear the complaint that a documentary without personal scenes seems dry and that boredom soon sets in. By interweaving personal emotions familiar to the spectator into the general themes, we allow him to discover the more complicated problems of our film. We urge him to think about them and compare and relate them to himself, his family, his home, his factories, and his surroundings. In short, we appeal not only to the mind, but also to the heart with the documentary film.

The development of the theme - in English they say 'the action' - is the road along which the documentary director guides the spectator to arrive at his conclusions. These conclusions should not all be fixed and ready by the first shot of the film, but we must lead the spectator toward them. And here typical personal scenes will help us strengthen the clear central line of the film, and give more depth and emotion to the content. We should not forget that during the viewing of a film, the audience will be provoked by the action to ask questions and the screen has to answer those during the denouement of the film. If some of these questions are answered in both a didactic and a personal way – of course, closely related to the general themes – then the film will have a stronger impact on the audience.

During my film work, like many documentary directors, I have often been faced with the a/m problem of effectively interweaving general events and personal scenes into the documentary. In 1937, for example, I was making a feature-length documentary film about the heroic fight of the Spanish people against the fascists, intended for an audience which had only seen fascist newsreels produced by Franco and had read only the most fantastic lies about the Spanish Republic. Our film had to convince this audience, which was at best indifferent, of the righteousness of the democratic cause, and to offer the truth about the people's fight in Spain. The general line of development of the film THE SPANISH EARTH is the interrelation between the fight at the front for a free, democratic Spain by the Republican army allied with the International Brigade, and the peaceful toiling of the peasants behind the front line, irrigating and cultivating the land that at last had become their own. By working this earth they help the soldiers at the front and they strengthen the future of their country.

This is the general development, the 'action', but in three places it finds its personification in a young Spanish peasant soldier. First, amidst the gunfire along the frontlines in the ruins of Madrid where Julian is writing a letter home. The second is in the middle of the film when he comes home to his village, Fuentaduenja, on the Tajo river, on three day's leave. The father is called from the fields, we view the embrace of father and son, the happiness of the mother, grandmother, and brother. The third scene reveals our soldier Julian training young peasant boys in the village square for future battles. All those scenes were real: Julian had fought in Madrid, he lived his whole life in Fuentaduenja, but of course, the scenes had to be reenacted in the sense as we have already explained above.

Why are people opposed to organized, re-enacted shooting in documentary films? Because they think it makes the film less truthful, it undermines the audience's confidence in its authenticity, or perhaps they are just clinging to narrow classifications and definitions of film art and end up declaring that asking people to act before the camera belongs solely to the domain of the fiction film. Of course, there are some dangers in applying re-enactment to documentary films, but we will come to that later. If persons opposed to re-enacted scenes consider the fact truthfully that everything must be filmed just as it is, just as it happens, then our films would show people constantly staring into the camera, because that is what really happens when you photograph people and that would be the truth, at least according to our opponents. So can we say that re-enactment starts with the interference of the director or cameraman into the 'natural' behaviour of people by insisting that they 'do not look into the camera'. But it is well known that in most documentary films the director goes further than this basic intrusion, he insists that actions be repeated, he organizes new circumstances or situations, especially in films where the personal element is an important aspect of the film.

Should repeating scenes and re-enactment in documentary film be tolerated? Does it harm the honesty or integrity of the film? This depends on what kind of scene or notion was chosen to be re-enacted. In order to express the truth, such scenes should be directly related to the central ideological theme, should be typical and characteristic for the situation, and should be acted convincingly, possibly by the same people at the same place of the original scene. I remember the value and strength of such personal, re-enacted scenes from the first showing of the film BORINAGE in Brussels. After the show, some people approached me excitedly, and said, 'That is not true, such situations do not and cannot exist in our country – it is faked.' I could calmly respond by saying, 'Please buy a train ticket to Mons tomorrow, proceed to the village of Monobloc and ask for the young mineworker Delplanc and see for yourself how he lives, what he earns, what worries his mother and when you come back, tell me that I did not film the truth.'

The young miner Delplanc appears in the film BORINAGE. He leaves the mine and comes home. He places the few coins he has earned that week on the table for his mother. The old woman divides the money; so much for the rent of the house, so much for food, just enough for potatoes and some lard, so much... and then there is no more. It is cold in the room because there is no coal in a miner's house in the Borinage. The water they use has to be retrieved from a dirty pit from the back of the house, and then has to be purified. The unbelieving spectator of Brussels will see all this for himself at the house of Delplanc, but many spectators had already decided to believe what they saw based on its penetrating, convincing documentary quality.

But this is not the whole truth, even if the audience discovers for itself that every scene and every shot is authentic. That is not sufficient. We need to show the interrelationship between the facts and general events and their revolutionary development. In BORINAGE, after the personal scene with Delplanc we show the general situation in Monobloc – of the four-hundred houses two-hundred are empty – the miners cannot pay their rent to the mining company and are evicted from their homes and forced to live in broken-down barracks near Jemappes which are left over from World War I. But they struggle against the evictions. A miner's family has to be evicted. And so when the sheriff enters their home to confiscate their furniture for public sale, neighbours and friends resist by sitting patiently for hours and hours on every piece of furniture, every table, the stove, even on the cupboard. The sheriff doesn't dare touch the people who are protecting the property of their comrade by occupying it. He does not want a scandal in the workers' section and he and his assistants finally decide to leave.

Another important point about giving a truthful, realistic picture of the Borinage was to find and to film typical events after the big strike of 1932. The strike was lost, betrayed by the social democratic leadership – none of the Belgian newspapers except the 'Drapeau Rouge' even mentioned it after the strike was lost. We observed a general exhaustion and indifference among the masses for any new action. Superficially, this indifference emerged the dominant ambience. Should we have filmed the fact that the

Henri Storck (right) and Joris Ivens, filming BORINAGE.

Organized or real demonstration? A gathering of miners in the Borinage.

general meetings were badly attended by the miners? Was this average state of affairs typical for the situation? Or should we have looked more thoroughly for other defining events. After the strike was lost we noticed the new, upcoming forces continuing the solidarity, the optimism and the militancy of the strike, carrying new hope for the coming battles for workers' rights. These forces could be discovered in the unspectacular, small workers committees, which sprung up all over the Borinage. These committees assembled around the simple and concrete daily needs of the miners' families. 'One bucket of coal for every family every week.' From the windows of their houses the miners could easily see enormous heaps of coal, the stocks of the mining company, rotting away, unsold, the price on the market per ton being too low – it was unprofitable to sell during the crisis years.

The heaping mounds of black coal are surrounded by barbed wire and armed guards. It is of this coal, the very coal the miner himself dug out of the earth of his Borinage, that he wants one bucket a week for his family. It is a just demand, around which every worker – liberal, communist, socialist, catholic – can unite.

It was these typical yet small, basic united-front actions which allowed one to witness the growth of a new revolutionary force. Naturally, we filmed some of the committee meetings. Often, in re-enacted scenes. Of course, the truthful filming of events and facts is still no guarantee that a documentary film will tell the truth. Single facts may be filmed truthfully, but by means of dishonest editing and a distorted commentary, big lies can be told, as we see in the films serving imperialist purposes which promote war. To tell the truth, we have to show facts and events, in conflict and in their interrelationships to create films in a socialist realist manner.

The composition and editing of the scenes has to be done honestly, realistically and in relation to the running commentary. We have to tell more than the superficial truth, we have to go below the surface of our theme, we have to reach the real 'big truth', which is not exactly a scientific expression, but hopefully you understand my point.

Allow me to add a personal note about BORINAGE. The film was a step forward in my development as a filmmaker. At the time of its production, I had just returned from the Soviet Union, where I had learned to work with the socialist realist method in the praxis of making SONG OF HEROES with the Komsomol in Magnitogorsk and in collaboration with the Moscow film workers. I gained a deeper insight and understanding regarding the task and responsibilities of the art of cinematography. BORINAGE was strengthened by the heroic struggle of the Belgian workers. And it is here that I took my first steps in the direction of socialist realism, having put behind me the flawed abstract theories regarding the function and formalist tendencies of art.

Let us now return to the question of the introduction of personal scenes into the treatment of documentary films. First, it should be stated that many documentary themes do not need personalization. I am thinking of the reportage films, such as the excellent front films which lately have been shot by the Korean cameraman. Add to that the so-called publicity films of Wernik. May I remind the reader of such broad films as Roman Karmen's SOVIET TURKMENISTAN, in which the theme of the Turkmenistan Canal resembles a romantic poem, while Kissiljow's Wolga-Don-Canal film also contains such episodes. Then there are the many films in which the general events speak so strongly for themselves in such a poetically dramatic or epic manner that no personal scenes are needed. Compare this with TRASA W-Z, the Berlin Festival Film, or NEW EARTH, among others. A more personal treatment should only be applied by a scriptwriter and director when it really deepens the content, when it improves its multi-faceted views, and when it enriches the form of expression and makes the development of the theme clearer when emphasis is placed on the people. Other factors to be considered are necessity to make the style a more popular one in order to reach a broader public.

There are documentary films in which the personal actions form a continuous line, where one or more persons are being seen throughout the enire film. A classic example of such a film is one of the first documentary films ever made, Robert Flaherty's NANOOK OF THE NORTH, made in 1922. It is the story of the hard life of an Eskimo and his family on the tundra and ice floes. Another recent example already mentioned is Vroctavski's film portrait of a village. The central theme is built around the story of Kujama. General aspects and particular points are interwoven and act upon each other along dramaturgical lines. Herbert Kline's FORGOTTEN VILLAGE, shot in Mexico, should also be mentioned. In such films, the director should always remain aware of the fact that the personal action should develop itself organically and logically out of the content. The personal story should emerge out of the underestimation of the possibilities of forms of expression which the theme by itself can give. In such cases the personal story becomes only a nice vehicle in which the theme is driven around to be admired by the public. The personal story should also not exceed the framework of the thematic material – nor should the spectator's interest be forcefully pushed in a direction of personal action because then the real theme and general notions are pushed too far into the background.

We see we are on dangerous ground here with our documentary films. One could even say we are closing in on the fiction film. Now, by overstepping our possibilities we risk obtaining false notes in our film and ultimately damaging the discipline and style of our documentary, thus placing doubts in the spectator's mind regarding the authenticity and integrity of our films. Because it seems that if the spectator smells the studio, the actor, or the sets in a documentary, he will also not believe the facts. It is evident that the personal story, and as a result, many re-enacted scenes, have to be handled with great care in the documentary. Discussions among filmmakers, writers, critics, and the public should clarify and help to open up its horizons and to mark the limits of the documentary, not in a dogmatic way, but in connection with the praxis of courageous production.

The Soviet filmmakers took such steps, and created a new style of documentary film - the artistic documentary. Great, monumental films about the heroic battles of the Red Army and the Soviet people in their great patriotic war such as the battle of Stalingrad and the fall of Berlin. In this connection, another classic, but older, Soviet film should be mentioned, Eisenstein's POTEMKIN. The interesting fact however is that in capitalist countries, another movement can be seen emerging, the tendency of the fiction film to resemble the documentary. In their so-called neo-realistic films the Italian directors apply many documentary methods, not only in finding original themes and script ideas, but also in the actual production. In films like THE BICYCLE THIEF, ROMA CITTA APERTA, PAISA, ROME 11 HEURES, many non-actors were used while real homes, streets, towns, villages, roads, and fields serve as locations. Filming was done in real rain; just like in authentic documentaries.

In this article, I have mainly linked re-enacted scenes to the obtaining of personal shots and scenes in our films but we should never forget that reality, the lives of the people, remains vibrant and constitutes a rich source for such personal scenes. With an alert cameraman, such scenes can be captured directly from life, and the director does not need to fall back on re-enactment. It is this kind of specific privilege that the documentary filmmaker – as contrasted with the fiction filmmaker – is in direct contact with life and that he has to utilize this privilege with daring. His documentary script should always have enough flexibility to include special scenes which cannot be foreseen.

Director, cameraman, assistants should always be on the lookout for personal, emotional scenes that belong to the province of the film that they are making, and spontaneously act upon these opportunities. Many times these sorts of natural scenes can even be anticipated, if the filmmaker himself is deeply involved in the action being filmed. In many such situations, the camera can be a hindrance to the normal activities of people. The fact that they are filmed annoys them and makes them act unnatural. Older people start to act like children, and children like older people. The director's and cameraman's experience and skills can avert this, of course, but the camera remains an intruder. I often wonder why, in cases of spontaneous scenes that the camera is not hidden or camouflaged. The hidden camera in a brief-case is not anything new, it was used years ago in experimental films – but more as an indiscretion to film people in funny situations on the streets or on sport places. It could, of course, be used for better purposes. In the years between 1930 and 1940, in my unit, the hidden camera was also used for other reasons, namely to avoid detection by the police while filming strike situations or militant demonstrations on the streets. Not only did the police not discover the camera, but we also got amazing, startling results of the natural activities of people, as in INDONESIA CALLING for example, among the dockerworkers and Indonesian seamen in Sydney's harbour.

Of course, not all aspects of re-enacted scenes can be covered here within the limitations of our articles. There is, for instance, the question of the specific dramaturgy when we introduce real people. It has to be different from fiction films, because the psychological aspects of character development are visually less developed in the documentary. The danger here is that people become more or less schematic, and their development mechanical. The documentary often shows that a person has changed along different stages of the film. But how he really evolved meaning through his thoughts, his doubts, his relation to other people, this is much more difficult to show. It takes a special dramaturgical and documentary treatment, a skillful use of commentary, to overcome those difficulties, to make people into real human beings in relation to other people and their work.

And if a writer or director wants to express this theme more personally, in a way which lies in the domain between documentary film and fiction film, he must realize that he is losing one of the qualities of the documentary film, that is that the audience can directly control the precision and integrity of the facts and real people. He not only enters with the form of expression of his artwork into the domain of fiction film but also into the realm of the different levels of truth which the audience experiences in seeing a fiction film. This is, somehow, how I see the function of the artistic documentary.

It is important for the future development of the documentary film that questions regarding re-enactment, personalizations, and, of course, also all other forms of expression and style, like the introduction of lyrical, poetic, epic, and didactic elements into our films, should be widely discussed and applied in the upcoming productions. In many countries, there are complaints that the development of the documentary is at present at a standstill, and that they are being made too much 'Schablone' like. Still, we should not forget that in 1952 our Polish documentary productions brought important and interesting results.

The effects of good documentaries can be so immediate and tremendous because they can be of such a great help to motivate the people into fulfilling the Five-Year Plan. Everything has to be done to win for the documentary film the popularity and prestige it deserves. Here, in the People's Democracies, the documentary film enjoys the full support of the government. How different this is in capitalist countries. There the commercial film companies which are controlled by the banks, are afraid of the documentary film because the real documentary tells the truth about daily life and the struggles of the people. Such themes are taboo over there, where the film, as a regular trade commodity, is busy hiding or falsifying those very themes.

In those countries, the documentary is only developing among the militant films, which capture the people's movement for peace and their struggle for independence. The film moguls fear truth and reality so much that they call the documentary 'poison'. But among progressive audiences and honest critics in the West the documentary has another name, 'the conscience of cinema'. An honourable name for the documentary in countries where the average fiction film production is dominated by Hollywood which tries its utmost, using the most loathsome methods, to condition the people for a third world war.

How different from the situation in the Soviet Union, in the Peoples Democracies, in People's China, where the newsreel, the documentary film, and the fiction film together fulfill their great mission in keeping the peace while helping to build a new world. There are young filmmakers from the film institute and from the field, who have joined the ranks of documentary filmmakers. Together with the more experienced film crews, assistants, scriptwriters and cameramen, they will solve the questions that I have mentioned in this article, and then they will make films, appropriate to the rapid development towards socialism, and simultaneously and effectively reaching an even broader audience. All of us should approach our tasks with more daring, and take risks with new concepts. We can afford to be daring because we have the goals and vision of socialist realism and the tradition, experience, and guidance of Soviet cinematic art behind us.

In the earlier days of documentary film, during the so-called avant-garde movement, a search for new expression often became abstract and an adventurous experiment led to a formalistic dead end. Socialist realism will not only protect us from that, but it will lead us to richer developments in both the content and form of our work.

Film and Progress (1963)

A speech by Joris Ivens presented during the forum of the III rd International Festival of Moscow, 12 July 1963

Film is a product of progress and has simultaneously become an active part of it. Film has become, in return, a force which can accelerate progress, but also slow it down. Film and progress have become intimately intertwined. Of course in the early days technical and scientific progress were important, it remains important. New documentary camera techniques are still rapidly developing. For raw film we are provided with better and faster emulsions. Projection techniques offer new sizes and the Czech filmmakers invented the Lanterna Magica, the multiple screen, while the Soviet Union has its Cinerama. But still we could do more.

We should not be modest in our demands for technical progress. I hope that some of the wonderful inventiveness and scientific research of the incredible equipment used in the sputniks will be made available to our technical camera and film equipment constructors.

Of course, nowadays books are not written any better because the typewriter has replaced the pen. But that is a different story with us filmmakers. The camera is our direct reproduction apparatus of reality. We documentary filmmakers daily face reality with our cameras, so we want to have the best tools known to men – in a word, we want our full share of technical progress.

Let us now turn our attention to our relation to social progress. Fundamental to this relation is the reality in which the film artist is living. Allow me also to reflect a moment on the idea of the artist and his reality. Reality is never static, it is dynamic, in flux. We are living in its midst, we are part of it. Our attitudes as filmmakers toward reality remain essential. Most of us, I think, consider reality as the real source of our artwork. Of course, it's not just the reproduction of reality, but in recreating it, enriching it, making it inspiring through application of our talent, creative imagination and technical skills. If we see our task as artist in this way and if we want to take part in the progress of humanity, then we must make honest appraisals of reality in order to fully comprehend our attitude toward that reality and the society we are living in. Here is where the consciousness and the awareness of his responsibility towards the people of the artist enters. This is the entry point for his ideology and our philosophy. Here everything becomes complicated and simple at the same time for an artist. It boils down to what do I want to say, in what way, to whom, and for what purpose. Does one become an introvert artist; do we become documentary filmmakers; or is fiction film our format; or do we want to share our emotions and experiences with the audience? Personal temperament also enters into this choice. Do we become a militant artist, a contemplating artist?

I remember what an artist's choice is. I know of a painter who once said, 'I want to have a practical palette with healthy colors.' That was the Dutch painter Van Gogh. As documentary artists we are very close to reality and the documentary film is married to progress. You could say also our profession deals directly with the daily events of life. We have to be close to the people we are going to film, live with them, and gain their confidence. Our work enters deeply into their struggles and activities; we reflect their aspirations. An artist has to live in the same way that history breathes. Our documentary work tries to remain in step with progress. How? The documentary filmmaker must always find new ways to make films, never remaining too satisfied with what he has done, and starting every new film fresh with new audacity, daring, and imagination.

During my work with the young filmmakers of Cuba, Chile, and Mali, I often urged them to attack reality. Not only in the conception of their film, but also during shooting. I urged them to insert their cameras into the action, in order to get away from over-used passive camerawork. This method of attacking reality was in order to push documentary filmmaking to a higher level.

For example, during the filming of the fishermen's harbour in Mansanilla, Cuba, we had to shoot the old dilapidated cabins the fishermen lived in and where the children played in the dirt and mud. This could not be filmed with a kind of neutral and sentimental camera eye looking for fine composition, but had to be filmed with a camera that moved around indignantly, accusingly, because the mud was not just wet earth, it was dirty, horrible, and unhealthy for children with bare feet. Through the camera eye, the audience should be aware of how awful and humiliating it is to live for generation after generation in these cabins where inside the wind just blows a little less than it does outside.

In France, in the USA, and in Canada, new ways of documentary filmmaking are being explored. These explorations go under the name of 'Cinéma Vérité', more correctly called 'Cinema Direct'. New ingenious lighting and noiseless 16mm cameras are used, microphones and synchronism without wires. In France, Jean Rouch and Mario Ruspolli are successfully exploring this method of filmmaking, and their method has been further developed, with higher artistic value, by Chris Marker, France's most outstanding documentarist, who produced the remarkable film about the citizens of Paris and Paris itself, LE JOLI MAI (THE PRETTY MONTH OF MAY).

Cinéma Vérité should not to be compared with such great film movements as neo-realism which developed in Italy after the war, but still, it offers new possibilities for the creation of documentary films. All these young movements and new artistic endeavors should be accepted and stimulated; they must go off the beaten track to explore new territory. An obstacle to the progress of film art however, is that films continue to be made in conditions that require a sphere of conformity or imitation of formats, once considered new. It is possible that our films will someday fall behind the desires and needs of the audience. It is also possible that the artist sometimes will not be in tune with current tastes. But progress will mitigate these situations.

An obstacle to artistic progress is censorship of the truth. A number of films made lately about the fight for independence in Cuba and Algeria, or about the action of trade movements, were prohibited and, therefore, did not reach large audiences. I come now to a point where progress is not some vague idea, but a very concrete one and directly linked to filmmaking – in Cuba, Algeria, Indonesia, Mali, Ghana, Tanganyika and other countries.

I was myself closely associated with the birth of documentary filmmaking in both Cuba and Mali. The film production at the Cuban Institute of Cinema Art and Industry, the ICAIC, is a perfect example of how film and progress are linked together. The Cubans never had a film industry before their revolution. And now, it is wonderful to see how quick the young people took filmmaking into their own hands. In four years of production, they have made eight feature films and about seventy documentaries, and a considerable number of educational films and cartoons to assist the healthy progress of their young nation.

We must now return for a moment to the relationship between the artist and reality. The artist not only deals with reality while he is making a film but also in the projection of his films for the people. When audiences see his films, this seeing becomes a real audience experience. The film, a work of art, if effective, enters into the daily reality of the people.

Director Gerassimov and critic Yureniev discussed filmmakers at the III International Film Festival of 'kinship with the people' that not only concerned the period of conception and realization of the film, but also the period in which a film as artwork lives among the people. This kinship should also be fostered in the dialogue of the filmmaker with the audience. The projected film should ask questions of the audiences and place them in an active relation to the actions and characters in the film. The filmmaker should sometimes agree and at other times disagree with the public – to deepen their understanding. The public in the silent and dark projection halls will ask emotional and intellectual questions.

There is a constant dialogue going on between filmmaker and the audience. This daily dialogue with millions of people on thousands of projection screens will influence social progress, the progress of mankind. So it is worthwhile for the film artist to have an honest, dynamic conversation with his audience; a stimulating conversation that raises their involvement to new unknown heights of emotions, knowledge, experience, and consciousness. Here lies our responsibility as film artists of the ethical and aesthetic value of our art, here should reign respect for the audience.

This dialogue forms a sort of potential emotional field full of currents, countercurrents, short cuts and tensions between the audience and the screen. We can spoil this dynamic aspect with a talkative, boring, all-explaining, all-knowing commentary that lulls the people to sleep. Such commentaries are the current affliction of many documentary films. With such texts we cannot conduct a proper dialogue with the audience.

Also, if we get lazy in our search for new forms for our films, we begin to cheat the audiences. After all, you invited them to an open dialogue, you asked them to see and pay to see your film! To serve progress, our films should not only look good in the cutting room, but they should come to life on the big screen for the audience. So with our cameras and projection lenses we should keep our films in focus – sharp and clear. We should be in focus with the times, with the present, in order to reveal the future. The French poet Paul Eluard wrote:

> *De l'horizon d'un homme, à l'horizon de toute humanité* – from the horizon of man to the horizon of all humanity.

Notes

Joris Ivens and the Documentary Project

1   Carlos Boker, *Joris Ivens, Film Maker*, UMI Research Press 1978. I am only referring to this specific assertion, made after a long discussion and theoretical interpretation of the Ivens path, and not to the otherwise important, thorough research included in the same book.

2   Here it is worth remembering that, when the documentary form was created, the classical narrative conventions had already been well established, generally forbidding the actor *to look at the camera*. So the fact that documentary could accept that look – exempted as it was, at least in part, from the aim of psychological identification – can be seen just as another sign of that new *balance of power*. While fiction establishes the act of looking as a *one way power*, documentary appears to give that power back, re-establishing a new equilibrium between those who film and those who are filmed.

3   Taking account what was said before, this notion of semi-automatic construction is of course well beyond the idea of documentary as a purely automatic gesture, or a primitive way of filming. By this time, cinema had in fact learned only too well that the use of the camera is the exercise of an unquestionable power, and therefore *control*. Moreover, *documentary was in fact a decisive part of what we could call the auteur* cinema, an area where one could express a personal view and *vision*. Therefore, the new stage was a further development, not a regression; an important step in the understanding of the specific mixture of objectivity and subjectivity that is part of all films.

4   CHRONIQUE D'UN ÉTÉ, directed by Jean Rouch and Edgar Morin (1961).

5   The first real collaborative film was in fact the episode of LOIN DU VIETNAM (1967), signed by Ivens but actually shot by Marceline in North Vietnam.

6   As many others of the supposedly *direct cinema* tradition in the sixties, LE 17ÈME PARALLÈLE is in fact a mixture of some synchronous sound recording and large post-synchronised bits, or a mix of direct and post-sync sound. However, in no way may this be used to question the nature of the revolution and the effective consequence of the new method on the whole construction of the film.

A Way of Seeing: Joris Ivens's Documentary Century

1   Eric Hobsbawm, *Age of Extremes: The Short Twentieth Century 1914-1991*(London, Michael Joseph 1995), p. 5.

2   Joris Ivens, *The Camera and I* (Berlin, Seven Seas Publishers 1969), p. 137.

3   See also Bill Nichols's chapter 'The Domain of Documentary in his *Representing Reality* (Indiana University Press, Bloomington/Indianapolis 1991), pp. 3-31.

4   Étienne Souriau (ed.), *L'univers filmique*, Flammarion, Paris, 1953. Souriau, a French 'Filmologue', introduced and defined these terms as part of a terminology to study film: the 'filmic' being everything that appears in the film; the profilmic is everything that exists in reality that receives a special destination in the film (like actors, props, decors) and leaves its traces on the celluloid. Digitally created elements e.g., do not have a profilmic existence. Distinct from the profilmic, the a-filmic refers to everything in reality that has no such destination, but can become profilmic (like locations and people in documentaries).

5   See Eva Hohenberger, *Die Wirklichkeit des Films: Dokumentarfilm – Ethnographischer Film – Jean Rouch*, Georg Olms A.G, Hildesheim, 1988, especially pp. 26-60; and Manfred Hattendorf, *Dokumentarfilm und Authentizität: Ästhetik und Pragmatik einer Gattung* (Verlag Ölschlager, Konstanz 1994).

6   Frank Kessler, 'Fakt oder Fiktion? Zum pragmatischen Status dokumentarischer Bilder', *Montage/AV*. (2 July 1998): p. 75; my translation.

7   See Paul Ricoeur, *Du texte à l'action: Essais d'herméneutique, II* (Paris, Éditions du Seuil, 1986), p. 115.

8   Maurice Merleau-Ponty, *Phénoménologie de la perception* (Paris, Éditions Gallimard 1945), pp. 376-377; my translation.

9   Hans Georg Gadamer, *Wahrheit und Methode: Grundzüge einer philosophischen Hermeneutik* (Tübingen, J.C.B. Mohr 1960/1990), p. 311.

10 Carl Plantinga makes the distinction between a fictive and an assertive *stance* to distinguish fiction from non-fiction. Carl Plantinga, *Rhetoric and Representation in Nonfiction Film* (London, Cambridge University Press 1997), pp. 15-21.

11 Siegfried Kracauer, *History: The Last Things Before The Last*, (New York, Oxford University Press 1969; Princeton, Markus Wiener Publishers 1995), p. 47 (page citations refer to the reprint edition).

12 Forsyth Hardy, ed., *Grierson on Documentary*, (Faber and Faber, London 1979 (first published 1946)), p. 37.

13 Kracauer, p. 47. The 'realistic tendency' and the 'formative tendency' are also the basic concepts Kracauer uses in his Theory of Film: The Redemption of a Physical Reality (Cambridge, Oxford University Press 1960).

14 Kracauer, *History*, p. 56.

15 Kracauer, *History*, pp. 90-91.

16 Basil Wright, 'Documentary Today', *The Penguin Film Review* 2 (January 1947); reprinted in Ian Aitken (ed.), *The Documentary Film Movement: An Anthology* (Edinburgh, Edinburgh University Press 1998), p. 238.

17 Joris Ivens, 'Documentary: Subjectivity and Montage', in this volume, p. 250-260

18 Aitken, o.c., p. 239.

19 Hardy, p. 113.

20 Paul Rotha, *Documentary Film* (London, Faber and Faber 1952 (first published in 1936)), p. 75.

21 See Hobsbawm, o.c., especially the chapters 'Into the Economic Abyss' and 'The Fall of Liberalism', pp. 85-141.

22 Ivens, see note 17.

23 Reviewers cited in William Alexander, *Film on the Left. American Documentary Film from 1931 to 1942* (Princeton NJ, Princeton University Press, 1981), p. 122.

24 Joris Ivens, 'Long Live Cinéma-Vérité' in Rosalind Delmar, *Joris Ivens: 50 years of filmmaking* (British Film Institute, London 1979), p. 111 (first published in French in *Les Lettres Françaises*, March 1963).

25 See page 4 and note 15.

26 Quoted from a titlecard by Hans Schoots, *Gevaarlijk leven: Een biografie van Joris Ivens* (Jan Mets, Amsterdam), p. 66; my translation. An English translation of this thorough and enlighting biography is in preparation and will be published by Amsterdam University Press.

27 Joris Ivens and Robert Destanque, *Aan welke kant en in welk heelal. De geschiedenis van een leven*, (Amsterdam, Meulenhof 1983), p. 116; my translation.

28 Ivens and Destanque, p. 101.

29 See Rotha, pp. 79-101. 'Broadly speaking, the documentary falls into four groups, each of which demands an individual estimate because each results from a different approach to naturally existing material.'

30 Rotha, p. 107.

31 Rotha, p. 88.

32 Ivens, *Camera and I*,1969, o.c., pp. 136-137.

33 Quoted in Schoots, p. 337.

34 Hobsbawm, p. 234.

35 Interview with Joris Ivens and Marceline Loridan in Rosalind Delmar, *Joris Ivens: 50 years of film-making*, (London, British Film Institute 1979), p. 71.

36 Joris Ivens in an interview with Hans Schoots, *De Groene Amsterdammer*, May 7, 1986, p. 12.

The Song of Movement

1 Joris Ivens in a letter to Miep Balgerie-Guérin, 14 January 1925, Collection Miep Balgerie-Guérin/European Foundation Joris Ivens, Nijmegen.

2 See note 1, 10 November 1926, MBG/ESJI.

3 Adress by Joris Ivens in the Nijmegen Museum 'Commanderie van Sint Jan' on the opening of the exhibition and the presentation of the catalogue *Rondom Joris Ivens, wereldcineast 1898-1934*, 16 November 1988.

4 L.J. Jordaan, *Joris Ivens* (De Spieghel, Amsterdam-Het Kompas, Mechelen 1931), p. 5.

5 Ibid., p. 11.

6   For information see: Urias Nooteboom and André Stufkens 'De bron, De familie Ivens en Joris Ivens jeugd in Nijmegen', in *Rondom Joris Ivens, wereldcineast 1898-1934*, pp. 12-32, Het wereldvenster/Nijmeegs Museum 'Commanderie van Sint Jan' 1988, The C.A.P. Ivens archives are in the Municipal Archives of Nijmegen.

7   C.A.P. Ivens, manuscript 'De fotografie in de laatste veertig jaren', Nijmegen 1927, written for *Veertig jaren fotografie*, gedenkboekje der NAFV 1887-1927, Amsterdam 1927.

8   *Provinciale Geldersche&Nijmeegsche Courant*, nr. 102, 2 May 1917.

9   Ibid., 5 May 1917.

10   Photo albums in the Collection Nooteboom-Ivens, Den Bosch.

11   Typed report in response to article by W.H. Idzerda, 'Herinneringen', Joris Ivens Archives/ESJI Nijmegen.

12   See note 4, p. 5.

13   Joris Ivens and Robert Destanques, *Aan welke kant en in welk heelal* (Amsterdam, Meulenhoff 1983), p. 66.

14   Address by C.A.P. Ivens for the first lustrum of 'Religion and Science', 20 February 1907. Collection C.A.P. Ivens in the Municipal Archives, Nijmegen.

15   C.A.P. Ivens and others, *Gedenkboek voor de Waaloverbrugging*, Nijmegen 1936.

16   Eric Hobsbawm, *Een Eeuw van Uitersten* (Age of Extremes) (Spectrum Utrecht 1995), p. 22.

17   See note 4, p. 7.

18   Interview of Joris Ivens by Hans Schoots, *De Groene Amsterdammer*, 7 May 1986.

19   See note 1, undated 'Tuesday evening'.

20   H.C.L. Jaffé, 'De Nederlandse Stijlgroep en haar sociale utopie', in *Over utopie en werkelijkheid in de beeldende kunst, Verzamelde opstellen van H.C.L.Jaffe (1915-1984)* (Amsterdam, Meulenhoff 1986), p. 125.

21   Quote from 'La vie mène la danse', unpublished autobiography of Germaine Krull, quoted in Kim Sighel, *Germaine Krull, photographer of modernity* (The MIT Press Cambridge, Massachusetts; London, England; Schirmer/Mosel Verlag/Museum Folkwang, Essen 1999).

22   Joris Ivens, 'Vor der Film – Die Brücke', a lecture delivered in Moscow, 1935, manuscript JIA.

23   See note 1, 1 November 1922, letter from Schöneberg-Berlin.

24   Hendrik Marsman, letter to Elisabeth de Roos, 20 May 1926, Literary Museum, The Hague.

25   Walter Benjamin in 'Kleine Geschichte der Photographie', 1931. Translation in *Het kunstwerk in het tijdperk van zijn technische reproduceerbaarheid* (SUN, Nijmegen 1985), p. 60.

26   Hans Schoots, *Gevaarlijk leven. Een biografie van Joris Ivens*, Jan Mets (Amsterdam 1995), p. 54.

27   Ibid., p. 55.

28 Thanking J.F. Haffmans, Utrecht.

29 Erich Wichman, film script, z.t., z.d. in Royal Library, The Hague and in the Wichman archives in the Central Museum, Utrecht. Quoted in J.F. Haffmans, *Geest, koolzuur en zijk*, 1999.

30 Joris Ivens in a letter to Menno ter Braak, 16 October 1927, collection Film League, Film Museum, Amsterdam.

31 Joris Ivens in a letter to Ed. Pelster on 25 October 1927, Collection Hans Wegner/European Foundation Joris Ivens, Nijmegen.

32 Joris Ivens, *Autobiografie van een filmer* (Born Publishers, Amsterdam/Assen 1970), p. 32.

33 Joris Ivens, 'Amateur cinematography and its possibilities', lectures delivered in the period from January 1928 - March 1929, among others for the Dutch Amateur Photographers Society (January 1928) and the International Exhibition for Film in The Hague (15 April 1928) organized by Piet Zwart. Publications in various magazines.

34 Ibid.

35 Menno ter Braak, *Cinema Militans*, De Gemeenschap, Utrecht, 1929.

36 See note 13, p. 76.

37 See note 4, pp. 10 and 11.

38 Joris Ivens in a letter to Arthur Lehining, 8 June 1927, See note 6, p. 41.

39 Joris Ivens, 'Autobiografie van een filmer', Born Publishers, Amsterdam/Assen, 1970, p. 28.

40 Joris Ivens, 'Zur Methode de Documentarischen Films, ins besondere des Films Komsomol', Moscow 1932. Translation in this volume, pp. 230-237.

41 Joris Ivens, 'Notes on the avant-garde documentary', Translation in this volume, pp. 224-226. See note 6, p. 180.

42 Joris Ivens, 'The artistic power of the documentary', address given at the International Congress for Photography in Leipzig, 1932; see note 6, p. 182, Translation in this volume, pp. 227-229.

43 See note 41.

44 Ibid.

45 Ibid.

46 Basil Wright, *The Long View*, London, 1974, p. 117.

47 Johan van der Keuken, lecture on the opening of the exhibition *Rondom Joris Ivens, wereldcineast 1898-1934*, Nijmegen Musem, 18 November 1988. Published in *Film and TV maker*, nr. 289, Amsterdam 1989.

48 Joirs Ivens, 'Fascism and the film', in *Links Richten*, nr. 8, 1 May 1933.

49 See note 34.

50 See note 21.

51 Bertolt Brecht, Notes on dialectical dramaturgy', in *Bertolt Brecht Theatrale experimenten en politiek*, SUN, Nijmegen, 1972, p. 32.

52 See note 26, p. 101.

53 Francois Furet, *Le passé d'une illusion, Essai sur l'idée communiste au XXe siècle*, (Editions Robert Laffont, Paris 1995).

54 See note 6, p. 169.

High-tech Avant-garde: PHILIPS RADIO

1   During the production of PHILIPS RADIO Ivens surrounded himself with a choice of young assistants, who learned the trade from him: Mark Kolthof and John Fernhout contributed extensively to the camera work; Helene van Dongen was production assistant and edited the film; Lou Lichtveld was responsible for the sound. In the meantime, others such as Willem Bon and Jan Hin worked on various film assignments Ivens had been given. This was Studio Joris Ivens as he himself called the group. The French cameraman Jean Dréville came to Eindhoven for additional shots.

2   Apart from Ivens, Philips gave another avant-gardist an assignment: Hans Richter, a German. The two filmmakers had different tasks. Richter was to show the role radio played in the people's lives, whereas Ivens was to make a portrait of Philips as a modern radio factory. The two films, PHILIPS RADIO and EUROPA RADIO, were simultaneously screened in Amsterdam on 28 September 1931.

3   Immediately after completing the editing, Ivens gave a summary of the film in a letter to his client, in which he also distinguished six parts and an introduction and an epilogue. Ivens to Philips/Numann, 10 June 1931 (Philips Company Archives PCA 185.1). I am grateful to Philips Company Archives (PCA) for allowing me full access to its holdings during my research.

4   Despite its short length, the communication section has its own place in the film. Not only is it a representation of the notion of communication that can be found in the exact centre of the film, but it is also the only fragment showing the purpose of a radio. Ivens considered this part a separate 'chapter' of the film (see note 3). It is possible to assume that its short length is the consequence of a cut, made before the first screening in September 1930. Philips wanted Ivens to restrict himself to what went on inside the factory. Philips had a good reason for this: Hans Richter was working on a film about the social role of radio communication, EUROPA RADIO. Philips (or Richter?) would not have allowed Ivens to enter Richter's territory.

5   'Shooting at Philips', in *NRC*, 7 February 1931.

6   K. Broos, 'Fifo 1929 – the New Photography', in F. Bool and K. Broos, *Fotografie in Nederland, 1920-1940* (The Hague 1979), pp. 28-43.

7   The original score is kept at the Bifi archives in Paris. I am grateful to Hans Schoots for supplying this information.

8   'Impressive industrial film of Philips', in *Haagse Post*, 3 October 1931.

9   L.J. Jordaan, 'Netherlands' first sound film', in *De Groene Amsterdammer*, 3 October 1931.

10 Ivens had thought of this scene rather early. See 'A Dutch radio sound film' in *NRC*, 8 February 1931. Elsewhere in the film a loudspeaker is shown and the command booms: 'Hello, hello, machine 2B, five hundred pieces,' while a hand writes the figures on a notice board.

11 Agreement between Ivens and Philips Radio Ltd, 1 September 1930 (PCA). The contract had been negotiated for some months (correspondence in PCA 185.1). Ivens promised to complete an 'institutional film' of about 800 metres' length, 'which will give an image of the production of radios in the factories in Eindhoven and elsewhere in the Netherlands by the client.' The contract price amounted to 9500 Dutch guilders. Philips guaranteed royalties of at least 2500 Dutch guilders. Travel and accommodation expenses were to be refunded by Philips, as were the cost of film titles and special effects.

12 Agreement between Ivens and Philips Radio Ltd, 2 May 1931 (PCA). Relevant correspondence can be found in PCA 185.1. It is an extension of the agreement of 1 September 1930. Philips ordered the 'composition, editing and production of a soundtrack'. Synchronization would take place at the Tobis studio in Paris. The soundtrack was to be ready 22 June 1931. The contract price amounted to 23,000 Dutch guilders, excluding 1,500 Dutch guilders for expenses.

13 'A Dutch radio sound film?', in *NRC*, 8 February 1931.

14 'For thirty metres of film', in *De Telegraaf*, 25 December 1930. It is not impossible that Lou Lichtveld wrote this report.

15 Conversation with Dr. L.A.M. Lichtveld, Hilversum, 30 November 1988. After his visit to Berlin Lichtveld wrote the article 'Fischinger musical films', in *De Groene Amsterdammer*, 31 January 1931.

16 'A Dutch radio sound film?', in *NRC*, 8 February 1931.

17 'The Philips radio film', in *De Maasbode*, 2 June 1931.

18 'The Philips radio film sonorized', in *NRC*, 30 May 1931. Dr. Vermeulen of Philips was to describe the same procedure as follows: 'Every microphone had its own amplifier in the central amplifying room, after which all were united in the mixing room, where 9 potentiometers and a general potentiometer for mixing and regulating have been installed'. Report of a journey to Paris, 26 May 1931 (PCA NL.563).

19 Lou Lichtveld, 'Music of labour', in *De Telegraaf*, 1 June 1931.

20 'The PHILIPS-RADIO film: a conversation with Lou Lichtveld', in *De Maasbode*, 2 June 1931.

21 Lou Lichtveld, 'Where sounds fall silent', in *De Telegraaf*, 30 May 1931.

22 'Joris Ivens's PHILIPS-RADIO film as sound film', in *Algemeen Handelsblad*, 30 May 1931.

23 'The Philips-film by Joris Ivens and Lou Lichtveld', in *NRC*, 29 September 1931. Later the same newspaper published a more favourable judgement: see *NRC* of 9 November and 12 December 1931.

24 M. Sluyser, 'People replaced by machines: Ivens kneels before his new idol', in *Het Volk*, 29 September 1931.

25 Herluf van Merlet, 'Philips' industrial film', in *De Tijd*, 29 September 1931.

26 Ibid.

27 L.J. Jordaan, 'The Netherlands first sound film', in *De Groene Amsterdammer*, 3 October 1931.

28 'Impressive industrial film of Philips', in *Haagsche Post*, 3 October 1931.

29 'In no way is my music independent. I only wanted to illustrate', Lichtveld said to a reporter in *Algemeen Handelsblad*, 30 May 1931. A similar statement in 'A film expedition to the Phohi', in *Algemeen Handelsblad*, 28 February 1931.

30 *Het Volk*, 29 September 1931.

31 Letter from Philips to Capi/Ivens, 6 January 1932 (PCA 185.1). This scene is included in the film print of PHILIPS RADIO kept by the Netherlands Film Museum. This print is practically identical to the film that was first performed in 1931. This can be concluded from what is known about the length and the structure of PHILIPS RADIO in 1931, and furthermore on the basis of the correspondence between Ivens and Philips (PCA 185.1). Ivens's letter to Philips/Numann dated 10 June 1931, in which Ivens describes the length and the structure of the film shortly after completing the picture and sound editing is important. This data corresponds to the print kept in the Film Museum. Also the length, which was '1000 metres' according to Ivens and 997 metres according to the Dutch censorship report of 24 September 1931, approaches that of the preserved print (980 metres). Only some intertitles were added with Ivens's consent.

32 The provincial press, with a large circulation in Eindhoven, made no attempt to disguise its disappointment. It disapproved of the one-sided attention to the machines. 'The Philips' industrial film', in *Eindhovensche en Meierijsche Courant*, 30 September 1931. 'How a filmmaker and a musician see and hear Philips', in *Dagblad van Noord-Brabant*, 30 September 1931.

33 Lou Lichtveld, 'Voice and music in sound film', in *Filmliga*, May 1932, p. 116. Also in Lou Lichtveld, *De geluidsfilm* (Rotterdam 1933), p. 73.

34 L.J. Jordaan. 'Richter – Ruttmann', in *De Groene Amsterdammer*, 22 February 1930.

35 Lou Lichtveld, 'Voice and music in sound film', in *Filmliga*, May 1932, p. 115.

36 Lichtveld characterizes his own work in this way in an interview. 'A film expedition to Phohi', in *Algemeen Handelsblad*, 28 February 1931. This view shows some parallels with the bruitism of the Italian Futurist Russolo.

LA SEINE A RENCONTRÉ PARIS and the Documentary in France in the Fifties

1 Robert Destanques and Joris Ivens, *Joris Ivens et la mémoire d'un regard*, Edition BFB, 1982 and *Joris Ivens, 50 ans de cinéma*, directed by Jean-Loup Passek, Paris, Centre Georges Pompidou, 1979.

2   Robert Grelier, Joris Ivens, Paris, Les Éditeurs Français Réunis, 1965, p. 100; 'LA SEINE A RENCONTRÉ PARIS est un des films les plus achevés de Joris Ivens, voire même un des plus grands films documentaires du cinéma contemporain'.

3   François Porcile, Défense du court-métrage français (Paris, Éditions du Cerf 1965), p. 100. In French, 'Désordonné, confus, il enfile les images les unes au bout des autres, sans aucune ligne de conduite, accumulant les redites, prenant le déjà-vu pour de l'insolite. Aucun rythme de montage ne vient organiser cet assemblage d'images disparates, pendant que Prévert réutilise ses procédés de langage depuis lontgemps éculés'.

4   A. Zalzman, Joris Ivens (Paris, Seghers 1963), pp. 12-17.

5   Manuscript BIFI, Ivens 08, B4.

6   In French: 'La Seine, tranquille et heureuse, court vers la mer à travers les champs et les vergers. La Seine se sent bien, elle ne sait pas ce qui l'attend!'

7   In French: 'Le jour est encore jeune. Avant d'entrer dans paris, la Seine à droite reçoit la Marne, s'élargissant générensement (rajoué dans l'interligne). A sa gauche, les grandes grues noires déchargent sans cesse les péniches de charbon. La lumière est étrange? Paris s'annonce.'

8   In French: 'Il semble que la Seine retarde son courant.. En coulant, elle salut [sic] les gens qui vit [sic] toute leur vie sur la Seine'.

9   Roger Odin, 'Le cinéma documentaire et le Groupe des trente', L'Âge d'or du documentaire/Europe années cinquante (Paris, L'Harmattan 1998), vol 1, pp. 19-51.

10 Estelle Caron, Michel Ionascu, Marion Richoux, 'Le cheminot, le mineur et le paysan', Roger Odin, L'Âge d'or du documentaire, Europe: années cinquante, op. cit., pp. 63-98.

11 Roger Odin, op. cit. pp. 42-44.

12 Gerard Leblanc, Georges Franju, Une esthétique de la déstabilisation (Paris, Maison de la Villette 1992).

Joris Ivens and Documentary in Italy

1   M. Lagny, La Seine a rencontré Paris and the Documentary in France in the Fifties, in this volume, p. 114-124.

2   C. Cosulich, Dieci minuti di troppo, in 'Cinema Nuovo', 93, 1956, p. 86.

3   The international cinematographers meeting held in Perugia, Italy, 24-27 September, 1949 was organised by a group of Italian filmmakers including Vittorio De Sica, Roberto Rossellini, Luchino Visconti, and Cesare Zavattini to discuss the question: 'Does today's cinematography reflect the problems of modern man?' Among the participants were the screenwriter Ben Barzman, film directors Alexander Ford, Vsevolod Pudovkin, Paul Strand and the critic and film historian Georges Sadoul. The 'Hollywood Ten' (the group of blacklisted filmmakers) also sent a message. U. Barbaro (ed.), Il Cinema e l'uomo moderno (Milano, Le edizioni sociali 1950).

4   J. Ivens, R. Destanque, *Joris Ivens ou la mémoire d'un regard* (Paris, Editions BFB 1982), pp. 247-250 (translated by the editor).

5   More details on Ivens's Italian trip can be found in V. Tosi, introductory essay to the Italian version of the first Ivens autobiography (J. Ivens, *Io-cinema, autobiografia di un cineasta*, Milano, Longanesi, 1979, and in the chapter 'La tournée di Joris Ivens' contained in V. Tosi, *Quando il cinema era un circolo – la stagione d'oro dei cineclub (1945-1956)*, Venezia, Scuola Nazionale di Cinema, Roma – Marsilio Editore, 1999, in press.

6   In my personal experience as a documentarist I have also witnessed the same. At the same time as the Joris Ivens Italian films were being made, working on the basis of an idea put forward by the Italian screenwriter Cesare Zavattini, I made a feature-length documentary about the contribution of the Italian Saving Banks to the economic development of the country (the film is entitled *Un quarto d'Italia*). State television agreed to screen my film on 31 October 1961, International Savings Day. As the complete film was too long for the TV schedule, RAI Television had prepared a shortened version (without contacting the author), systematically excluding all the sequences presenting social difficulties or poverty. In this case the sponsors (the Saving Banks Association) helped me to intervene personally in order to shorten the film in accordance with my own views, having discussed the controversial sequences with RAI Television.

7   In his second autobiography, Ivens gives another version, saying that he himself brought a copy of the complete film out of Italy (J. Ivens, R. Destanque, *Joris Ivens ou la mémoire d'un regard* (Paris, Editions BFB 1982), p. 256.)

8   Directed by Stefano Missio, produced by Scuola Nazionale di Cinema, Roma, 1997, 44', 16mm.

9   Manuscript in the Joris Ivens Archives in Nijmegen.
   ... c'est-à-dire du monopolisme americain: c'est-à-dire un aspect le plus fort, de la polémique avec Mattei et ses idées 'socialistes' et italiennes. Le film était (h)orrible et le commentaire lourd et faux. Mais on a dit un tas de choses que sous l'aspect politique-économique sont important(es) pour la bataille que Mattei conduit. C'est evident que la projection a été faite dans ces jours profitant que les films de l'ENI n'étai(e)nt pas prêts et c'est évident aussi que ça répond à un pla polémique du quel vous, qui êtes *politique* outre que poète et artiste, ne pouvez pas ignorer. Nous devons penser que Mattei doi(t) dans nos films dire et demontrer le plus qu'est possible. E(t) ça *non parce que il paye, mais aussi parce que il ne pourra pas avoir d'autre soirées à la télévision*, (puisque) elle est – il ne faut pas l'oublier – monopole de ses ennemis.

10 Original in the Joris Ivens Archives in Nijmegen.

11 Manuscript in the Joris Ivens Archives in Nijmegen. The quoted draft of the letter was partly written in Paris and completed in Havana (Cuba).
   Cher ami, comment allez-vous? C'est longtemps que je n'ai pas de vos nouvelles. Pendant plus qu'un an nous avons eu seulement quelques communications télégraphiques des différents coins du monde. La vie de notre film: Italie n'est pas un pays pauvre a été assez impétueuse, si je comprend bien, au Festival de Venise 1960 et autre. Après que j'avais fais le film en 3 parties (chaque environ 45 minutes) on nous a forcé de couper, mutiler le film, ça a heurté son contenu et sa forme d'expression. Ces coupures et cette mutilation ont été demandé par les autorités réactionnaires et par

des gens avec une incompréhension artistique. Je suis insulté et en même temps malheureux qu'on a détruit mon oeuvre [crée] selon une conception pure, correcte, honnête, accepté par tous au début de la réalisation. Je suis fier du film intégral que j'ai fait avec votre aide et dans votre maison de production.

12 Joris Ivens in an interview by Andrea Vannini which took place on 18 March, 1989 and was partially published in 'La Repubblica' (Florence) on 22 March, 1989. – The socialist leader Pietro Nenni, having known Joris Ivens during the Spanish Civil War, was, at the time, vice-premier of the Italian government.

13 Lezione di cinema – Joris Ivens al Centro Sperimentale di Cinematografia, edited by Stefano Missio, presented by Virgilio Tosi, produced by Scuola Nazionale di Cinema-Cineteca Nazionale, Roma, 1998, 40', video.

14 Joris Ivens, *Io-cinema autobiografia di un cineasta*, presented with an essay by V. Tosi, Milano, Loganesi, 1979.

15 Joris Ivens, R. Destanque, *Joris Ivens ou la mémoire d'un regard* (Paris, Éditions BFB 1982), pp. 344-345.
Si demain je pars à Florence pour y réaliser un nouveau film, ce sera une autre étape. La dernière peut-être? [...] J'ai imaginé que ce film allait être la rencontre d'un vieux documentariste et d'une ville, qui elle aussi a beaucoup vécu. Chacun a son histoire, son musée, ses richesses, et sa mémoire. C'est un jeu de miroir et une double interrogation: celle d'un homme qui veut saisir la ville dans sa réalité, celle d'une ville qui s'interroge sur l'homme qui vient la filmer. C'est un duel et je suis impatient qu'il débute. Mais quand va-t-il commencer? [...] Décidément, rien n'est jamais acquis au cinéaste!

Joris Ivens and Marceline Loridan: A Fruitful Encounter

1 Joris Ivens, Robert Destanque, *Joris Ivens ou la mémoire d'un regard* (Éditions BFB, Paris 1982).

2 Joris Ivens, 'Vive le cinéma vérité!' in *Les lettres françaises*, 17 mars 1963, p. 7.

3 Interview with the author.

4 Joris Ivens, Robert Destanque, p. 73.

The Documentary and the Turn from Modernism

1 For comments and suggestions pertinent to this article I thank Alla Effimova and Warren Sack. Catherine Soussloff offered generous feedback on earlier drafts of this essay that led to considerable revision and clarification. Akira Lippit provided useful suggestions on the history of the *stammbaum* model. I am greatly indebted to them for their contributions.

2   Kazimir Malevich, 'On New Systems in Art', Troels Andersen, ed., *Essays in Art*, I (London, 1967), p. 88. Cited in Charlotte Douglas, 'Biographic Outline', Galina Demosfenova, ed., *Malevich: Artist and Theoretician* (Paris, Flammarion 1991), p. 12.

3   Douglas, 'Biographical Outline', p. 16.

4   My discussion of the *Stammbaum* v. wave theory of language is primarily indebted to Geoffrey Sampson, *Schools of Linguistics* (Stanford, Stanford University Press, 1980). I first encountered the application of wave theory to a broader set of issues in a collo-quium conducted by Daniel Boyarin at the University of California Berkeley on the permeable interactions among second and third century Jews and Christians in Fall 1998.

5   Sampson, pp. 19-20.

6   Ivens himself, during an interview with Carlos Böker, said, 'I see the cinemato-graphic art as two currents, actualities, on the one side, on the side fiction; in the mid-dle, documentary swims, is sometimes very linked to fiction film, but sometimes very near actualities.' Böker, *Joris Ivens, Filmmaker: Facing Reality* (Ann Arbor, UMI Press, 1978), p. 2.

7   Bill Nichols, *Representing Reality: Issues and Concepts in Documentary* (Bloomington, Indiana University Press, 1991). See especially chapter 2 for a description of four modes of documentary representation (expository, observational, interactive and re-flexive), and Nichols, *Blurred Boundaries* (Bloomington, Indiana University Press, 1994), chapter 5, which introduces a fifth mode of performative documentary. Al-though I caution that modes are like the 'dominants' of a text and can easily blend and blur together, there is nonetheless a hint of progression toward 'better' modes in the style of the narrative account I offer. A wave theory of film history works to de-flate this evolutionary tendency.

8   Fredric Jameson, 'Beyond the Cave: Demystifying the Ideology Modernism', *The Ide-ologies of Theory: Essays*, vol. 2 (Minnesota, University of Minnesota Press, 1988), p. 121.

9   Jameson, p. 122.

10 Cited in Charlotte Douglas, 'Malevich and Western European Art Theory', Galenia Demosfenova, ed., *Malevich: Artist and Theoretician* (Paris, Flammarion, 1991), p. 59.

11 I use the masculine, third person pronoun throughout since the individuals central to this discussion are all male and questions of gender play no significant role in their conceptualization of their work. To the extent that women serve as subjects of repre-sentation they do so in highly conventional, even stereotypical ways. The use of 'he' and 'him' here points to what can only be seen as a significant absence.

12 Cited in Irina Karasik, 'Malevich as His Contemporaries Saw Him', in *Malevich*, p. 198.

13 Karl Marx, *Capital*, vol. 1, in Lawrence H. Simon, *Karl Marx: Selected Writings* (India-napolis, Hackett 1994), p. 277.

14 Emelio Marinetti, 'The Founding and Manifesto of Futurism', *Selected Writings* (New York, Farrar Strauss 1971), p. 42.

15 Marinetti, p. 41.

16 I owe this speculation to Warren Sack who first proposed it in conversation.

17 Carlos Böker, *Joris Ivens, Film-maker: Facing Reality* (Ann Arbor, UMI Press 1978), p. 76.

18 Thomas Waugh, *Joris Ivens and the Evolution of the Radical Documentary: 1926-1946.* (unpublished Ph.D. dissertation 1981), p. 172.

19 Marx, *Capital*, p. 279.

20 Marinetti, 'Manifesto', p. 42.

21 The details of the shift entailed by Ivens's choice of realism are superbly recounted in Waugh, *Joris Ivens and the Evolution of the Radical Documentary*. I am deeply indebted to this work for much of my general perspective as well as for those particular insights that footnotes can acknowledge specifically.

22 For further discussion of the transition toward Socialist Realism in the late twenties see Denise Youngblood, 'The Advent of Sound and the Triumph of Realism (1928-1935)', *Soviet Cinema in the Silent Era 1918-1935* (Austin, University of Texas, 1991); James Goodwin, *Eisenstein, Cinema, and History* (Urbana and Chicago, University of Illinois Press, 1993); Jay Leyda, *Kino* (London, George Allen and Unwin, 1963); Peter Kenez, *Cinema And Soviet Society* (New York, Cambridge University Press, 1992).

23 Grigory Seryi cited in Douglas, 'Biographical Outline', in *Malevich*, p. 18.

24 Douglas, 'Biographical Sketch', in *Malevich*, p. 22.

25 Douglas, 'Biographical Sketch', in *Malevich*, p. 22.

26 These terms were provided to me by Warren Sack, who first heard them introduced by Paul Virilio during an interview Sack conducted with him in Summer 1998. Virilio meant them to apply to software designs intended to serve problem, solving functions versus designs that were not goal-oriented but open-ended in how they operate. The latter were, for Virilio, rare in the current technological landscape but also of much greater interest.

27 Ivens claimed he was 'just seeing things' in his early films. See Waugh, *Joris Ivens*, p. 236. *Zaum* refers to things 'beyond reason' or 'beyond the logical mind.'

28 Ivens, 'Collaboration in Documentary', in Delmar, *Joris Ivens*, p. 100.

29 Waugh, *Joris Ivens*, p. 211.

30 For further discussion of these issues see Peter Wollen, 'The Two Avant-Gardes' and "Ontology' and 'Materialism' in Film', in *Readings and Writings* (London, Verso 1982).

31 This encapsulation is a modified version of Waugh's summary of Ivens's approach to filmmaking. See *Joris Ivens*, p. 168.

32 Michel Foucault, *The Order of Things* (New York, Vintage, 1973); Slavoj Zizek, *Looking Awry: An Introduction to Jacques Lacan through Popular Culture* (Cambridge, MIT Press 1992).

33 Most of the technical resources to produce what I term 'performative documentaries' in *Blurred Boundaries* (Bloomington, Indiana University Press 1994) such as *Tongues Untied, History and Memory, Sari Red*, or *Bontoc Eulogy* were available by 1935 but the aesthetic-political framework for doing so was nowhere to be seen. The 1930s are indicative of a general tension between situated, engaged filmmaker and his effort to

give rhetorical voice to a distinct perspective on social issues. This effort, though, once coupled to the disembodied, universalizing mechanisms of narrative realism (continuity editing; third person, omniscient narration, plausible characters and audience identification) idealized the film-maker, deflecting considerations of the conditions and categories limiting his knowledge and point of view. The documentary filmmaker more clearly stands for 'man' than he stands for gendered, ethnically or racially differentiated men.

34 The first phrase comes from Waugh, *Joris Ivens*, p. 434.

35 See my *Blurred Boundaries* (Bloomington, Indiana University Press 1994) for further discussion of the middle voice.

36 'Strategic location' is Edward Said's term for the position of an author in relation to the material he re-presents: *Orientalism* (New York, Vintage 1979), p. 20.

37 Brian Winston, 'The Tradition of the Victim in Griersonian Documentary', in Alan Rosenthal, *New Challenges for Documentary* (Berkeley, University of California Press 1988), pp. 269-287.

38 See Jack Ellis, *The Documentary Idea*, whose historical account discusses no films of Ivens's after THE POWER AND THE LAND (1941), Richard Barsam, *Nonfiction Film*, who discusses nothing after THE 400 MILLION (1939), and that only in passing. Only Erik Barnouw's more internationally attentive *Documentary: A History of the Non-Fiction Film* (New York, Oxford University Press 1993) gives extended covered to Ivens's later work and even here there is minimal sense of Ivens's overall development as a filmmaker (Barnouw provides the dates of several postwar films without giving their titles [p. 206]). He only appears in the narrative when his films serve as one of the examples of larger tendencies Barnouw finds at work.

39 Douglas, 'Biographical Sketch', p. 26.

'Honest, Straightforward Re-enactment': The Staging of Reality

1 Joris Ivens, *The Camera and I*, Seven Seas Books, Berlin, 1969, p. 90.

2 Ibidem.

3 Idem, p. 38.

4 Richard Barsam, *Nonfiction Film*, E.P. Dutton, New York, 1973, p. 1.

5 Gideon Bachman, 'The Frontiers of Realist Cinema: The Work of Ricky Leacock', *Film Culture* vol. 19-23, summer 1961, p. 19.

6 Jennings Collection: item 6.

7 Barrett, at piano, strikes up 'One Man Went to Mow' as Johnny enters. He clowns to the music, then leans over the piano singing and instructing Barrett as to who enters next:
Barrett plays... for each, as they come and join in: 'The Colonel' (Rumbold), Walters, Jacko, Joe Vallance, B.A. ('Make it snappy! says Johnny.) B.A. bows, turns and says:

And here come the headmaster! Sub walks across... (Siren... begins as music ends.) Barrett says: What about number eight? Johnny replies, That's you mate! You're riding with us tonight! They conclude the song 'Eight men went to mow', the siren rising above their voices until it dominates the soundtrack. Hodgkinson, A.W. and R.R. Sheratsky. *Humphrey Jennings – More Than a Maker of Films.* (Hanover, University of New England 1982), p. 143.

8   Jackson, K. (ed.), *The Humphrey Jennings Film Reader*, (Manchester, Carcanet P 1993), p. 40.

9   Jennings Collection: item 6.

10 *Heart of Britain: Omnibus.*

Joris Ivens and the Legacy of Committed Documentary

1   Thomas Waugh, ed., *Show Us Life: Toward a History and Aesthetics of the Committed Documentary* (Metuchen, NJ, Scarecrow Press 1984; 1988).

2   Thomas Waugh, *Joris Ivens and the Evolution of the Radical Documentary 1926-1946* (Ph.D. dissertation, Columbia Univ. 1981), esp. pp. 290-301, 338-352.

3   Jeremy Murray-Brown, 'False cinema: Vertov and early Soviet film', *The New Criterion*, Vol. 8, No. 3 (Nov. 1989), pp. 21-33.

4   Guy Hennebelle, 'French Radical Documentary After May 1968', introduction by Thomas Waugh, 1983 Foreword by Hennebelle, *Show Us Life*, pp. 168-171.

5   Joris Ivens, 'Quelques réflexions sur les documentaires d'avant-garde', *La revue des Vivants* (Paris), No. 10, October 1931; similar terms return somewhat later in 'Mijn Lezing in Parijs', *Filmliga*, Vol. 6, No. 6 (1933), p. 171.

6   Joris Ivens, *The Camera and I* (Berlin and New York, International Publishers 1968), p. 193.

7   Patricia Zimmerman and John Hess, 'Transnational Documentaries: A Manifesto', *Afterimage*, Jan/Feb 1997, pp. 10-14.

8   Les Rencontres internationales du documentaire de Montréal, December 2-6-1998, now become an annual event.

9   Two production operations that epitomize the activist documentary aspirations of the North American New Left of the late sixties, in the US and Canada (the National Film Board), respectively.

10 *Camera and I*, p. 92.

11 Two superb non-Indian examples I have in mind are THE DAMNED (Lee de Bock, Belgium, 1998, on China's Three Gorges project) and Magnus Isacsson's and Glen Salzman's POWER (Canada, 1997, on the Great Whale project in Northern Quebec).

12 Manjira Datta, unpublished screening diary, 1993, courtesy the author.

13 *Camera and I*, pp. 58-61.

A Special Relationship: Joris Ivens and the Netherlands

1 *Nieuwe Revue*, 28 June 1995.

2 Robert Destanque, Joris Ivens, *Joris Ivens ou la mémoire d'un regard*, Paris 1982, pp. 53-61.

3 It is an interesting question why Ivens went to such great pains to keep up his reputation in the Netherlands. He remained a Dutch citizen throughout his life and was proud of the fact that he spoke Dutch without an accent. Yet he had not lived in his fatherland since 1934. Is it possible that though he was a world citizen the fear of being stateless was too big? Was his Dutch citizenship compensation for the fear of bonding which he showed in other spheres of life?

4 All the biographical data in the text have been derived from: Hans Schoots, *Gevaarlijk leven. Een biografie van Joris Ivens*, Amsterdam 1995.

5 Cf. Germaine Dulac, *Le Monde*, 12 January 1929; Vsevolod Pudovkin, *Rote Fahne*, 17 March 1931.

6 Remarkable is the number of former FTL students among the teachers at the first officially recognized training course, the Netherlands Film Academy, at the end of the fifties.

7 L.J. Jordaan, *Joris Ivens* (Amsterdam/Mechelen 1931), p. 20.

8 See, for instance, the following 'Monografieën over Filmkunst', C.J. Graadt van Roggen, *Het linnen venster*, Rotterdam 1931, Menno ter Braak, *De absolute film*, Rotterdam 1931, L.J. Jordaan, *Dertig jaar film*, Rotterdam 1932, Henrik Scholte, *Nederlandsche filmkunst*, Rotterdam 1933.

9 Cf. Menno ter Braak, op. cit.

10 Cf. Bert Hogenkamp, Henri Storck, *De Borinage: de mijnwerkersstaking van 1932 en de film van Joris Ivens en Henri Storck* (Amsterdam/Leuven 1983).

11 The communist distributor IFO probably judged that there would be a big chance that the film would be rejected by the judging committee. Besides IFO had more experience with showing (Soviet) films in union meetings than exploiting them in commercial cinemas.

12 *Nieuwe Rotterdamsche Courant*, 8 March 1934.

13 Cf. Reinhard Müller (Hrsg.), *Die Saüberung. Moskau 1936: Stenogramm einer geschlossenen Parteiversammlung* (Reinbeck bei Hamburg 1991), p. 295 and pp. 323-324.

14 Dossier THE SPANISH EARTH (issue E 2180), Central Committee for Film Censorship, General State Archives, The Hague.

15 Dick Vriesman, *Film: behandelende historische, economische, sociale en kunstzinnige problemen van de film*, Amsterdam 1938, p. 164.

16 Joris Ivens, *Joris Ivens ou la mémoire d'un regard*, o.c., p. 228.

17 See Nicole van den Bosch, *Joris Ivens vs De Overheid: reputatieonderzoek, 1945-1985*, doctoral thesis film and television science, University of Amsterdam, 1995.

18 In *De Waarheid* of 4 August 1951 Ivens mentioned 'forced emigration'.

19 Hans Schoots, *Gevaarlijk leven, Een biographie van Joris Ivens*, Amsterdam 1995, p. 313.

20 Cf. *Joris Ivens ou la mémoire d'un regard*, o.c., p. 9.

21 See Nicole van den Bosch, *Joris Ivens vs. De overheid: reputatieonderzoek, 1945-1985*, doctoral thesis film and television science, University of Amsterdam, 1995.

22 *Intermediair*, 4 October 1985.

23 *Hervormd Nederland*, 24 September 1988, pp. 14-17.

24 Eric van 't Groenewout, *Indonesia Calling. Het verhaal van schepen die niet uitvoeren*, historical dissertation, State University Leiden, 1988. Van 't Groenewout had already published an article based on this research in the weekly, *Vrij Nederland*, 23 May 1987.

25 Nicole van den Bosch's dissertation, *Joris Ivens vs. De Overheid: reputatieonderzoek, 1945-1985*, is a good example. This student of film and television science wanted to graduate on a subject relating to Ivens. The fact that the Ivens collection was not available in 1994 forced her to choose a subject on which sufficient source material was available elsewhere.

26 See Bram Reijnhoudt, *The Difficult Road to Restoration of the Films of Joris Ivens*, NFM Themareeks No.28, Amsterdam 1994.

27 *De Gelderlander*, 18 November 1998.

28 Bart Tromp in *De Gelderlander*, November 1998.

29 *Algemeen Dagblad*, 29 October 1998; *Vara TV Magazine*, 21 November 1998; *Trouw*, 19 November 1998 gave an opposing view: 'All that was influenced by Ivens' was the headline.

30 See Nicholas Pronay, 'John Grierson and the Documentary – 60 years on', in *Historical Journal of Film, Radio and Television*, Vol. 9 No. 3 (1989), pp. 227-246; later Brian Wilson contributed in *Claiming the real: the documentary film revisited*, London 1995.

Music and Soundtrack in Joris Ivens's Films

1   Walter Benjamin, *Poésie et révolution*, Éditions Denoël, Paris 1971.

2   Joris Ivens, Robert Destanque, *Joris Ivens ou la mémoire d'un regarc*, Éditions BFB, Paris, 1982.

3   Ibid.

4   Ibid.

5   Hanns Eisler, 'Hochofenmusik', manuscript.

6   From the film's commentary by Chris Marker.

The Key to the Metaphysics of the Wind

1   This article is based on Sylvain De Bleeckere, *Une histoire de vent. Een filmsymphonie over de adem van de aarde.* Kampen, Kok, 1997.
    References:
    CAPI Films (ed.), *Une histoire de vent.* (Venice Press file 1988) Paris, 1988
    Ivens, J., Destanque, R., *Aan welke kant en in welk heelal. De geschiedenis van een leven* (Amsterdam, Meulenhoff 1989).
    The Yellow Emperor, *De vier geschriften van de Gele Keizer.* (translation Mansvelt Beck, B.J.) (Utrecht/Antwerpen, Kosmos-Z&K 1995).
    Mall, R.A., *Philosophie im Vergleich der Kulturen: interkulturelle Philosophie- eine neue Orientierung* (Darmstadt, Wissenschaftlicht Buchgesellschaft 1995).
    Naquin, S., Chün-Fang, Y., *Pilgrims and Sacred Sites in China.* (Studies on China 15) (Taipei, University of California Press 1992).
    Schoots, H., *Gevaarlijk leven. Een biografie van Joris Ivens* (Amsterdam, Jan Mets 1995).
    Wing-Tsit Chan, *A Source Book in Chinese Philosophy* (Princeton, Princeton University Press 1963).

Notes on the Avant-garde Documentary Film (1931)

1   Originaly published as 'Quelques réflections sur les documentaires d'avant-garde' in *La revue des vivants*, nr. 10 1931, pp. 518-520.

The Artistic Power of the Documentary Film (1932)

1   International Congress for Photograpy, Leipzig, 1932. Translation by Elles Erkens.

On the Method of the Documentary Film – in Particular the Film KOMSOMOL (1932)

1   Original text: *Zur Methode des dokumentarischen Films – in besondern des Films* KOMSOMOL, European Foundation Joris Ivens/Joris Ivens Archives, Inv.nr. JIA 190. Translated from the German by Kees Bakker.
2   The Litotdel was the Literature Department of Mesjrabpom Film. Joris Ivens wrote this article in order to obtain approval for the production of the 'Komsomol' film, later entitleD PESN O GEROJACH (SONG OF HEROES).

3 Magnitostroj (Magnet Mountain) is the area where the blast furnace and the town Magnitogorsk were built while Joris Ivens was making his film there.

Documentary: Subjectivity and Montage (1939)

1 This article is an elaboration of an unpublished lecture at the Museum of Modern Art, New York, December, 13 1939, in the framework of a course at Columbia University on 'The History of the Motion Picture'.

2 Joris Ivens refers here to POWER AND THE LAND.

A Short Biography of Joris Ivens

1898
Born 18 November: George Henri Anton Ivens at Van Berchenstraat in Nijmegen, the second son of photographic supplies dealer Cees Ivens and Dora Muskens.

1911
Makes a juvenile film about Indians and a farmer's family, titled THE WIGWAM, in Nijmegen.

1911-1917
Pupil at the municipal Dutch High School in Nijmegen.

1917-1919
Trains as officer in the mounted field artillery.

1919-1921
Studies economy at Higher Commercial College in Rotterdam, becomes student president.

1921-1924
Studies photographic technique in Berlin, apprenticeship in several photography laboratories, befriends the poet Marsman and Arthur Lehning.

1924-1933
Works in the Amsterdam branch of his father's photo shop called CAPI; studies avant-garde films; befriends the German photographer Germaine Krull. They get married in 1927.

1927
Co-founder of Film Liga, begins his first film experiments.

1928
His film THE BRIDGE makes Joris Ivens the pioneer of Dutch film art and attracts international attention. Befriends painter Anneke van der Feer and Helene van Dongen, then a secretary. Van Dongen soon becomes a film editor. Ivens marries her in 1944.

1928-1931
Makes form and movement studies such as RAIN and the first Dutch artistic sound film: PHILIPS RADIO (also called INDUSTRIAL SYMPHONY).

1932-1934
Makes controversial social films at the time of Depression such as NEW EARTH (about reclamation of polder in the Zuiderzee) and BORINAGE, after which he leaves Holland for Russia.

Joris Ivens in 1946 (Photo: Marion Michelle).

1936-1945

Settles in America and makes anti-fascist films such as THE SPANISH EARTH in Spain together with Ernest Hemingway and THE 400 MILLION in China; collaborates in Canada and America (among others, for the USA War Department) on films about the war against Japan and Germany. American photographer Marion Michelle becomes his partner, scriptwriter and camerawoman.

1946

Resigns as film commissioner for the Dutch government, in solidarity with the Indonesian Republic. Makes INDONESIA CALLING.

1947-1957

Stays in Eastern Europe and makes some trade union films such as SONG OF THE RIVERS in colaboration with, among others, Brecht and Sjostakovic. The Polish poetess Ewa Fiszer becomes his third wife in 1951.

1955

Is awarded World Peace Prize.

1957

Settles in Paris, wins Golden Palm in Cannes and Golden Gate Award in San Francisco with LA SEINE A RENCONTRÉ PARIS.

1957-1965

Films in France, China, Italy, Cuba, Mali, and in Chile documenting the recovery of the land, but also makes lyrical films such as POUR LE MISTRAL and ...A VALPARAISO.

1963

The French filmmaker Marceline Loridan becomes his partner, together they make 20 films, and get married in 1977.

1964

First festive reception in Amsterdam to carefully restore the split with his father-land.

1967

Is awarded International Lenin Prize for science and culture in Moscow.

1969

Minister Marga Klompé commissions Ivens to make a film about Holland.

1965-1970

Devotes himself to the capturing of the liberation of Vietnam and makes several films against the American war of aggression.

1971-1977

Large film project about the cultural revolution in China; HOW YUKONG MOVED THE MOUNTAINS is shown in many countries including on Dutch television, and is bought by the Museum of Modern Art in New York.

1978

Is awarded honorary doctorate from the Royal College of Art in London.

1980-1988

Large film project about the history of Florence, developed but not realized. In China he makes a film about the wind, UNE HISTOIRE DE VENT.

1984

Is made Commander of the Legion d'Honeur, presented by French president Mitterand.

1985

Is awarded the Golden Calf, the top Dutch Film Prize, by Minister Brinkman; is made Grand Officer of the Republic of Italy and is presented with the golden medal For Merits for the Fines Arts by the Spanish king Juan Carlos.

1987

Is awarded the Che Guevara Prize in Cuba.

Joris Ivens during the filming of UNE HISTOIRE DE VENT.

1988
Is awarded the Golden Lion for his complete oeuvre at the Venice Film Festival.
Is also made honorary citizen of Nijmegen.

1989
Is decorated with a Knighthood in the Order of the Dutch Lion; dies in Paris on
28 June; Marceline Loridan is awarded the Felix for their joint film, UNE HISTOIRE
DE VENT.

Filmography

The films mentioned below are listed in chronological order. We have given the original title of the film and the current English and French distribution titles (if the titles are not in English or French originally), and the basic information of the film. It concerns, mostly, the finished films Joris Ivens has directed, or in which production he had a major role. More background information about the films (credits, short description) can be found at the website of the European Foundation Joris Ivens: www.ivens.nl.

1910-1930
FAMILIE-FILMS IVENS
Home movies Ivens family / Films de famille Ivens:
– ZANDBAK, VAN BERCHENSTRAAT (originally without title)
Sand-box, van Berchenstraat / Bac à sable, van Berchenstraat
(2 minutes, b/w, silent, 35 mm, circa 1910)
– 'T ZONHUIS
The Sunhouse / Maison du soleil
(6 minutes, b/w, silent, 35 mm, 1921)
– O, ZONNELAND
Zonneland / Zonneland
(7 minutes, b/w, silent, 35 mm, 1922)
– 'T ZONHUIS
The Sunhouse / Maison du soleil
(2 minutes, b/w, silent, 35 mm, 1925)
– THEA'S MEERDERJARIGHEID ZONNELAND
Thea's Age of Majority, Zonneland / La majorité de Thea, Zonneland
(12 minutes, b/w, silent, 35 mm, 1927)
– ZONNELAND
Zonneland / Zonneland
(circa 8 min, b/w, silent, 35 mm, 1930)

1912
DE WIGWAM (Brandende Straal)
Wigwam (Shining Ray) / La Hutte (Flêche ardente)
(with the Ivens family; Holland, 8 minutes, b/w, silent, 35 mm)
1927-1928
FILMEXPERIMENTEN
Film experiments / Expériments cinématographiques:

– PROEF-OPNAMEN CHARLOTTE KÖHLER
Test-shooting Charlotte Köhler / Prises provisoire Charlotte Köhler
(Holland, b/w, silent, 35 mm, lost)
– DE ZIEKE STAD
The Sick Town / La ville malade
(with Erich Wichman; unfinished, b/w, silent, 35 mm, 1927, lost)
– KINOSCHETSBOEK
Film Sketchbook / Album à dessin cinématographique
(Holland, b/w, silent, 35 mm, 1927, lost)
– DIE STRASSE
The Street / La rue
(unfinished, Holland, b/w, silent, 35 mm, 1927, lost)
– ZEEDIJK FILMSTUDIE
Filmstudy Zeedijk / Études sur le Zeedijk
(Holland, 10 min, b/w, silent, 35 mm, 1927, lost)
– DEMONSTRATIEFILMS MICROCAMERA,UNIVERSITEIT LEIDEN
Instruction films micro camera, University Leiden / Films d'instruction micro-
camera, Université Leiden
(Holland, b/w, silent, 35 mm, 1928, lost)

1927
ÉTUDES DES MOUVEMENTS À PARIS
Studies in Movement in Paris
(Holland, 4 min, b/w, silent, 35 mm)

1928
DE BRUG
The Bridge / Le pont
(Holland, 11 min, b/w, silent, 35 mm)

1929
BRANDING
Breakers / Les Brisants
(Dir: Mannus Franken; Holland, 33 min, b/w, silent, 35 mm)

1929
IK-FILM
I Film / Moi-film
(Holland, 10 min, b/w, silent, 35 mm, lost)

1929
SCHAATSENRIJDEN
Ice Skating / Les patineurs
(Holland, 8 min, b/w, silent, 35 mm, lost)

1929

ARM DRENTHE (DE NOOD IN DE DRENTSCHE VENEN)
Poor Drenthe (The Misery in the Peat-mores of Drenthe) / Pauvre Drenthe (La misère aux tourbes de Drenthe)
(Holland, 15 min, b/w, silent, 35 mm, lost)

1929

REGEN
Rain / La pluie
(with Mannus Franken; Holland, 12 min, b/w, silent, 35 mm)

1929

HEIEN
Pile Driving / Pilotis
(Holland, 10 min, b/w, silent, 35 mm)

1930

WIJ BOUWEN
We Are Building / Nous batissons
(Holland, 110 min, b/w, silent, 35 mm) also as independent parts:
– NVV-CONGRES
NVV Congress / Congrès du NVV
– JEUGDDAG
Day of Youth / Journée de la jeunesse
– NIEUWE ARCHITECTUUR
New Architecture / Nouvelle architecture
– CAISSONBOUW
Caisson Building / Caissons armés de Rotterdam
– AMSTERDAMSE JEUGDDAG
Amsterdam Day of Youth / Journée de la jeunesse à Amsterdam
– ZUIDERZEEWERKEN
Zuiderzee Works / Zuiderzee
– ZUID-LIMBURG
South Limburg / Sud Limbourg

1930

JEUGDDAG VIERHOUTEN
Day of Youth, Vierhouten / Journée de la jeunesse, Vierhouten
(Holland, b/w, silent, 35 mm, lost)

1930

ZUIDERZEE
Zuiderzee / Zuiderzee
(Holland, 50 min, b/w, silent, 35 mm)

1930

VVVC-JOURNAAL
VVVC News / Ciné-journal VVVC
3 parts:
– VVVC-JOURNAAL
VVVC News / Ciné-journal VVVC
(Holland, 15 min, b/w, silent, 35 mm, lost)
– NO. 1: FILMNOTITIES UIT DE SOVJET UNIE
Nr. 1: News from the Soviet Union / No. 1: Journal de l'Union soviétique
(Holland, 20 min, b/w, silent, 35 mm, lost)
– NO. 2: DEMONSTRATIE VAN PROLETARISCHE SOLIDARITEIT
Nr. 2: Demonstration of Proletarian Solidarity / No. 2: Démonstration de solidarité prolétaire
(Holland, 20 min, b/w, silent, 35 mm, lost)

1930

BREKEN EN BOUWEN (Tribune film)
Tribune Film / Tribune film
(Dir.: Mark Kolthoff; Holland 20 min, b/w, silent, 35 mm, lost)

1931

DONOGOO-TONKA
Donogoo-tonka / Donogoo-tonka
(Holland, b/w, silent, 35 mm, lost)

1931

PHILIPS RADIO
Philips Radio / Symphonie industrielle
(Holland, 36 min, b/w, sound, 35 mm)

1932

CREOSOOT
Creosote / Créosote
(with Jean Dréville; Holland, 80 min, b/w, silent, 35 mm)

1933

PESN O GEROJACH (KOMSOMOL)
Song of Heroes, or Komsomol / Komsomol, ou Le chant des héros
(Russia, 50 min, b/w, sou, 35 mm)

1933

NIEUWE GRONDEN
New Earth / Nouvelle terre
(Holland, 30 min, b/w, sou, 35mm)

1934

MISERE AU BORINAGE

Borinage

(with Henri Storck; Belgium, 34 min, b/w, silent, 35 mm)

(in the same year a Russian re-edited sound version was made)

1934

SAARABSTIMMUNG UND SOWJETUNION

Saar Referendum and Soviet Union / Référe

(with Gustav Regler; Soviet Union, b/w, sou, 35mm, lost)

1936

BORZY (KÄMPFER)

The Fighter / Le Lutteur

(Dir.: Gustav von Wangenheim; Soviet Union, b/w, sou, 35mm)

1936

DE RUSSISCHE SCHOOL IN NEW YORK

The Russian School in New York / L'école russe à New York

(United States, b/w, sou, 35mm, lost)

1937

THE SPANISH EARTH

Terre d'Espagne

(United States, 52 min, b/w, sou, 35 mm)

1939

THE 400 MILLION

Les 400 millions

(United States, 53 min, b/w, sou, 35 mm)

1941

POWER AND THE LAND

L'électrification de la terre

(United States, 33 min, b/w, sou, 35 mm)

1941

OUR RUSSIAN FRONT

Notre front russe

(with Lewis Milestone; United States, 38 min, b/w, sou, 35 mm)

1942

OIL FOR ALLADINS LAMP

La lampe d'Aladin

(United States, b/w, sou, 35 mm)

1943

ACTION STATIONS !

Alarme! ou Branle-bas de combat

(Canada, 50 min, b/w, sou, 35 mm)

1945

THE STORY OF G.I. JOE

Le récit de G.I. Joe

(Dir.: William Wellman; United States, 97 min, b/w, sou, 35mm)

1946

INDONESIA CALLING

L'Indonésie apelle

(Australia, 22 min, b/w, sou, 35 mm)

1949

PIERWSZE LATA

The First Years / Les premières années

(Czechoslovakia, Poland, Bulgaria, 99 min, b/w, sou, 35 mm)

1951

POKÓJ ZWYCIECY SWIAT

Peace Will Win / La paix vaincra

(with Jerzy Bossak; Poland, 90 min, b/w, sou, 35 mm)

1952

FREUNDSCHAFT SIEGT !

Friendship Triumphs / L'amitié vaincra

(with Ivan Pyriev; Russia, GDR, 95 min, colour, sou, 35 mm)

1952

WYSCIC POKÓJU WARSZAWA-BERLIN-PRAGA

Peace Tour 1952 / La course de la paix Varsovie-Berlin-Prague

(Poland, GDR, 44 min, col, sou, 35 mm)

1954

LIED DER STRÖME

Song of the Rivers / Chant des fleuves

(GDR, 90 min. b/w, sou, 35 mm)

1956

MEIN KIND

My Child / Mon enfant

(Dir.: Vladimir Pozner, Alfons Machalz; GDR, 22 min, b/w, sou, 35mm)

1956

DIE ABENTEUER DES TILL EULENSPIEGEL / LES AVENTURES DE TILL L'ESPIEGLE
The Adventures of Till Ulenspiegel
(Dir.: Gérard Philipe; GDR/France, 90 min, col, sou, 35 mm)

1957

DIE WINDROSE
The Windrose / La rose des vents
(Dir.: Alberto Cavalcanti a.o.; GDR, 110 min, b/w, sou, 35mm)

1957

LA SEINE A RENCONTRÉ PARIS
The Seine Meets Paris
(France, 32 min, b/w, sou, 35 mm)

1958

BEFORE SPRING
Lettres de Chine
(China, 38 min, col, sou, 35 mm)

1958

SIX HUNDRED MILLION WITH YOU
600 millions avec vous
(China, 12 min, col, sou, 35 mm)

1960

L'ITALIA NON È UN PAESE POVERO
Italy is not a Poor Country / L'Italie n'est pas un pays pauvre
(Italy, 110 min, b/w, sou, 35 mm)

1960

DEMAIN A NANGUILA
Nanguila Tomorrow
(Mali, 50 min, col, sou, 35 mm)

1961

CARNET DE VIAJE
Travel Notebook / Carnet de voyage
(Cuba, 34 min, b/w, sou, 35 mm)

1961

PUEBLO ARMADO
An Armed People / Peuple armé
(Cuba, 35 min, b/w, sou, 35 mm)

1962

MARC CHAGALL

Marc Chagall

(Dir.: Henri Langlois; France, colour, sou, 35mm; film was not released)

1963

...À VALPARAÍSO

(France/Chile, 37 min, b/w and col, sou, 35 mm)

1963

LE PETIT CHAPITEAU

The Little Circus

(France/Chile, 6 min, b/w, sou, 35 mm)

1964

LE TRAIN DE LA VICTOIRE

The Victory Train

(Chile, 9 min, b/w, sou, 35 mm)

1965

POUR LE MISTRAL

The Mistral

(France, 30 min, b/w and col, sou, 35 mm and cinemascope)

1966

LE CIEL, LA TERRE

The Threatening Sky

(France, 30 min, b/w, sou, 35 mm)

1966

ROTTERDAM-EUROPOORT

Rotterdam Europort

(Holland, France, 20 min, col, sou, 35 mm)

1967

LOIN DE VIETNAM

Far From Vietnam

(Collective; France, 115 min, col, sou, 35 mm)

1968

17ème PARALLÈLE

The 17th Parallel

(with Marceline Loridan; France, 113 min, b/w, sou, 35 mm)

1970

LE PEUPLE ET SES FUSILS
The People and Their Guns
(Collective; France, 97 min, b/w, sou, 35 mm)

1970

RENCONTRE AVEC LE PRÉSIDENT HO CHI MINH
Meeting With President Ho Chi Minh
(with Marceline Loridan; France 8 min, col, sou, 35 mm)

1976

COMMENT YUKONG DEPLAÇA LES MONTAGNES
How Yukong Moved the Mountains
(with Marceline Loridan; France, 12 hours, col, sou, 16 mm) 12 parts:
– AUTOUR DE PETROLE: TAKING (84 min)
The Oilfields
– LA PHARMACIE NR. 3: SHANGHAI (79 min)
The Pharmacy: Shanghai
– L'USINE DE GÉNÉRATEURS (131 min)
The Generator Factory
– UNE FEMME, UNE FAMILLE (110 min)
A Woman, A Family
– LE VILLAGE DES PÊCHEURS (104 min)
The Fishing Village
– UNE CASERNE (56 min)
An Army Camp
– IMPRESSIONS D'UNE VILLE: SHANGHAI (60 min)
Impression of a City: Shanghai
– HISTOIRE D'UN BALLON: LE LYCÉE NO. 31 À PÉKIN (19 min)
The Football Incident
– LE PROFESSEUR TSIEN (12 min)
Professor Tsien
– UNE RÉPÉTITION A L'OPÉRA DE PÉKIN (30 min)
Rehearsal at the Peking Opera
– ENTRAÎNEMENT AU CIRQUE DE PÉKIN (18 min)
Training at the Peking Circus
– LES ARTISANS (15 min)
Traditional Handicrafts

1977

LES KAZAKS – MINORITÉ NATIONALE – SINKIANG
The Kazakhs, National Minority, Xinjiang
(with Marceline Loridan; France, 50 min, col, sou, 16 mm)

1977

LES OUIGOURS – MINORITÉ NATIONALE - SINKIANG

The Uigurs, National Minority, Xinjiang

(with Marceline Loridan; France, 35 min, col, sou, 16 mm)

1979

COMMÉMORATION À PARIS DE LA MORT DE MAO ZE DONG (Journal)

Commemoration of the death of Mao Ze Dung (News-item)

(with Marceline Loridan; France, col, sou; made for Chinese television)

1988

UNE HISTOIRE DE VENT

A Tale of the Wind

(with Marceline Loridan; France, 74 min, col, sou, 35 mm)

Selected bibliography

This bibliography lists the major publications regarding Joris Ivens and his work: autobiographies, biographies, monographs and the most important doctoral and PhD theses.

A lot more has been written regarding Joris Ivens's films and other specific subjects, but it would be too much to mention all these publications here. All texts, and many articles not mentioned below, can be found in the Joris Ivens Archives, and can be consulted at the European Foundation Joris Ivens.

Autobiographies

Joris Ivens, *The Camera and I*, Seven Seas Books, Berlin, 1969.

Joris Ivens, *Autobiografie van een filmer*, Born, Amsterdam/Assen, 1970 (elaborated translation of *The Camera and I*).

Joris Ivens, *Die Kamera und Ich: Autobiografie eines Filmers*, Rowohlt, Reinbeck, 1974.

Joris Ivens, *Io di cinema*, Biblioteca Longnesi, Milano, 1979.

Joris Ivens and Robert Destanque, *Joris Ivens ou la mémoire d'un regard*, Éditions BFB, Paris, 1982.

Joris Ivens and Robert Destanque, *Aan welke kant en in welk heelal. De geschiedenis van een leven*, Meulenhoff, Amsterdam, 1983.

Biographies, monographs, works of reference

Bakker, Kees, *Inventaris van het Joris Ivens Archief*, Europese Stichting Joris Ivens, Nijmegen, 1998 (also in English: *Inventory of the Joris Ivens Archives*, European Foundation Joris Ivens, Nijmegen, 1999).

Bertina, B.J., *Joris Ivens, revolutionair*, IVIO, Amsterdam, 1969.

Bleeckere Sylvain De, *Une histoire de vent. Een filmsymfonie over de adem van de aarde*, Uitgeverij Kok, Kampen, 1997.

Brunel, Claude, *Joris Ivens*, Cinémathèque française, Paris, 1983.

(collective, ed.), *Joris Ivens*, Cinéma Politique: no. hors série, Paris, 1978.

Costa, José Manuel, *Joris Ivens*, Cinemateca Portuguesa, Lisboa, 1983.

Delmar, Rosalind, *Joris Ivens, 50 Years of Film-making*, British Film Institute, London, 1979.

Devarrieux, Claire, *Entretiens avec Joris Ivens*, Albatros, Paris, 1979.

Drobashenko, S., *Kinorezisser Joris Ivens*, Iskusstvo, Moscow, 1964.

(The Film Archive of China, ed.) *Joris Ivens and China*, New World Press, Bejing, 1983.

Gambetti, Giacomo, *Joris Ivens, cinquant'anni di cinema*, Marsilio Editori, Modena, 1979.

Grélier, Robert , *Joris Ivens*, Éditeurs Français Réunis, Paris, 1965.

Hogenkamp, Bert , Henri Storck, *De Borinage. De mijnwerkersstaking van 1932 en de film van Joris Ivens en Henri Storck*, van Gennep, Amsterdam, 1983.

Ivens, Joris, Marceline Loridan, *Le 17ème parallèle, la guerre du peuple (deux mois sous la terre)*, Éditeurs Français Réunis, Paris, 1968.

Ivens, Joris, Vladimir Pozner, *Lied der Ströme*, Tribüne, Berlin, 1957.

Jordaan, L.J., *Joris Ivens*, De Spieghel, Amsterdam, 1931.

Klaue, W., M. Lichtenstein, H. Wegner (ed.), *Joris Ivens*, Staatliches Filmarchiv der DDR, Berlin, 1963.

Kreimeier, Klaus , *Joris Ivens, ein Filmer an den Fronten der Weltrevolution*, Overbaumverlag, Berlin, 1976.

Kreimeier, Klaus, *Il cinema di Joris Ivens*, Mazotta, Milano, 1977.

Meyer, Han , *Joris Ivens, de weg naar Vietnam*, Bruna, Utrecht, 1970.

(Nederlands Filmmuseum, ed.) *Joris Ivens, 50 jaar wereldcineast*, Nederlands Filmmuseum, Amsterdam, 1978.

Passek, Jean-Loup , Jacqueline Brisbois (ed.), *Joris Ivens, 50 ans de cinéma*, Centre Georges Pompidou, Paris, 1979.

Reijnhoudt, Bram , *The Difficult Road to Restoration of the Films of Joris Ivens*, Nederlands Filmmuseum, Amsterdam, 1994.

Saaltink, Hans , *Joris Ivens 65 jaar*, Nederlands Filmmuseum, Amsterdam, 1964.

Schoots, Hans , *Gevaarlijk leven. Een biografie van Joris Ivens*, Jan Mets, Amsterdam, 1995.

Schoots, Hans, *Dangerous Life. A Biography of Joris Ivens*, Amsterdam University Press, Amsterdam, 2000 (edited translation of 1995).

Stufkens, André (ed.), *Passages, Joris Ivens en de kunst van deze eeuw*, Museum Het Valkhof/Europese Stichting Joris Ivens, Nijmegen, 1999.

Stufkens, André, Jan de Vaal, Tineke de Vaal (ed.), *Rondom Joris Ivens, wereldcineast. Het begin, 1898-1934*, Het Wereldvenster/Nijmeegs Museum 'Commanderie van Sint Jan', Nijmegen, 1988.

Wegner, Hans, *Joris Ivens, Dokumentarist der Wahrheit*, Henschelverlag, Berlin, 1965.

Zalzman, Abraham, *Joris Ivens – Cinéma d'aujourd'hui*, nr. 9, Seghers, Paris, 1963.

Dissertations

Andreotti, Francesco, *Il cinema di Joris Ivens e la messa in scena della realtà*, Università degli studi di Pisa, Facoltà di lettere e filosofia, Pisa, 1996.

Böker, Carlos, *Joris Ivens, Filmmaker: The Mythical Presentation of a Dialectically Interpreted Reality*, University of Iowa, Philosophy of Speech and Dramatic Art, 1978.

Bosch, Nicole van den, *Joris Ivens vs. de overheid: reputatieonderzoek, 1945-1985*, University of Amsterdam, Film and Television Studies, Amsterdam, 1995.

Caffarena, Attilio, *"Il Ponte" di Joris Ivens e le avanguardie cinematografiche degli anni venti. Trascrizione grafica e analisi semiologica*, Università degli studi di Genova, Facoltà di magistero, Genova, 1976.

Cassiers, Willem, *Joris Ivens. Het filmmedium als politiek uitdrukkingsmiddel*, Vrije Universiteit Brussel, Faculteit Letteren en Wijsbegeerte, Brussels, 1974.

Groenewout, Eric van't, *Indonesia Calling. Het verhaal van schepen die niet uitvoeren*, Rijksuniversiteit Leiden, Vakgroep Geschiedenis, Leiden, 1988.

Hiller, Norbert , *Ein Dokumentarfilm im Auftrag der Industrie – Joris Ivens und sein Film "Philips Radio"*, Universität Köln, Philosophischen Fakultät, Köln, 1983.

Stölting, Winfried, *Untersuchung unterschiedlicher Konzeptionen des Dokumentarfilms am Beispiel der Berichterstattung über die VR China (Filmvergleich: Ivens/Loridan: "Wie Yü-Gung Berge versetzte", 1977; Antonioni: "China", 1972*, SHfBK, Fachbereich Kunstpädagogik, Braunschweig, 1977.

Tendler, Silvio, *La relation cinéma et histoire vue à travers l'étude de l'oeuvre de Joris Ivens*, École des Hautes Études en Sciences Sociales, Paris, 1976.

Waugh, Thomas, *Joris Ivens and the Evolution of the Radical Documentary 1926-1946*, Columbia University, Ann Arbor, 1981.

About the Authors

Kees Bakker studied Film and Performing arts at the University of Nijmegen. He has teached Film History and Film Theory at this same department, and works since 1994 at the European Foundation Joris Ivens as coordinator of the Joris Ivens Archives. He recently published the *Inventory of the Joris Ivens Archives*, and has published several articles on film theory and documentary film. Kees Bakker is currently preparing a dissertation on the hermeneutics of representation and interpration of reality in audiovisual media.

Sylvain De Bleeckere is philosopher and teaches Art Philosophy and Anthropology at the department of Architecture of Hogeschool Limburg, Belgium. He is editor of the periodical *CineMagie*. He has published on philosophy of culture, metaphysics, and art, on Nietzsche, and on the films of Tarkovsky and on UNE HISTOIRE DE VENT by Joris Ivens and Marceline Loridan.

Claude Brunel teaches Film and Music in the Department of Médiation Culturelle of the Université de la Sorbonne Nouvelle (Paris III). She initiated a Joris Ivens exhibition in Paris in 1983 and published a monograph on Joris Ivens. Claude Brunel is also a documentary filmmaker and the vice-president of the European Foundation Joris Ivens.

José Manuel Costa is Deputy Director of the Portuguese Film Archive, teaches Film History and Documentary Film at the University of Lisbon, and was president of the Association des Cinémathèques Européennes. He is author of monographs on D.W. Griffith, Robert Flaherty, Frederick Wiseman, and Joris Ivens.

Karel Dibbets is historian and teaches at the department of Film and Television Studies at the University of Amsterdam. He is co-editor of the Media History Yearbook, and has published extensively on the subject of film history, among which *Film and the First World War*, which he edited with Bert Hogenkamp, and *Talking Pictures: The Introduction of Sound Films in the Netherlands, 1928-1933* (in Dutch).

Bert Hogenkamp is Professor of Media History at the University of Utrecht, and heading the Research Department of the Netherlands Audiovisual Archives. He is co-editor of the Dutch *Journal of Media History*, and has published several books on Dutch documentary, on Film and the Workers Movement in Great Britain, and edited with Karel Dibbets *Film and the First World War*.

Günter Jordan worked for more than twenty years for the DEFA Documentary Film Studio. He studied at the Friedrich Schiller University in Jena, and studied for director at the Potsdam-Babelsberg Film Acadamy. Since 1991 he works as an independent author and director. He published several articles and books on documentary film and edited with Ralf Schenk *Schwarzweiss und Farbe. DEFA Dokumentarfilme 1946-1992* on the DEFA Documentary Film Studios.

Michèle Lagny is professor at the department of Médiation Culturelle of the Université de la Sorbonne Nouvelle (Paris III). She directs researches on French documentaries of the fifties and works on the project 'Film as document for historians and the writing of history by the cinema'.

Alfons Machalz was director and programme editor for German television. He worked several decades for the DEFA Documentary Film Studio, where he made numerous ethnographical and biographical television documentaries – among them portraits of artists like Goethe, Händel, Dziga Vertov and Joris Ivens.

Bill Nichols is Professor of Cinema Studies at San Francisco State University, and author of numerous books and articles on documentary film. He edited the two anthologies *Movies and Methods* and published on the subject of representation in audiovisual media, among which his *Ideology and the Image*, *Representing Reality* and *Blurred Boundaries*.

Jean-Pierre Sergent is writer-journalist. He had a role in CHRONIQUE D'UN ÉTÉ by Jean Rouch and Edgar Morin, made with Marceline Loridan in 1963 the film ALGÉRIE ANNÉE ZÉRO on the independence of Algeria, and collaborated with Joris Ivens and Marceline Loridan on some of their films, like LE 17ÈME PARALLÈLE and LE PEUPLE ET SES FUSILS.

André Stufkens studied Art History at the Acadamy for the Arts in Arnhem, and is a teacher of Art and Art History at the Municipal Comprehensive School of Nijmegen. He also works as coordinator at the European Foundation Joris Ivens. He initiated a Joris Ivens exhibition in Nijmegen and published a volume on Joris Ivens's early works: *Rondom Joris Ivens, wereldcineast. Het begin 1898-1934*.

Virgilio Tosi is director of documentary films, particularly in the field of scientific cinematography. He is also Director of Research of audiovisual technologies, and teaches Scientific Cinematography and History of Documentary Film at the Scuola Nazionale di Cinema in Rome.

Thomas Waugh has taught Film Studies at Concordia University, Montreal, since 1976. He is author of *Joris Ivens and the Evolution of the Radical Documentary 1926-1946* (dissertation), and editor of *Show Us Life: Toward a History and Aesthetics of the Committed Documentary*, and many articles on Canadian, American and Indian documentary.

Brian Winston began his career at Granada Television in 1963. He currently is Head of the School of Communication, Design and Media at the University of Westminster. He published several works on documentary filmmaking and media technology, like *Claiming the Real, Technologies of Seeing* and *Media Technology and Society*. In 1985 Brian Winston won an Emmy for documentary script writing. He is also a governor of the British Film Institute.

Illustrations

All illustrations have their source in the different collections of the European Foundation Joris Ivens (Joris Ivens Archives, Marceline Loridan-Ivens Collection, Marion Michelle Collection, Hans Wegner Collection), with the exception of the reproductions of the Malevich paintings which come from the Stedelijk Museum Amsterdam. We want to thank Marceline Loridan-Ivens, Marion Michelle and the Stedelijk Museum, for their permission to reproduce these photos in this volume. Copyright for the photos: Joris Ivens Archives / European Foundation Joris Ivens, with the exception of the photos mentioned below.

p. 8   Joris Ivens in the Blue Mountains; Australia, 1946. Photo: Marion Michelle (MMC/EFJI).
p. 14   Portrait Joris Ivens. Photo: Chris Marker (JIA/EFJI).
p. 33   below. Photo: Podzuweit (JIA/EFJI).
p. 51   Joris Ivens with camera, about 1910. Family Archives: Nooteboom-Ivens.
p. 143   Kazimir Malevich. Stedelijk Museum Amsterdam.
p. 151   Kazimir Malevich. Stedelijk Museum Amsterdam.
p. 157   Kazimir Malevich. Stedelijk Museum Amsterdam.
p. 161   above filming the eviction scene. Photo: Willy Kessels (JIA/EFJI).
p. 189   Joris Ivens and Holland. Photo: Elisabeth Lotar (JIA/EFJI).
p. 213   Still from UNE HISTOIRE DE VENT. CAPI Films, Paris (MLI/EFJI).
p. 219   above and below. Stills from UNE HISTOIRE DE VENT. CAPI-Films, Paris (MLI/EFJI).
p. 267   above and below. Photo: Willy Kessels (JIA/EFJI).
p. 296   Joris Ivens, 1946. Photo: Marion Michelle (MMC/EFJI).
p. 298   Photo: Nicolas Philibert/CAPI Films (MLI/EFJI).

Index